How refreshing to find a college textbook that remembers that at the heart of good writing is a *human* heart, one attached to a writer with experiences, reflections, attitudes, and perceptions worthy of sharing. *You've Gotta Have Heart* is structured with humor, humanity, and a keen understanding of the starts and stops that accompany almost every writer's process. Filled with student-composed essays, examples, and anecdotes from the author's real life, and encouraging quotations from other writers and artists, *You've Gotta Have Heart* focuses on carefully guiding students through the writing process. Furthermore, the text helps students build confidence in their writing by advocating a portfolio approach, different kinds of peer reviewing, and metacognitive strategies for writers. Students should find a textbook that validates their own experiences and voices extremely beneficial and enjoyable.

--Angela M. Gulick, Professor of English and Critical Studies, Parkland College, Champaign, IL

You've Gotta Have HEART—
in Your WRITING

SIXTH EDITION

by

James L. Brimeyer

Northeast Iowa Community College

Uncial Press   Aloha, Oregon

2018

You've Gotta Have Heart—in Your Writing

Sixth Edition
Copyright 2018 by James L. Brimeyer

ISBN 13: 978-1-60174-240-7

Cover Design © 2018 by Judith B. Glad

Published by Uncial Press
    An imprint of GCT, Inc.
    2550 SW 204th Ave.
    Aloha, Oregon 97003
    http://www.uncialpress.com
    Printed in the United States of America

———

The Library of Congress has cataloged the earlier edition as follows:
Brimeyer, James L., 1947-
  You've gotta have heart-in your writing / by James L. Brimeyer. -- 4th ed.
    p. cm.
  Includes bibliographical references and index.
  ISBN 978-1-60174-089-2
  1. English language--Rhetoric--Study and teaching. 2. Creative writing--Study and teaching. I. Title.
  PE1404.B736 2009
  808'.04207--dc22

                    2009044486

This book is dedicated to:
*my wife Kay, for her unending support and love
over the years
my family—Joe and Amy, Ellen and Luke,
Mariah, Kayla, Evan, Hannah, Paisley—
Grandpa's treasures—my teachers all
my teaching colleagues over the years, whose dedication and creativity
have inspired me
my students—past, present, and future—who have taught me far more
than I have taught them.*

About the Author

Jim Brimeyer has taught writing courses at Northeast Iowa Community College since 1989. Before that, Jim taught high school English for 25 years. He received his BA and MA in English Education from Loras College in Dubuque, Iowa. Jim has also written *Taming the Writing Tiger: A Handbook for Business Writers* (2014, third edition) and *A Tradition of Excellence: Bernie O'Connor and Wahlert Athletics*, a biographical tribute to his high school English teacher. Jim's booklet, *Response and Self-Reflection: The Heart and Soul of My Writing Classroom*, was published in 2002 by the Iowa Writing Project. Jim's articles have been published in NCTE's *Teaching English in the Two-Year College*, *The Successful Teacher*, *The Teaching Professor*, *Portfolio News*, *Iowa Language Arts News*, and *Julien's Journal*. He has given countless pedagogical presentations from coast to coast.

Jim Brimeyer's honors include the ICTELA Iowa Literacy Award, the National Council of Instructional Administrators Award for Community College Teaching, the NISOD Teaching Excellence Award from the University of Texas at Austin, the University of Notre Dame Educator Award, the University of Chicago Outstanding Teacher Award, and the Iowa State University Excellence in Teaching Award. In 2005, Jim was selected Iowa Professor of the Year by the Carnegie Foundation for the Advancement of Teaching and the Council for Achievement and Support of Education. In 2006, Jim was named the Iowa Community College Teacher of the Year by Iowa's Community College Board of Trustees Organization.

Preface

This book, a combination writing guide and handbook written for both English Composition I and II, offers students strategies that will serve them in developing the types of written communication and thought essential to academic, working world, and personal success. The book focuses on writing as process and is intended to help students identify and refine their own personal writing processes. The chapters are divided into three parts: a composition section based on writing projects, a stylistic section for writing improvement, and a portfolio section to support ongoing learning.

The book is based on a number of premises. First, every student can write. In my 40-plus years as a writing facilitator, I have found that every student has a story to tell and uniqueness to share. Initially, many students may not see themselves as writers, but after discovering their ability and potential, they find that they, too, can write clearly and effectively.

Second, chapters end with a focus on developing an on-going, learning Portfolio in Progress (formative assessment), which leads to a Demonstration Portfolio (summative assessment) submitted near the end of the courses. The portfolio component offers students the opportunity to extend the writing process by putting their pieces of writing aside for a time and returning to them with "fresh eyes" as they revisit and revise essays throughout the course. Students then select pieces of writing for their Demonstration Portfolios and organize them to show their growth. In addition, students continually self-analyze their writing and progress through self-reflective opportunities and conclude with a metacognitive self-evaluation of their performance in the courses.

Third, the book is based on the teaching theory of "diagnosis and prescription." Instructors continually diagnose student writing and prescribe areas in the writing that need attention or improvement. Instructors can then facilitate learning by referring individual writers to sections of the book that might help the writer improve or by using sections of the book to teach "mini-lessons" on specific skills to the entire class or smaller groups of the class. The skills presented in each chapter are not intended to be used in any specific order, but rather implemented based on the needs of the student writers.

Fourth, the book uses student samples as models rather than professional writers' essays for three reasons. One, student writings aim at the goals of the writing projects in this book. In contrast, professional examples would require fitting the prompts to the professionals' writings. Two, student examples give student writers confidence that they can accomplish the goals of the writing projects rather than feel intimidated that they could never write like professionals anyway. Three, rather than imitating a professional writer's voice and style, student writers are encouraged to develop their own personal voices and write from their hearts.

Anna, the main character in the musical *The King and I*, sings "Getting to Know You," which begins, "It's a very ancient saying but a true and honest thought, that if you become a teacher, by the students you'll be taught." Over my 40-plus years in the writing classroom, I have learned often and much from my students. Through their writings, my students have taken me on countless journeys to places around the world. They have shared stories about themselves. Some have doubled me over in laughter, and others have bent me over in tears. Students have expanded my horizons by sharing their hobbies, talents, and treasures. And students have convinced me to broaden my thinking about real and important life issues. But most of all, writing students have taught me that they all can write, and when they search their hearts, they all find valuable ideas to share.

Acknowledgements

I cannot say thank you enough to those who have helped me bring this dream of a book to reality. I especially thank my Northeast Iowa Community College colleagues—Corlas Bildstein, David Daack, Becky Kamm, Larry Kruse, Marzieh Shahrivar, Linda Ressler, Else Schardt, Peter Schenck, Patricia Seelye, and Chris Timmerman—for reviewing the early drafts and offering invaluable response and help.

Thanks to the former students who have willingly given me permission to include their writings in this volume.

Finally, I express my sincere appreciation to Professor Katherine Fischer, Professor Angela Gulick, Dr. Kevin Koch, and Dr. Rodney Smith, master teachers who have inspired me and endorsed this text.

You've Gotta Have HEART— In Your Writing

Table of Contents

About the Author...i

Preface.. iii

Acknowledgements...v

CHAPTER 1: First You've Gotta Have Heart 1

Why Write?...3
Journal...5
Extended Writing Process...6
Writing Portfolio...16
Portfolio Checklist...19

CHAPTER 2: Use Your Uncommon Senses......................................23

Writing Project 2-1: Your Significant Place...24
Sample Student Essay — *My Second Home* by Tara Pohlman 25
Sense Imagery..28
Figurative Language 29
Essay Structure: Titles, Openings, Middles, Closings 32
Be Specific!..42
Expanded Writing Process—Sharing Stage: Peer Response 45
Self-Reflection Questions 46
Sample Entry Slip—*Forever Young* by Keri West.............................47

CHAPTER 3: "That's the glory of, that's the STORY of…" 49

Writing Project 3-1: Your Significant Event 50
Sample Student Essay—*Brace Face* by Andrea Kedley 51
The Mechanics of Writing Dialogue..54
Developing a Strong Style Through Action Verbs...............................58
Conciseness/Cut the Deadwood...63
Unnecessary Shifts in Tense, Voice, Person..68
Portfolio Introductions: Luetta Bockenstedt
Kara Pickel Schroeder, Amanda Mathe, Regina Shafer 71

CHAPTER 4: Hey, Expert, Explain Yourself! 75

Writing Project 4-1: You're the Expert 76
Sample Student Essay—*A Hard Act to Follow* by Jennifer Basten.......76
Writing Project 4-2: Study Advice..79
Writing Project 4-3: Ritual or Ceremony..80
Writing Project 4-4: Marvel at Yourself..80
Hot Tips for Writing Sentences...80
Fractured Fragments 81
Ruptured Run-Ons 83
Parallelism 86
Mangled Meaning: Misplaced, Dangling, Squinting Modifiers 89
Demonstration Portfolio 91
Sample Student Writing—*Portfolio Metacognitive Essay*....................92

CHAPTER 5: Be Convincing 95

Writing Project 5-1: Letter for Change 96
Sample Student Essay—*The Destructive Invasion*
    by Elias Langois...97
Writing Project 5-2: Letter to the Editor 100
Sample Student Essay—Letter to the Editor of *Glamour* Magazine....100
Writing Project 5-3: Letter to Legislator...103
Writing Project 5-4: Problem-Solution 103
Writing Project 5-5: War 103
Using Modifiers Correctly 104
Case Out the Pronouns...108
Portfolio in Progress 113

CHAPTER 6: "Comparatively-Contrasting" 117

Writing Project 6-1: Compare/Contrast. 119
Sample Student Essay—*Four-year or Two-year Nursing
    Degree: Two-year Works for Me* by Jane Reymer 120
Writing Project 6-2: College vs. High School.....................................123
Writing Project 6-3: School Days 123
Writing Project 6-4: You've Changed? 124
Writing Thesis Statements 124
Voice: Active and Passive 127
Portfolio in Progress 130
Sample Student Writing—Entry Slip: *The Customer is
    Always Right* by Kristen Runde 130

CHAPTER 7: Cement an Abstract Term in Concrete 133

Writing Project 7-1: Make an Abstract Concrete 134
Sample Student Essay—*The Fruit of Friendship*
by Elliott Zelinskas 135
Writing Project 7-2: Connotation 137
Writing Project 7-3: Fool 138
Writing Project 7-4: Pride 138
Writing Project 7-5: Hero/Heroine 138
May We Come to Agreement? 139
Subject-Verb Agreement 139
Pronoun-Antecedent Agreement 143
Portfolio in Progress 146

CHAPTER 8: Let's Get Critical, Critical 149

Writing Project 8-1: Critical Writing 151
Sample Student Writing—*Definition of Love* by Brenda Jasper 152
Sample Student Writing—*Critical Writing Response to*
Definition of Love by Jamie Byremis 153
Writing a Critical Essay About Literature 158
Writing Project 8-2: Critical Writing—Literary Analysis 161
Sample Student Writing—*Flaubert's Treatment of Women*
in Madame Bovary by Rebecca Stroschein 161
Word Usage 166
Portfolio in Progress 171

CHAPTER 9: More Student Writings 173

Significant Place—*The Mississippi's View of Life* by Stacia Riccio 173
Significant Event—*Send to Me My Spring* by Angela Frohling 177
You're the Expert—*Bringing Pictures to Life* by Missy Richard 182
Letter for Change—*Not Nagging, Just Advising*
by Luke Wiederholt 185
Letter to the Editor—*Money Doesn't Grow on Trees*
by Nikolai Doffing 187
Comparison-Contrast—*My Heroic Nuisance* by Kelsey Kieler 191
Definition of Abstract Term—*Freedom: Never to be*
Taken for Granted by Carissa Oberbroeckling 194
Research Essay—MLA Format: *Defining and Treating ADD*
by Rachel Hellewell 198

CHAPTER 10: Research Writing 213

Writing Project 10-1: Research Writing...............................214
Setting a Timetable 214
Selecting a Topic...215
Locating Sources...216
Citation Styles...218
Working Bibliography 220
Taking Notes 221
Writing Project 10-1A: First Draft Without Sources...222

CHAPTER 11: Writing the Draft—With Sources – MLA...............................225

Sample Student Essay—*Stop the Madness* by Deanne Wuflekuhle 240

CHAPTER 12: Writing the Draft—With Sources – APA...............................247

Sample Student Research Paper—APA Format
The Slippery Climb by Carol Wissing...260

CHAPTER 13: Good MECHANICS
Keep Writing Motors Running Smoothly 267

Comma Placement 267
Apostrophe...276
Semicolons...279
Colons 279
Dashes...280
Parentheses...280
Italics...281
End Punctuation...281
Quotation Marks 281
Capitalization 282
Spelling 283
Glossary of Editing FUNdamentals...283

Works Cited...289

Index 293

CHAPTER 1

First You've Gotta Have Heart

The Devil in the Broadway musical *Damn Yankees* must know a lot about writing because the best writing comes from an author's heart. Many consider writing an art that touches only certain "gifted geniuses," like William Shakespeare or Mark Twain or Annie Dillard or Stephen King or JK Rowling. So, too, many students and writers feel that the rest of us "regular folks" were never touched at birth by the Muse's magic; therefore, we will never be able to write well. True, few will reach the artistic level or success of a Twain or Rowling, but everyone is blessed with the skill to write well enough to find personal, academic, and professional writing success. And the key to that writing success is "you've gotta have heart" in your writing. More than just correct rhetorical and grammatical skills, you must write honestly, sincerely, passionately from "your heart." Author Marjorie Holmes states, "When you write from the heart, you not only light the dark path of your readers, you light your own way as well" (*Chicken Soup* 163).

This skill or craft of writing can be developed with practice, and like any other skill, the more you write and practice, the better you become as a writer. Writing, as a skill or craft, resembles practicing the piano or shooting baskets or practicing ballet or hitting a golf ball. The more you practice writing, the better you become, and the better you become, the more confidence you gain as a writer.

Now this does not imply that improving as a writer comes easily. Any writer of any significance will tell you that writing demands time and effort. Author Sinclair Lewis states, "Writing is just work—there is no secret. If you dictate or use a pen or type with your toes, it is still work" (Murray, *Shoptalk* 57). So be prepared to work hard, to write, rewrite, and revise a lot. But this personal and academic challenge will lead you to writing competence and confidence. And maybe you will even realize the meaning of Thomas Paine's words: "the greater the challenge, the greater the triumph." Remember, triumph means the "umph" added to TRY! Yes, you can write. Let your ideas, feelings, and opinions come from your heart.

~ ~ ~

"If you don't want to work your ass off, you have no business trying to be a writer" (144).
—Stephen King

~ ~ ~

Many students enter college writing courses fearful of their writing abilities, but, in reality, every student can write and has valuable ideas, feelings, and opinions to share in writing. Students are born with the potential to use writing as a clear means of communication and to improve as writers. But so often students enter composition classes convinced from previous experiences or unrealistic thinking that they are not capable of writing. Students enter writing classes at various degrees of writing competence. Some enter college as competent, confident writers; others need longer to develop their writing competency and confidence. But every student can improve as a writer, no matter the level of competence he or she brings to a writing course. So as the old saying goes, "If you're good, get better. If you're better, become the best you can be" as a writer.

In *National Geographic*, Joel L. Swedlow writes, "Writing is humankind's most far reaching creation, its forms and designs endless. Yet the purpose of writing remains unchanged: to convey meaning, whether playful, mundane, or profound" (110). Hopefully, you will search the far-reaches of your heart, soul, and mind to let ideas, feelings, and opinions drawn from your experiences come through your personal writing voice into your writing. Through this personal search into yourself, hopefully you'll discover things about yourself, your life, and your writing that you may never have realized or considered before. And possibly you'll find this search to be an engaging, enlightening, and enjoyable experience.

~ ~ ~

"Clear writing is the sign of a clear mind, and those who capture their ideas on paper stand out as fluent, confident and persuasive" (1).
—Andersen & Hinnis

~ ~ ~

WHY WRITE?

• Thinking. Writing offers many advantages to those willing to pursue this craft. First, writing develops thinking skills. The more you develop as a writer, the more you will also develop as a thinker. Writing and thinking go hand in hand. In their book *Promoting Active Learning*, Chet Meyers and Thomas Jones write, "Part of our task as teachers is to help students learn to write so that they will become better thinkers. Nothing replaces writing as a unique mode of learning" (26-27).

In the same vein, reading greatly enhances writing and thinking skills. The more you read, the more it can influence your writing and writing improvement. In his book *On Writing*, famous novelist Stephen King states, "If you don't have time to read, you don't have the time (or the tools) to write. Simple as that. Reading is the creative center of a writer's life" (147). So along with your writing skills, work toward developing your reading skills. Writing and reading are joined at the hip. Both help us become better writers and thinkers.

• Power. Writing certainly serves as a powerful means of communication, which can either heal or hurt. Many people build others up by sending personal or congratulatory notes or even love letters. On the other hand, writing, some of which is sent anonymously, can be used for complaints or dissatisfaction. News writing, for example, can powerfully enhance a person's reputation with positive reporting of achievements or destroy a person's reputation with defaming news.

• Writing to Learn. Writing has become a strong and effective learning/teaching strategy for many instructors in all disciplines. Most college campuses have implemented or are implementing Writing Across the Curriculum and Writing to Learn strategies to enhance learning. More often than ever before, instructors in science, math, and technology, for example, use writing as a teaching tool to help students comprehend facts, retain information, and apply concepts as they learn. Writer-teacher Judith Langer suggests, "The more students write about content, the better it will be remembered. There is comparatively little recall of content that has not been written about. Writing focuses student attention on less information, but deeper and more varied thinking is invoked, and the material is remembered longer" (54 in Davis). You are likely to experience more essay exams, writing assignments, and writing journals than college students of fifteen or twenty years ago. Improving your writing skills, then, can help you learn better in all disciplines and help you reach your academic goals as a college student.

• Job Market. Writing applies to the working world. Most jobs require some level of writing skill in correspondence using paper or computer or e-mail. Furthermore, writing, via letter or application and resume, usually serves as the initial introduction of a prospective employee to the employer. Employers and personnel directors make evaluations of capability and sometimes intelligence based on the writing quality of job applications. So clear, effective writing can enhance your chances for job interviews. During the interview, you will obviously need to call on your own verbal and inter-personal skills to make a positive impression. However, anticipating and writing out answers to frequently asked questions can help you prepare for an interview and build up your confidence.

• Make Sense of Life. Writing helps people deal with life. Many counselors, psychoanalysts, and psychiatrists now use writing to help their clients deal with issues they are struggling with. Counselors ask clients to write about past or present experiences and feelings in order to clarify and deal with these issues in their lives. "Recent studies have documented that writing about feelings can alleviate depression, boost the immune system, and lower blood pressure" (122), writes Joel L. Swerdlow in his article "The Power of Writing." Many times when people use writing as a stress release or a means to unload some emotional "baggage," they are better able to cope with life's hurdles and move on in a more positive, productive way. A growing number of people, maybe you, are using journals to record life experiences and to help clarify their feelings and thinking about personal issues.

• Enjoyment. Writing can be fun and rewarding! Some writers enjoy expressing their creativity through poetry, fictional or non-fictional writing, or humorous writing. Many of these same writers have earned a healthy living using their talents. Some students have also used their writing skills in various writing competitions for publications, prizes, or scholarships, which might bring financial as well as personal rewards.

You can undoubtedly add to this list of ideas on the importance of writing.

JOURNAL

Keeping a journal helps writers grow. Some instructors require a journal as part of their course requirements. Even if your instructor does not require it, you can help yourself as a writer by keeping your own journal. The journal offers writers a private place to record their thoughts and feelings without worrying about correctness or a grade. Because the journal is not intended for an outside audience, writers feel free to write in their own personal voice, a key factor in a writer's development. And because writers feel free to write without worry about correctness, they naturally seem to develop more fluency in their writing style.

The journal offers writers a private place to write about things they are interested in and care about. The journal also gives you a place to store ideas, observations, and insights. You might also save words, phrases, ideas, lines from poems or songs, unpolished thoughts, passages from your reading, titles, topics—anything that may be used in your writing at a later time. Furthermore, student writers may use journal writing to create topics; to refine, expand, or change topics; to experiment with different writing strategies and styles; and generally to improve themselves as writers. Journaling gives you the freedom to think, dream, hypothesize, doubt, question, create, and write freely.

Try to journal consistently, if not daily, at least several times each week. Don't worry about correctness. Grammar and usage do not count in your journal. Write as freely and uninhibitedly as possible. Let your ideas flow. Periodically reread your journal entries to see if any feelings, thoughts, or ideas might be developed into topics for future writing.

~ ~ ~

"The journal becomes an invitation to open up, to explore, to dip into that stream of language. Good journal writing is fishing in the river of your mind" (46).
—Dan Kirby

~ ~ ~

EXTENDED WRITING PROCESS

During the last quarter of the twentieth century to the present time, writers, teachers, and researchers have studied and emphasized the notion of writing as a process rather than simply as an end product. By examining the writing process as a series of recursive stages, writing experts have been able to help students improve as writers. In thinking of writing as a process, writers should recognize that the process will vary for each writer depending on his or her personality, previous experiences, and habits. For example, some writers prefer a quiet, secluded place to write while others may like soft, background music. Some use pen or pencil for early stages and drafts while others prefer word processing from the outset. No one way to use the process or develop a piece of writing works for everyone. Each writer needs to reflect on and use what works best for his or her needs.

Generally, the writing process can be identified as a series of stages. Note the word "stages" rather than steps because the writing process occurs in a recursive fashion vs. a linear, step-by-step procedure. Sometimes, writers may circle back more than once to an earlier stage to develop a piece of writing. Furthermore, a writer's process may vary depending on the task at hand. For example, writing for a composition class may require use of a full process over an extended period of time while writing an essay exam under time constraints may demand a modified writing process.

One advantage of using a process approach to writing is that writers need not overload their brains by trying to create, clarify, and correct the writing all at the same time as in a "one shot" product focus. The writer can focus on generating and planning ideas in the early stages, drafting and revising in the middle stages, and editing and proofreading in the later stages. This approach seems to reduce the pressure and stress on writers who overload their brains by doing too many writing tasks at once.

We will look at the writing process as a series of three stages: developing, sharing, and polishing—with many sub-stages within those three main stages. The developing stage consists of brainstorming/planning, pre-writing, drafting, revising, and editing. The sharing stage involves peer response, revision, writing center response, instructor response, and peer proofreading. The polishing stage involves final proofreading, along with self-reflections and metacognition (awareness of our thinking process) for the Demonstration Portfolio.

Brainstorming/Planning

Writers begin the brainstorming stage the second they begin to think about the assignment or topic or their purpose in writing. Many times assignments are given in classes, and students' brains immediately begin a mental search for topics and ideas before they write anything on paper or type anything on a screen. This unlocking of the brain is natural and fruitful. You may think of writing ideas as you drive to or from home or school or work. You may even think of writing ideas in your sleep. Or you may talk about your topic and ideas with family, friends, or classmates and even choose to record your conversation. Importantly, however, you must capture your creative thoughts so these ideas can't escape. This leads to the next sub-stage.

As you determine your writing needs, you formulate a working plan to identify the specific topic, purpose, and audience for your writing. You may choose your own topic in some instances while in other instances, the topic may be assigned. You also need to identify your audience. Who will read your writing? How much do they already know or believe about your topic? Many times your style and content will vary depending on your audience. For example, if your roommate went to Cancun for spring break and left you her Porsche to drive and you got into a fender bender, you would write letters in a different style and tone to your friend, her parents, your parents, your insurance agent, and the police investigator. Your purpose will determine your goal, slant, or position on the topic you choose. Maybe you need to explain, share a story, or persuade your audience to sympathize with you about your recent fender bender.

Pre-writing

Once you have developed a working plan, you prepare for the writing by capturing ideas on paper and by generating more ideas using pre-writing strategies, such as slash outline, cluster, fishbone, free write, or formal outline. Getting started may present problems for some writers, and the more they think about the topic or assignment, the more pressure they feel. Pre-writing helps writers get started on paper. Pre-writing might be compared to loosening up your brain muscles so you can think freely about ideas and ways to gather them. The pre-writing strategy you choose will depend on your topic and your preference as the writer. No one strategy works best for all writers. The key is to unlock your brain, to generate as many ideas as possible about your topic, and to capture those ideas. Once you begin to write a draft, you may choose to use most of the ideas you generate or choose to dispose of some that don't seem to fit. In addition, you may add or delete ideas once you begin the drafting itself.

Slash Outline

Autobiography

In using a slash outline, you simply list every idea that comes into your brain about your topic. By writing ideas on paper, you may generate as many ideas as possible and gain control of your topic so that you don't later forget good ideas you initially generated.

birth

family

school

jobs

marriage

hobbies

future

plans

Cluster (Web or Mind-map)

The cluster, also called web or mind-map, allows writers to generate ideas that expand like a growing bush. Place your topic in the middle of your page and write every idea that your brain generates as off-shoots of the topic. This strategy also allows your brain to begin to organize ideas into sections or clusters. As writers see where their brain takes them in generating ideas, they are subconsciously stimulated to expand on ideas that fit into each section or cluster.

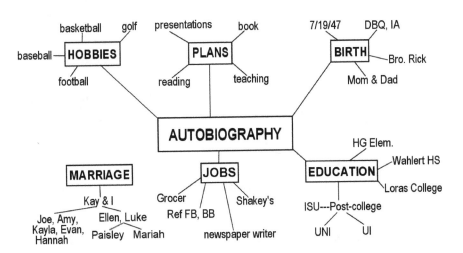

Fishbone

The fishbone resembles the cluster, but takes a lateral format. Place your topic on the left side of your paper. Then on a lateral line, write every idea that your brain generates about your topic.

		college	teaching	walk
	place	high school	college	golf
	date	elementary	teen	read
BIRTH	**EDUCATION**	**JOBS**	**HOBBIES**

AUTOBIOGRAPHY

FAMILY	**MARRIAGE**		**PLANS**
parents	Kay & I		teaching
sibling	Joe, Amy, Kayla, Evan, Hannah	book
Bro. Rick	Ellen, Luke, Mariah, Paisley	presentations

Free Write

Free writing might be used in a couple of ways—time or length. If you choose the time option, put a segment of time on the clock, twelve minutes, for example. Then write non-stop for that amount of time. Get on paper every idea that your brain generates, even if ideas don't seem to fit your topic. Your brain may naturally wander to other things in a stream-of-consciousness manner, but try to get all ideas down; then sort them out later. Don't worry about correctness or sentence structure. Free write to unlock your brain, to generate ideas. One problem that sometimes occurs with free writing is keeping up with your brain as it generates ideas so quickly.

The second free writing option, length, closely resembles the time method. You choose a certain length, one or two sides of a paper, that you will fill by writing non-stop every idea that your brain generates, whether applicable to your topic or not. Later you can pick and choose which ideas to keep and which to eliminate.

12 Minute Free Writing

I need to fish for ideas for my autobiography. Start at birth. Born on July 19, 1947 in DBQ, IA to Leon Brimeyer of North started at Dyersville Beckman in 1969. Then spent 25 years at Wahlert HS. Then came Buenie and Grace Link of Balltown. Poor as a kid. Dad never made $20 thousand in his life. Mom and Dad deceased. Grew up no spent first 6 years in Buenie. Moved to DBQ at age 7. Stuck! Stuck! Stuck! Stuck! Now attended Holy Ghost, Wahlert, and Loras. Got MA in 76 and attended Iowa, Iowa State, UNI, Carleton for further studies. Love Iowa Writing Project. Stuck! Stuck! Married to Kay with son Joe in Seattle and daughter Ellen in Cedar Falls with our granddaughter Mariah. Pause. Love teaching I to NICC since then. Now what? I love to read—mostly educational books, lots of Shakespeare. I enjoy walks—four miles a day. I enjoy golf—when I play well!! I love music, especially playing piano. I have 4 minutes to go. In school,—grade school—I had a early morning paper route. In HS—I delivered groceries for a corner market. In college I played piano at Shakey's ₵ for our church and for weddings. I also wrote sports department for the Telegraph herald and the Witness. I also reffed high school and college football and basketball. I enjoy teaching and love the community college variety of students and ages. I love to read such interesting and exciting topics in their essays. I learn more from students than I teach, I suspect. Time up. I'm whipped.

Formal Outline

Some writers choose the formal outline because they have worked with it in their earlier school experiences. By using Roman numerals, letters, and numbers, writers generate ideas while beginning to organize these ideas at the same time. This pre-writing strategy works for some. However, many writers find that its formal structure doesn't allow the flexibility and freedom of other pre-writing strategies. But if a formal outline works for you, use it.

Autobiography

I. Birth
    A. Mercy Hospital
    B. July 19, 1947
    C. Family
        1. Leon Brimeyer
        2. Grace Link
        3. Brother—Rick

II. Education
    A. Elementary—Buenie & Holy Ghost
    B. Wahlert
    C. College—Loras
    D. Post-college—Loras, Iowa, Iowa State, UNI, Carleton

III. Employment
    A. Teen—newspaper carrier
    B. Grocery delivery
    C. College—music-Shakey's
    D. TH sports writer, Ref FB &BB

IV. Marriage
    A. Kay
    B. Kids—Joe and & Ellen
    C. Grandchildren

V. Hobbies
    A. Reading
    B. Golf
    C. Walking

VI. Plans
    A. Enjoy teaching & life
    B. Book

Writers have used other pre-writing strategies than these. From your previous writing experiences, you may have developed a different pre-writing strategy which helps you unlock your brain. Don't re-invent the wheel. Use what works for you and gives you confidence. As you become more experienced as a writer, you may want to experiment with other pre-writing strategies to see which one will work best for you in different writing situations. Also, note that you are not restricted to using just one pre-writing strategy. Maybe more than one will help generate even more ideas.

Drafting/Writing

Once you feel you have given enough time to generating ideas through pre-writing, you will need to move to the keyboard or take up your pen to begin drafting. You will use ideas you generated with your pre-writing strategies to help you compose. As you write, you may add ideas as they come to you. Most importantly in this drafting stage of the process, write freely from your heart. Let your words and ideas flow freely onto the paper. Write freely and naturally. You are using this drafting stage to begin to formulate your piece of writing, not to finalize it. So let it happen. Don't worry about organization, sentence structure, word choice, usage, spelling, or punctuation. Get your ideas onto the page. Many times writer's block occurs because writers try too hard to get it correct the first time. They worry more about correcting their writing than creating their writing and unconsciously block the flow of ideas. So let the ideas flow from your heart. You can attend to correctness in the editing stage. Also, don't worry about that splendid title and/or introduction to grab your readers' attention and keep them engaged. You can return to those parts of the essay later after you see where your writing takes you. Remember the key: **you've gotta have heart!**

~ ~ ~

"Writing and rewriting are a constant search
for what one is saying" (Murray, *Shoptalk* 114).
—John Updike

~ ~ ~

Revising/Rewriting

After you have written your draft, you are ready to move to the next developing stage, revision. As the word RE-VISION suggests, with your readers in mind, you will take another look at your writing, another "vision," to see how you might develop and improve the piece. During this revision stage, the focus remains on ideas, content, organization, tone, and vocabulary which can enhance your topic. During the revision stage, you might add or delete ideas, rearrange them, provide more details or examples; do anything that might clarify and strengthen your piece. According to noted American writer Bernard Malamud, "Rewriting is often the best part of writing. Writing is never completed; it's abandoned. One must always learn in rewriting to shape the work as if one were squeezing the best out of it. Rewriting is a form of having a second chance to distill something or to think over something, and there are some writers who find that their most imaginative ideas come to them as afterthoughts" (qtd. in Cheuse and Debanco xxi). At this point in the process, do not worry about editing correctness. That step will come. Revise to focus on the clear meaning and organization of your text. And remember: **you've gotta have heart in your writing!**

~ ~ ~

"Most people hate reworking their writing.
It is human nature. The pressure and agony of
writing is one reason why alcohol has been humorously
dubbed 'the occupational hazard of professional writers.'
It is not the writing per se, but the rewriting and redrafting
process that can drive a person to drink. Worse is the
reality of knowing that even before you begin to write—no matter how well
you write—your writing will require revision" (195).
—Elizabeth Danziger

~ ~ ~

Editing

At some point, you will need to focus on correctness to assist your audience in reading clearly and easily. In this stage, you will check not only the clarity of your ideas but also your sentence development, word choice, grammatical usage, spelling, and punctuation. You might wish to use a few techniques which work well during the editing stage.

First, get an editor. Find a friend, roommate, fellow student, family member; use anyone whom you trust to help you improve your piece of writing. Then be open to suggestions and changes. Many times instructors build response groups into their class schedules for writers to receive feedback from their peers during a workshop format. You might also schedule time to take your piece of writing to the college Writing Center, a valuable asset to any college campus, to receive reaction from individuals trained in one-on-one writing response techniques. The more responses and reactions you get from others, the better you will sense what works and does not work in your writing. Then you can make necessary revisions and corrections.

Second, read your piece aloud. This allows you to "plug in" two extra senses—speaking and hearing—to help clarify and clean your writing. Many times you will feel, see, sense, and catch areas of your writing that don't sound right or don't feel right or don't look right. Then you can make necessary changes. You might also consider reading your piece of writing into an audio tape-recorder and playing it back. Many times you will hear what sounds out of place or choppy or incorrect. Then you can adjust or fix those areas.

Third, read your piece of writing in reverse. Start with the last sentence of the piece and work your way backward to the beginning. This helps you isolate each individual sentence, and you can correct it separately for meaning, plus usage, spelling, punctuation, and the like. When you read from the beginning to the conclusion in natural order, your brain tends to focus on ideas because it naturally knows what you have written and jumps ahead looking for those ideas. You then may miss the cosmetic features of your writing that make it correct and easy to read.

Finally, always take advantage of technology, which offers spell-check programs and grammar checkers built into computer programs. However, remember that the spell checker will not catch every misspelled word. It will not distinguish homonyms and recognize the difference between its-it's, your-you're, there-their-they're, to-two-too, etc. And your grammar checker may locate but not distinguish between correct word usage, for example good vs. well or pronoun cases.

Throughout your process, keep in mind the advice of writer and teacher Joseph Williams, who says, "We write and revise our earliest drafts to discover and express what we mean, but in drafts thereafter, we write and revise to make it clear to our readers. At the heart of the process is the principle whose model you probably recall: Write for others as you would have others write for you" (220).

~ ~ ~

"...Biting my truant pen, beating myself for spite:
Fool! Said my Muse to me, look in thy heart and write."
—Sir Phillip Sidney, Astrophel and Stella

~ ~ ~

YOU'VE GOTTA HAVE HEART

The most important aspect of writing is choosing a subject to write on that you truly care about. This will help bring enthusiasm, passion, and personal voice to the forefront and will make your writing more interesting to read. Famous author Kurt Vonnegut writes, "Find a subject you care about and which in your heart you feel others should care about. It is the genuine caring, and not your games with language, which will be the most compelling and seductive element in your style" (*Chicken Soup* 123).

~ ~ ~

"Have you ever gotten the impression that writing well
in college means setting aside the kind of language you
use in everyday conversation? That to impress your
instructors you need to use big words, long sentences,
and complex sentence structures? If so, then we're here
to tell you that it ain't necessarily so. On the contrary,
academic writing can—and in our view should—be relaxed,
easy to follow, and even a little bit fun... Relaxed, colloquial
language can often enliven academic writing and even
enhance its rigor and precision" (115-116).
--Gerald Graff and Kathy Birkenstein

~ ~ ~

STRUT YOUR STUFF!

Your instructor may assign a piece of writing to get to know you and your writing from the choices that follow or provide another topic or let you choose your own topic. Plus, the instructor will probably specify the length. Use all sub-stages of the Developing Stage of your writing process—brainstorming/planning, pre-writing, drafting, revising, editing—to develop your piece of writing. Save all stages of writing on your computer because you will be using multiple stages of responding and revising throughout this course and book to develop your portfolio, your demonstration of writing progress. Above all, remember: **you've gotta have heart in your writing.**

Writing Topics:

1-1 Autobiography. Compose your life story. Share important and meaningful aspects and times of your life, such as family, schooling, employment, hobbies and interests, significant accomplishments, and more. As you provide information, try to be as specific as possible. Give details to help your reader visualize you as a person.

1-2 Greatest Accomplishment. Explain your greatest accomplishment in your life to date, and explain why you consider this your greatest accomplishment. Do not be shy. If you need to boast, please do so. Remember: "if it's the truth, it ain't braggin'."

1-3 Student Portrait. Describe yourself as a student. How do you learn best—through lectures, small groups, individual study, hands-on projects? Provide examples from your previous educational experiences that exemplify your qualities as a student. Relate any ideas that will help your readers see you as a student.

1-4 Writer's Profile. Focus on your past experiences as a writer. Explain your attitudes toward writing, and share your feelings about being in this writing course. As you provide information, be as specific as possible. Give details and examples to help your readers visualize you as a writer.

1-5 Time Travel. You can travel back in time and change any event. Identify the event you would change, the ways you would change it, and the reasons you would change it.

1-6 Wish Granted. You find a magic lamp, and the genie grants you a wish. Explain the best and the worst things that could happen.

WRITING PORTFOLIO

~ ~ ~

"Portfolios mean more than evaluation or assessment.
They are tied to our definition of literacy. When we
read and write constantly, when we reflect on who we
are and who we want to be, we cannot help but grow" (xii).
—Bonnie Sunstein (*Portfolio Portraits*)

~ ~ ~

A portfolio presents a purposeful collection of your student work in English Composition I and/or II and demonstrates your efforts, progress, and achievements throughout the course(s). The portfolio should also show your ability to analyze, synthesize, and evaluate your writing and others' writings. Hopefully, this project will empower you as a student because you will select specific pieces to include and to be evaluated in your portfolio. You will also organize the portfolio to reflect yourself as a student and person. Furthermore, this portfolio project will also help you become a more self-directed learner as you assess and self-reflect on your own work and determine ways in which you can improve your writing and your approach to future academic and working-world challenges. Your portfolio will enhance your learning and "accommodate a wide variety of learning styles. A portfolio is not merely a collection device; it is a learning tool because it requires that students actively reflect on and judge their own work" (Schmit & Appleman in Sunstein, *The Portfolio Standard*, 188).

Throughout these courses and book, you will be working on your Portfolio in Progress, which will lead to your final Demonstration Portfolio. The Portfolio in Progress, sometimes referred to as a Working Portfolio, involves your ongoing learning while using the writing process and revisions, plus your on-going self-reflections on your writing progress and learning. Your Portfolio in Progress will become your storehouse of writings and reflections from which you will choose those you put into your Demonstration Portfolio.

The Demonstration Portfolio, submitted near the end of the writing course, will allow you to demonstrate your overall progress, growth, and learning, rather than using each writing project as its own separate and finished product. The Portfolio extends the writing process by encouraging continuous revision and improvement of your writings throughout the course. Since a piece of writing can always be revised, you may return to any essay for revision as you learn new strategies and improve your writing skills. Rather than isolated assignments and a stop-and-go approach, the portfolio offers a full recursive writing process, which allows you to return to and revise earlier pieces of writing and to demonstrate your writing and learning growth over the course of the semester.

~ ~ ~

*"One goal for portfolios in writing classrooms is
that students continue to work on pieces of writing as
their capacity to explore subjects insightfully becomes
more sophisticated over the course of a term"* (84).
—Marilyn Barry (qtd. in *Sunstein*)

~ ~ ~

Your English Composition I or II Portfolio should include the following parts:

- **Student Introduction**

    Write an introduction to your portfolio that introduces its contents and establishes an organizational sustained metaphor/theme that unifies your portfolio. This theme or sustained metaphor should be reinforced in your Table of Contents and Entry Slips. No entry slip required. (See the final pages of Chapter Three.)

- **Table of Contents**

    Provide an <u>annotated</u> (short explanation or commentary) list of all entries in your portfolio along with page numbers. (See the end of Chapter Five for an example.)

- **Entry Slips—Reflections on Writing**

    For each item (excluding Introduction and Metacognitive Essay), include a minimum one-page, three paragraph, word-processed, and double-spaced entry slip, which provides a reflection (analysis) of the piece of writing and the process you used to develop it. Focus entry slips on higher order concerns of your writing process. Tie the title or opening paragraph to your portfolio's sustained metaphor/theme. (See the "Portfolio in Progress" section at the end of Chapter Two for specific ideas on developing self-reflective entry slips. Also, see a sample entry slip at the end of Chapters Two and Six.)

- **Writing Process Entry–Required—English Composition I & II**

    Include your choice of one major project plus its entire process for evaluation. This includes pre-write, drafts, revisions, final product; along with all peer responses and/or instructor responses. **Entry Slip Required.**

- **Research Essay Process–Required—English Composition II**

    Include your revision plus your instructor's initial response copy and the evaluation scale. **Entry Slip Required.**

- **Remaining Major Projects—Required—English Composition I & II**

Include your other revised major projects. (Your instructor may ask for track changes and a previous version, as well). **Entry Slip Required.**

- **First Writing—Diagnostic—Required—English Composition I & II**

  Include the instructor evaluated draft, along with your revision, track changes, and Entry Slip. **In this minimum three-paragraph entry slip, reflect on the change (improvement) in your writing since this first piece written at the beginning of the course. Consider such issues as use of process, stylistic awareness, and editing improvement.**

- **Optional Inclusions (0-4):**

  Include any of your other writings written this semester. These might include personal essays, a writing assignment from another class in which you demonstrate writing strategies you've developed in either English Composition I or II, a piece of your newly created poetry (one page minimum), a piece of your creative writing (seven paragraph minimum). **Entry Slip Required for each Optional Inclusion.**

- **Metacognitive Essay**

  Assess your performance in this course. Don't evaluate the course, but rather assess how you performed. Reflect on your growth as a writer, learner, and thinker during this course. Although you may need to mention some weakness or strength of the course, focus on how you reacted to that weakness or strength. What do you know now that you didn't know before? What can you do now that you couldn't do before? If you've made gains, list the kinds – gains in writing skill, confidence, study habits, organizational skills... Or if you've gained little, list the reasons why – lack of time, lack of interest, getting off to a bad start... No entry slip required. (See a sample metacognitive essay at the end of Chapter Four.)

PORTFOLIO CHECKLIST

Use the following checklists as you prepare your Demonstration Portfolio.

ENG 105: Composition I

☐ Introduction: establishes a sustained metaphor/theme that introduces and unifies the entries of the portfolio—five paragraph minimum.

☐ Table of Contents: page numbers and an <u>annotated</u> explanation of the contents of each portfolio entry.

☐ Entry Slips: writer's reflection on each entry. Focus on HOC issues (LOC focus for diagnostic essay only). Tie title or opening paragraph to the portfolio introduction—one page/three paragraph minimum.

☐ Portfolio-evaluated Essays: 3-1 Event and 5-1 Persuasive Letter—track changes and new copy required.

☐ Revised essays previously evaluated: 2-1 Place and 4-1 Expert—track changes and new copy required.

☐ Revised Diagnostic Essay: previously evaluated copy, track changes, and new copy required.

☐ Optional Personal Inclusions: four maximum—written this semester (prose—seven paragraph minimum; poetry—one page minimum) entry slips and track changes required for each.

☐ Full Process—Author's Choice of 3-1 or 5-1. This ONE entry includes pre-writes, drafts, revisions, peer responses, track changes, first evaluated copy (if applicable), with clean copy on top for evaluation. Note: full process is also required for any essays when peer response was missed.

☐ Metacognitive Conclusion: Evaluate your performance—seven paragraph minimum.

ENG 106: Composition II

☐ Introduction: establishes a sustained metaphor/theme that introduces and unifies the entries of the portfolio—five paragraph minimum.

☐ Table of Contents: page numbers and an <u>annotated</u> explanation of the contents of each portfolio entry.

☐ Entry Slips: writer's reflection on each entry. Focus on HOC issues (LOC focus for diagnostic essay only). Tie title or opening paragraph to the portfolio introduction—one page/three paragraph minimum.

☐ Portfolio-evaluated Essay: 7-1 Definition—track changes and new copy required.

☐ Revised essays previously evaluated: 6-1 Compare-Contrast and 8-1 Critical Analysis—track changes and new copy required.

☐ Revised Research Paper: previously evaluated copy, evaluation sheet, and new copy required.

☐ Revised Diagnostic Essay: previously evaluated copy, track changes, and new copy required.

☐ Optional Personal Inclusions: four maximum—written this semester (prose—seven paragraph minimum; poetry—one page minimum) entry slips and track changes required for each.

☐ Full Process—Author's Choice: For ONE entry, include pre-writes, drafts, revisions, peer responses, track changes, first graded copy, with clean copy on top for evaluation. Note: full process is also required for any essays when peer response was missed.

☐ Metacognitive Conclusion: Evaluate your performance—seven paragraph minimum.

CHAPTER 2

Use Your Uncommon Senses

~ ~ ~

"Next to knowing how to write about people,
you should know how to write about a place.
People and places are the twin pillars on which
most nonfiction is built" (88).
—William Zinsser

~ ~ ~

Often writers depend on only the sense of sight to develop pieces of writing. They forget some equally powerful descriptive tools in their bag of tricks—the other four senses. By activating and using all senses (sight, sound, taste, smell, and feel), writers can provide more imagery and evoke sounds, flavors, aromas, and textures, which help bring writing to life. Descriptive use of sense imagery often enhances other purposes for writing such as telling a story, explaining something, or persuading and arguing. Using descriptive sense imagery allows writers to accentuate vivid details and focus on **"the show,"** not "the tell" in writing.

Most of the time, writing calls for description of a place, object, or person. But as natural storytellers, many writers slip into relating a narrative or explanation when the purpose calls for description. In descriptive writing, the writer creates a dominant impression to leave in readers' minds. Maybe the writer wants to create the dominant impression of an object's vast size or complexity or a place's awesome beauty or a person's appearance or sense of humor. The writer then uses sense imagery to develop this dominant impression by creating a mood or establishing a feeling. The writer "**shows**" rather than "tells."

Let's say that your assignment calls for you to describe a place, such as your doctor's office, and you choose to create the dominant impression of anxiety as you wait in that little room for the doctor's arrival. From this vantage point, you will describe what the doctor's office looks like, sounds like, tastes like, smells like, and feels like. You will "**show**," not tell, your anxiety through sense imagery. Many times, if possible, writers will return to the place they intend to describe so that they experience all the senses and can more easily capture them in writing.

Writers must also decide how to keep the description coherent by providing a natural organization for the reader to follow. For example, you might describe the doctor's office from top to bottom or from right to left or left to right. Or you might choose to organize the description by dividing the writing into sections, focusing on one sense at a time. Writers must continually keep the audience in mind as they move from one image to another so as not to confuse or lose readers in the transition.

Your writer's tool box also contains figurative language which adds strength, vividness, and freshness to your descriptions. Figurative language offers a powerful tool to use in accentuating sense imagery. When you write description, see how many figures of speech you might naturally incorporate, without forcing them, into your writing to help bring your images to life.

STRUT YOUR STUFF!

Writing Project 2-1: Your Significant Place   Think of a significant place in your life, maybe the most beautiful, comfortable, secure, peaceful, exciting, awe-inspiring place you care about; or maybe the most fearful, disturbing, alarming, bewildering, annoying place that you detest. Visit that place, preferably by going there. If you find a visit impossible, try to find pictures or a video. If these methods are unavailable, visit the place in your memory. Unlock your five senses to capture the sensations and details of that place.

Write a description of your significant place that causes readers to feel as if they can experience the place even though they've never visited it. Establish a stationary narrating position (your narrator cannot move), a consistent point of view (first or third person), and consistent tense (past or present) for your description. Use sense imagery and figurative language to help create a dominant impression or feeling that you wish to establish throughout your essay. Let readers see the significance of the place. Above all, remember: **you've gotta have heart in your writing**. Writing Checklist:

☐　1. Does the essay describe a place rather than an event or person?

☐　2. Is the dominant impression clearly developed? Are sense imagery and figurative language used effectively?

☐　3. What camera angle (point of view) is used? Does the narrator remain stationary throughout the essay? Is the narration consistent regarding person (I, we, he, she, they)? Avoid indefinite reference (you) unless "you" is identified.

☐　4. Do the title and opening grab readers' attention? Does the conclusion bring adequate closure to the essay?

☐　5. Are the sentences varied in beginnings and lengths?

☐　6. Are verbs vivid? Is the tense (present or past) used consistently throughout the essay?

~ ~ ~

"If you are describing a beach...find details that are significant...They may be useful, colorful, or comic, or entertaining. But make sure they are details that do useful work" (90).
—William Zinsser

~ ~ ~

SAMPLE STUDENT WRITING

Significant Place
My Second Home
by Tara Pohlman

I sit at my usual table in the corner of Hazel's Café in Manchester, Iowa. The café offers a homey feeling to those who visit. The little, cream-colored swirls on the tabletop draw my attention like a hundred bathtub drains. The silver trim is peering from the rough, rounded edge. The bright red, lopsided chair I sit on feels uncomfortable, but the padding supplies a touch of home. I try to find the most comfortable position for my brief stay.

The walls around me tell several stories. Covered in newspaper ads, these walls reveal many historic events in our small town. Pictures of Elvis, Hazel's favorite musical artist, and other famous musicians watch over the customers. Further down the wall, pictures of various artists like Toby Keith and Dwight Yokem catch my eye. At one time, these artists played at the Delaware County Fair and stopped here at Hazel's for some good food.

I watch the servers bustle about, trying to keep the many customers satisfied. The bus boy, with beads of sweat forming on his forehead, is cleaning table after table. I chuckle at the waitress wearing a t-shirt that says, "I'm not listening," across the front. She tries to keep tabs on the many customers strewn about the booths and tables. They sit in chairs of various colors—red, yellow, and brown. The chairs look tired after their many years of service.

On this unusually busy Monday morning, all the customers look as though they are fleeing to the comforts of the café. On a typical Monday, patrons get a slow start, and not as many frequent Hazel's. Some middle-aged, working folks are eating breakfast here to start their day. Others, probably retired, simply look for a way to pass the time. I sit back to watch the activities going on around me.

I notice the couple in front of me, an older pair with silvery gray hair that seems to glisten in the light. The slender woman owns a stunning smile. I smell her perfume, reminding me of a field of wild flowers. I can't catch a glimpse of her man's face, but his roundness offsets her trimness. She laughs at the sign on the pink poster behind the register that reads, "If you want credit here, please go to Helen Waite." The man slightly bounces as he laughs.

Next to them sits a woman clad in a pair of sweats and a baggy sweatshirt. A mother of three shows patience with her children as she softly hushes them. They range in age from about three to eight and act as if they're starring in *Planet of the Apes*. The little, blonde-haired boy laughs as his younger brother dumps the salt shaker on the floor. The cute, little, brown-haired sister, off in her own world, tears napkins into small pieces, leaving a pile of snow on the floor in front of her.

The waitress rushes past my table carrying plates loaded with eggs and heaps of hash browns. One plate of bacon is still spattering from the heat of the grill. The other plate contains brown, circular patties of ground sausage. I catch a whiff of buttery hash browns and can almost feel the heat rising from the plate. The people across the room look anxious as their meal approaches their table.

Through the door comes an older gentleman with a beard as bushy as the shrubs outside my house. His bowler's cap sits cockeyed on his head. Cold air swarms in around him as if it is searching for warmth. Each head turns to look at him as if he's committed a crime. He slowly strides through the maze of tables to the stool-lined counter. His legs creak with each step. He orders a cup of coffee. The steam rising from the cup carries a fresh coffee scent that works its way around the room.

I gently shift positions as my bottom begins to ache. At the same time, I catch a warm breeze from the small, brown heater humming in the corner. The waitress comes up beside me and begins to pour a stiff, dark stream of black-as-coal liquid into my cup. I smile at her and quickly take a sip of the warm, refreshing coffee. It goes down smoothly, and I feel the comfort travel through my being. She smiles again as she hurries past me heading back to the kitchen. With a nod, I reassure her of my satisfaction.

Through the swinging doors that make a quiet swoosh each time they are pushed open, I catch a glimpse of a short, round, elderly lady in the kitchen. She wears a bright-red apron as she stands over a number of small, black, frying pans heating on the stove. A man, dressed in a blue denim shirt and baseball cap, stands over the grill. I can see small amounts of gray hair sticking out the sides of his cap. The dishwasher, with a wet apron around her middle, looks bushed.

I hear the searing of potatoes and the crackling of bacon on the grill. I listen to the crisp sputter of sausage frying on the pan, waiting to be rescued from the heat. The eggs pop from the underside, gasping for air in the frying pan. The clanking of dishes smacks against the sides of the stainless steel sink as if they are running a race. Standing ever so still in the corner, the refrigerator opens and shuts only on demand. The burst of the toaster shoots out two newly toasted slices of bread.

I return from my daze when the waitress sets my plate of light brown, finely shredded, buttery hash browns in front of me. I pick up my fork and dig in, taking a large bite and enjoying the softness in my mouth. Then I bite into the greasy, crunchy bacon. The over-easy eggs display bright yellow centers and feel soft and mushy on my tongue. I experience the soft crispness of the toast as I bite into the tanned triangle.

With the rush of breakfast now ending, the room begins to calm. A few people remain. Trying to convince her children to put on their multi-colored coats, the young mother packs up her clan. At the counter, a young man wearing blue jeans and a racing shirt gulps his food as if he's got somewhere to go. Laughter from the kitchen help rings in my ears. I stretch my legs, feeling as if I were sitting for a decade. My belly is so full I know I can drag it on the floor.

The waitress comes by and asks, "How was everything?" I tell her the usual, "It was great." We talk for a few minutes before she wanders off to another table. Before paying my bill, I chat with the cook who has come out of the kitchen to visit. As another customer leaves, cold air rushes at me and tempts me to stay at my small table in Hazel's Café, my second home and one of my favorite places in the world.

Discussion Questions:

1. What is the author describing, and what camera angle does the writer take?

2. What dominant impression does the writer try to establish in the piece?

3. Point out specific examples of sense imagery and figurative language. Analyze the effectiveness of the writer's use of sense imagery and figurative language.

4. Analyze the effectiveness of the title, introduction, and conclusion. How well do they support the topic?

5. Does the writer "have heart" in the essay? What specific aspects of the piece support your response?

6. Evaluate the strengths of this essay. What improvements for the piece would you suggest?

7. Evaluate the effectiveness of the piece holistically and provide rationale for your evaluation.

SENSE IMAGERY

Try to make the description of your significant place come alive by using all five senses in your writing. Go to the place you plan to describe. Take along a notebook and pen. When you get there, sit silently and let your senses work. Note what you see. Then close your eyes and let your sense of hearing dominate. After a time, jot down all the things your sense of hearing captures. Then close your eyes and let your sense of smell dominate. After a time, jot down all the things your sense of smell captures. Continue the process with touch and taste. Activate those senses that you normally do not use in your writing. Next, use a pre-writing strategy to capture more sensations, or write a draft if you feel ready, but concentrate on the power of sense imagery to help bring your writing to life and to help engage your readers.

Noted author Ray Bradbury writes, "Why all this insistence on the senses? Because in order to convince your reader that he is there, you must assault each of his senses, in turn, with color, sound, taste, and texture. If your reader feels the sun on his flesh, the wind fluttering his shirt sleeves, half your fight is won. The most improbable tales can be made believable, if your reader, through his senses, feels certain that he stands in the middle of events. He cannot refuse, then, to participate. The logic of events always gives way to the logic of the senses" (41). So work to activate your senses to enhance your writing and to engage your readers.

FIGURATIVE LANGUAGE

~ ~ ~

"The use of simile and other figurative language is one of the chief delights of fiction—reading it and writing it, as well" (178).
—Stephen King

~ ~ ~

- **Simile**—compares using the words <u>like</u>, <u>as</u>, <u>than</u>.
  Example, "My doctor looks like Attila the Hun behind his incognito, gray-black beard."
- **Metaphor**—compares without using <u>like</u>, <u>as</u>, <u>than</u>.
  Example: "My doctor is Attila the Hun behind his incognito, gray-black beard."
- **Personification**—gives human characteristics or sensibilities to inanimate objects, animals, ideas, or abstractions.
  Example: "The dentist's suction device swallowed me up—teeth, tongue, and tonsils."
- **Onomatopoeia**—uses words to suggest sounds.
  Example: "The buzz of the dentist's drill prepared me for an all-out assault on my right molar."
- **Hyperbole**—uses exaggeration to produce heightened effect, usually comic.
  Example: "As I lay on the doctor's table staring upward into his glasses-shielded eyes, my bodily furnace kicked in so heatedly that I thought I would sweat to death within twenty seconds."
- **Litotes (understatement)**—an irony which says less than one means.

Example: "As the doctor hid his sword-like needle behind his right calf, he barked, 'This will feel like a tiny mosquito bite!'"

- **Allusion**—a casual reference to a historical or literary figure or event.

Example: "The Brobdingnagian center grabbed all the rebounds."

Caution: When you use figurative language, be sure that your figures of speech add life, vividness, and freshness to your writing. Avoid overused, trite, or dead images, such as "hard as a rock," "pulling my leg," "over the hump," "bend over backwards," which distract from rather than enhance your writing. Also, avoid mixing metaphors whereby one metaphor follows another but does not logically complement the other. For example, "I was in such hot water that I couldn't find a leg to stand on." Work to create fresh, new, unique figures of speech that flow with your context rather than feel "forced" or overused.

~ ~ ~

"Of all devices of language, metaphor is the most powerful, the most convincing, the most persuasive" (215).
—Joseph Williams

~ ~ ~

PRACTICE 2A: Recognizing Figures of Speech   Identify the figures of speech in the following examples. Then evaluate the effectiveness of each example.

1. Jay Gatsby had broken up like glass against Tom's hard malice, and the long secret extravagance was played out. (*The Great Gatsby* 148)
2. Only wind in the trees, which blew the wires and made the lights go off and on again as if the house had winked into the darkness. (*The Great Gatsby* 82)
3. "Perhaps you know that lady," Gatsby indicated a gorgeous, scarcely human orchid of a woman who sat in state under a white-plum tree. (*The Great Gatsby* 106)
4. At his lips' touch she (Daisy Buchanan) blossomed for him (Jay Gatsby) like a flower and the incarnation was complete. (*The Great Gatsby* 112)
5. After Macbeth's brutal murder of King Duncan, he states to his wife, Lady Macbeth, "Will all great Neptune's ocean wash this blood clean from my hand?" (Shakespeare, *Macbeth* 2.2.58-59)

6. To which Lady Macbeth replies, "A little water clears us of this deed" (Shakespeare, *Macbeth* 2.2.66).
7. After Macbeth is informed of his wife's death, he responds, "Out, out, brief candle! Life's but a walking shadow, a poor player that struts and frets his hour upon the stage and then is heard no more" (Shakespeare, *Macbeth* 5.5.23-26).
8. Love is a many splendored thing. It's the April rose that only grows in the early spring; Love is nature's way of giving a reason to be living, the golden crown that makes a man a king. (Song lyrics to "Love Is a Many Splendored Thing" by Paul Francis Webster, 1955)
9. Robert Frost wrote a poem about a boy whose hand was cut off by a buzz saw; the boy died as a result of the accident. Frost's poem is entitled, "Out, Out—"
10. The buzz saw snarled and rattled in the yard. (Frost l.1)
11. At the word, the saw as if to prove saws knew what supper meant, leaped out at the boy's hand...(Frost ll. 14-16)
12. At the start of the summer came the permanent rain and with the rain came the cholera. But it was checked and in the end only seven thousand died of it in the army. (Ernest Hemingway, *A Farewell to Arms* 4)
13. "Now is the winter of our discontent / Made glorious summer by this sun of York" (Shakespeare, *Richard III* 1.1.1).

PRACTICE 2B: Writing Figurative Language   For each of the following, write a sentence or more that expresses an idea through figurative language. Use a different figure of speech for each item.

1. a tornado siren
2. a turkey
3. jazzercise
4. snow in Texas
5. full moon
6. Mall of America
7. earthquake
8. college tuition
9. three-hour lecture
10. rugby scrum

ESSAY STRUCTURE:
TITLES, OPENINGS, MIDDLES, CLOSINGS

Writers may use any number of strategies to capture readers' attention in the title and opening paragraph, maintain that attention throughout the body of support and evidence, and bring closure to an essay. Ineffective writing of any of these parts of the essay may cause readers to feel disjointed, disappointed, or disillusioned. An interesting opening lures readers into the essay while an effective closing ushers readers out, hopefully with more knowledge and insight than before reading the essay.

TITLE

The title of your essay gives the first impression of your writing skill. The title works like good bait to get your catch, the readers, to "nibble" at your essay. If your audience is not intrigued by your title, they may not want to read on. A title may not make a paper, but it gives readers the initial impression that the topic and the writer are worth "nibbling" at. The title needs to be informative and also arouse interest. However, the title may not be the first part of the essay you write. You might delay creating the title until you see where the writing takes you. Many times a title will appear as you write the middle or closing paragraphs of an essay.

~ ~ ~

"Titles are one of the most important forms of meta-commentary, functioning rather like carnival barkers telling passersby what they can expect when they go inside. Titles should give readers some sense of your argument rather than merely announcing your topic" (127-128).
--Gerald Graff and Kathy Birkenstein

~ ~ ~

Fishing for Readers

One of the following strategies may help you develop an intriguing, informative title. Of course, you may create a much more effective title than the ones suggested here, so don't feel restricted to limiting your creativity to this list of strategies for titles.

- **Ask a question. The essay will answer the question.**
  Who will win Saturday's intrastate showdown?
- **Use alliteration.** Start words with the same consonant.
  Wee Willie Winkie
  One Misty, Moisty Morning
  Georgie Porgy, Pudding and Pie
- **Use a pun, a play on word**s.
  Tweedle-Dum and Tweedle Dumber
  Man Struck by Lightning Faces Battery Charge
  Bush Wins on Economy, but More Lies Ahead
- **Use rhyme.**
  A Tear in My Beer
- **Create an allusion, a reference to another text, book, or poem; to a historical event or person; or to a myth or legend.** Writers have borrowed effectively from Shakespeare's *Macbeth*.
  By the Pricking of My Thumbs,
    a novel by Agatha Christie
  Something Wicked This Way Comes,
    a novel by Ray Bradbury
  Tomorrow and Tomorrow and Tomorrow,
    a novel by Kurt Vonnegut
  "Out, Out—," a poem by Robert Frost
  The Sound and Fury, a novel by William Faulkner
- **Use directional titles that present both your topic and your position, punctuated with a colon.**
  Love: That Elusive Feeling
  War: Never an Option
  Drinking: A Teen Epidemic

AVOID:
Underlining, italicizing, using quotation marks, or capitalizing all letters in titles.

OPENING

If the title of a piece of writing gets readers to "nibble," the beginning paragraph tries to get them to "bite" so that they continue reading your essay. Besides "catching" readers' attention, the opening announces and limits your subject, indicates an organization for the essay, and establishes an appropriate tone and point of view that will accomplish your purpose. The opening of an essay gives the reader an impression of what will follow. A lively, catchy beginning engages readers and urges them to continue reading. On the other hand, a dull, boring beginning can make readers stop immediately. Like the title, writing the opening may be delayed or radically revised after the body is written since later paragraphs or the conclusion of the essay may suggest an effective opening.

~ ~ ~

"A lead should be provocative. It should
have energy, excitement, an implicit promise
that something is going to happen or that some
interesting information will be revealed. It should
create curiosity, get the reader asking questions" (33).
—Gary Provost

~ ~ ~

No one best technique to open an essay has been established, but any number of strategies may work well, depending on your topic, purpose, audience, and personal preference. Check the possibility of using one of the following strategies as an opener for your essay.

- **Use an interesting QUOTATION.** This might be a fresh quotation from a character you deal with in your essay, or it may be a quotation from an authority on your topic or a recognized author, historical figure, philosopher, politician, or religious leader. To find an appropriate quotation to begin your essay, you need not read every book in the library. The internet or your library houses many reference books, such as *Bartlett's Familiar Quotations, The Oxford Dictionary of Modern Quotations, The Oxford Dictionary of Humorous Quotations,* and *The International Thesaurus of Quotations,* which can help you locate a meaningful, striking quotation to begin your essay. Then tie the quotation to the first sentence of your text.

"Everyone can write...It is possible for anyone to produce a lot of writing with pleasure and satisfaction," states writing expert Peter

Elbow. *Although most students believe that certain people are born with writing talent and creativity while most are not, Elbow has struck a chord with many writing teachers.*

"Now is the winter of our discontent." Like Shakespeare's Richard III, I am feeling discontent with my writing, except my discontent has lasted winter, spring, summer, and fall.

- Use a **Statement** by an **EXPERT** or **AUTHORITY** (not necessarily a famous writer, but rather a doctor, a member of the police force, a social worker, etc.)

"Psychologist Izzy Real believes a full-time student should not work a full-time job."

- Use a surprising or startling **FACT** or **STATISTIC**.

Two years ago the Board of Regents raised tuition at the Regents universities 18%. This past spring the Board raised tuition another 17%. Few college students at colleges and universities can afford such drastic tuition hikes.

- Use a **RHETORICAL QUESTION.** The paper then answers the question.

Why are so many college students choosing a community college for their post-secondary education?

- Use an **ANECDOTE**, a short narrative.

I started my first writing project for composition class last Thursday. After I finished my first draft, I pitched it into the wastebasket and started again. On Friday, I developed such a case of writer's block that I couldn't even come up with a topic. On Saturday at 11 p.m., I finally thought of a topic but could only produce one paragraph. On Sunday, I was so discontented with my writing that I rested. Will I ever be able to write?

- Open with the thesis, the **CENTRAL IDEA** or claim. Immediately go for the "jugular."

I work full-time at Wally World and take a full class schedule of 15 credits, so finding time to write essays presents quite a challenge.

- Provide interesting **BACKGROUND** or show the **SIGNIFICANCE** of the topic.

I work a fulltime job of 40 hours per week in the snack bar at Wally World, and I attend NICC full time with a class load of five classes worth three credits each. I'm nearing the brink of a nervous breakdown.

- Use **FIGURATIVE LANGUAGE**—simile, metaphor, allusion.

Working full time and attending college seem like a lifetime sentence packed into two years.

- Use **CONTRAST**.

Many great pieces of literature are written in jest, but they can't measure up to the number written in earnest.

- Use **HUMOR**.

"How come your son is doing so well in his college composition class?"

"Well, wine makes him sick; he's afraid of women; he hates to play games; he's allergic to the sun, and he can't sing, so he just stays home and writes."

- Use **DESCRIPTION**.

An archway carved with impish cherubs grows from the outer edges of the stage at the refurbished Five Flags Theatre. Under this portico hangs a heavy, red velvet curtain adorned with gold-braided piping. Gently, the curtain brushes the stage, swaying ever so slightly from the breeze of the open doorways like the hem of a prom dress dancing on a gymnasium floor. Faint whispers and an occasional thud give a hint of the activity behind the heavy, ornate curtain. A single spotlight shines on the curtain displaying a caricature of a small, disheveled child, a representation of Les Miserables.—Deanna Allan

- Use **a line of POETRY or SONG lyrics.**

You may locate poems by title, first line, author, or subject in The Columbia Granger's Index to Poetry located in the library.

"You've gotta' have heart, miles and miles and miles of heart." *The devil in the Broadway musical "Damn Yankees" must know a lot about writing because the best writing comes from a writer's heart.*

SOME OPENING "JUNK" TO AVOID

1. Avoid opening **ANNOUNCEMENTS**.

In this essay, I am going to discuss why my full time job and my full time college course load don't leave me much time to write essays for my composition course.

2. Avoid **APOLOGIES**.

I am not sure this is exactly correct, but this is my opinion about how much writing NICC students do in their classes.

3. Avoid **OVERWORKED EXPRESSIONS.**

The handwriting is on the wall about my college writing skills. The expectations at Lake Okoboji Community College are a drop in the bucket compared to the expectations at Northeast Iowa Community College.

4. Avoid **QUALIFIERS,** such as **definitely**, **really**, **very**. They suggest a lack of confidence in your knowledge of or position on your topic.

In this essay, I am going to really discuss why my full time job and my full time college course load definitely don't leave me very much time to write essays for my composition course.

5. Avoid **DICTIONARY DEFINITIONS.**

According to Webster's Collegiate Dictionary, a writer is "an author who puts ideas on a page for a reader."

6. Avoid Shakespeare's **"To be or not to be"** line. It's been overused.

To write or not to write tonight, that is the question.

PRACTICE 2C: Titles and Openings   Analyze and evaluate the effectiveness of the following titles and openings; then, write a sentence or two explaining your opinion.

Titles:
1. My Views on Smoking
2. Things Fall Apart
3. Who Passes? Who Fails? Who Cares?
4. Equal Opportunity, Equal Pay
5. Abortion
6. Professional Athletes—Masters of Greed

Openings:
1. I am sitting down at the computer to write you a letter.
2. College professors are educators who talk in someone else's sleep.
3. In this essay, I am going to relate the reason why I feel so stressed out with my college classes.
4. Call me Ishmael.
5. The purpose of the curriculum is to prepare students to cope with the problems of today. Examples of courses which will be helpful in this regard are "Principles of Hellenistic Art," "French Poetry of the Renaissance," and "Music of the Baroque and Pre-Classical periods" (Ebersole 107).

6. "Hey, Mom," asked our son Dan as he was filling out a questionnaire, "what class are we?"

I thought for a moment. What class? "Seniors," I said sophomorically. "Or shall we be juniors? Which class has more fun?"

"Aw, Mom, be serious," Dan said. "I gotta know; what class are we? Upper? Middle? Lower?" (Ebersole 14).

PRACTICE 2D: Titles and Openings: Write both openings and titles—attention grabbers—for the following topics:

a. description of a beautiful mountain range
b. opposition to raising college tuition
c. autobiography for a college application
d. comparison/contrast of Saturday and Sunday
e. convincing youngsters not to start smoking
f. explanation of your "tricks" for studying

PRACTICE 2E: Magazine Articles: Locate magazine articles that demonstrate various strategies for effective titles and openings. Also, try to find other methods that magazine article writers use to attract readers' attention. Cut them out or copy them and bring them to class to share with your peers. Write a short explanation of what makes each title and opening effective.

MIDDLE

~ ~ ~

"A lot of nonsense has been written in writing textbooks about paragraphs, much of it not only wrong but harmful. Much of the nonsense arises from the false notion that every paragraph should be a short essay and that the thesis for the essay should be expressed in something called a topic sentence" (90).
—Richard Marius

~ ~ ~

After you have teased readers into "nibbling" on your title and gotten them to "bite" on your opening, you need to "hook" readers and "reel 'em in" with the middle, or body, paragraphs, which support, develop, or prove the topic or thesis of your essay. Writers develop the middle, supporting paragraphs to provide evidence through such strategies as examples, arguments, statistics, or quotations from authorities. Paragraph indentations signal changes to readers. A writer may indent to shift to a new incident or supporting piece of evidence, to move to a different idea or a different slant, or maybe to restate or emphasize an idea. Paragraph indentations usually occur naturally rather than accommodating the "old formula" of requiring a topic sentence and supporting sentences because "a paragraph is a miniature essay with a beginning, middle, and end." In fact, in her book, *A Rhetoric for Writing Teachers*, Erika Lindemann states that researchers found topic sentences in paragraphs "only 13% of the time" (152).

So rather than fitting paragraphs into the "old formula," consider developing the length and depth of your paragraphs for reading ease. Write paragraphs between five and eight sentences of varied length and syntax. Or you might look at paragraphing this way: the length of a paragraph should not exceed its width. This guideline, not rule, provides sufficient length to develop a main idea but does not allow paragraphs to ramble on, causing readers to lose focus. Sometimes a special purpose, such as dialogue or emphasis, may call for shorter paragraphs than the suggested five sentences. In *Writing With Style*, John R. Trimble suggests that paragraphing properly requires audience awareness and common sense rather than a formula. "Long paragraphs send off alarms in most readers' minds; very short paragraphs suggest insubstantiality and flightiness; a long succession of medium-length paragraphs indicates no imagination and proves monotonous. Moral: vary your pacing to keep your piece alive and vital" (81).

Paragraphing helps writers put order to their thoughts and break down ideas into manageable units. For readers, paragraphs make writing easier to follow, provide relief for readers' eyes, and give readers confidence they can absorb the piece one smaller block at a time. Consider indenting a new paragraph when a shift takes place for a: (1) change in emphasis or ideas, (2) change in time, (3) change in speakers, (4) change in place or setting. For clarity in paragraphs, use specific nouns early in each paragraph as antecedents for later pronouns, and avoid using vague nouns (a person, people) and pronouns (one, you, he, she, it, they). Also, maintain consistency in verb tense (present, past), person (first, second, third), and number (singular, plural).

Writers should consider two aspects of paragraphing, unity and coherence, in developing their paragraphs. Unity suggests that all ideas and sentences in a paragraph deal with the same idea or topic. Some writers use a "fishhook" technique to ensure unity. Each paragraph "fishhooks" into the thesis, and each paragraph "fishhooks" into the preceding and succeeding paragraphs. And each sentence "fishhooks" into the sentence before it and after it. Coherence implies a smooth, clear flow from idea to idea, paragraph to paragraph, and sentence to sentence. Most of the time, coherence happens naturally as writers use transitional words or repeat words or ideas as a means of flow.

However, a pattern of short, choppy sentences that seem to lack smooth flow could indicate a coherence problem stemming from a lack of transitions. To improve smoothness and transitions, a writer may repeat key words, use synonyms, use a pronoun referring to a preceding noun, or provide transitional words. The following chart of transitional words gives readers directional signals to help provide coherence in a piece of writing. But remember: don't overuse transitional words. Readers naturally sense changes and look for them in writing.

TRANSITIONAL CHART

Addition:	also, and, besides, finally, further, furthermore, in addition, likewise, moreover, then, too
Compare:	also, as well, in like manner, in the same way, likewise, similarly
Contrast:	although, but, despite, even though, however, nevertheless, still, on the contrary, on the other hand, otherwise, yet
Exemplification:	for example, for instance, in fact, in other words, specifically, that is
Place:	above, adjacent to, behind, below, beyond, close by, far, here, in front of, near, nearby, next to, north (south, east, west), of, on one side, opposite to, over, surrounding, through, within
Purpose:	to this end, for this purpose, with this object
Result:	accordingly, as a result, because, consequently, for this reason, so, then, therefore
Summary:	and so, finally, in brief, in short, therefore
Time:	after, afterward, at the same time, before, between, earlier, formerly, gradually, in the future, in the past, later, longer, meanwhile, now, since, soon, suddenly, then

CLOSING

The final paragraph of your essay, the conclusion, should "put your catch into your bucket" for keeps. Your essay should not come to a screeching halt, but rather allow you, the writer, to exit gracefully. The closing paragraph should bring closure to your essay and leave the reader with a satisfying, final impression. It reminds readers of your main point and hopefully gives them something to think about. The conclusion may even offer a recommendation or make a call to action. The conclusion may seem like completing a circle since it should relate to or connect to the opening or thesis without restating it.

Many of the strategies suggested for openings—quotations, rhetorical questions, humor, emphasis of significant point(s), etc.— will also work well for closing your essay. During the drafting stage, some writers like to set aside some prime ideas or phrases to use in their closing. You may wish to experiment with this trick. Also, examine the following techniques that sometimes work in bringing closure to essays.

- **Suggest the importance of your topic.**

Maintaining a full time job and full time course load is not working for me. I need to cut back work hours, or I will jeopardize my academic accomplishments and my mental health.

- **Suggest a call to action.**

To keep sane and to find academic success, college students need to weigh the advantages and disadvantages of working full time while taking a full course load.

- **Summarize important points only for long or complicated papers.**

Three major issues, then, are involved in a college student's decision to work: first, the number and rigor of courses the student is taking, second, the time the full time job requires, and third, the student's ability to handle pressure and stress.

SOME CLOSING "JUNK" TO AVOID

1. **Avoid restating your thesis.**

   As I said in my thesis, a full time college course load and full time job can bring a student to the brink of insanity.

2. **Avoid wasted phrases like, "In conclusion," "In closing," "Let me close by saying," "To sum up."**

In conclusion, let me say that I believe that college students should not work full time while taking a full load of courses.

3. **Avoid apologizing.**

Although I'm only a first-year college student, I have realized that college students should not work full time while taking a full load of courses.

4. **Avoid summaries in short papers.** However, summaries may be needed for long or complicated papers.

PRACTICE 2F: Conclusions: Write a conclusion for the topics listed in Practice 2D.

PRACTICE 2G: Magazine Articles: Locate magazine articles that demonstrate various strategies for effective conclusions. Also, try to find other methods that magazine article writers use to bring closure to their articles. Cut them out or copy them and bring them to class to share with your peers. Write a short explanation of what makes each conclusion effective.

BE SPECIFIC!

In your writing, try to be as exact and specific as possible to give readers the clearest picture of the meaning you intend. Note the following examples:

Vague:	The disgruntled composition teacher entered the classroom a little late.
Specific:	Professor Waldo Wright ripped open the door to his 8 a.m. English Composition I classroom at 8:12 and threw his attaché case on the desk.
Vague:	The lady bought lots of items at the mall for which she paid too much.
Specific:	Sarah Spends left Kennedy Mall with three dresses, two hats, two pairs of slacks, and five pairs of earrings for which she paid $812.

PRACTICE 2H: Be Specific   Substitute specific wording for the following nouns:

1. person	4. college	7. vehicle	10. song
2. city	5. food	8. smell	11. cap
3. musical group	6. athlete	9. restaurant	12. teacher

PRACTICE 2I: Be Specific   Substitute specific action words for the following verbs:

1. eat	4. drink	7. talk	10. look
2. touch	5. run	8. hit	11. catch
3. complain	6. sing	9. start	12. ask

~ ~ ~

"Not only does specific language serve as clarification and evidence, but it also adds interest. It can spice up a passage that might otherwise be bland" (37).
—Robert Miles

~ ~ ~

PRACTICE 2J: Be Specific   Rewrite the following sentences to make them specific and exact.

1. The young man read a magazine until very late yesterday evening.
2. The person placed his tools in the truck.
3. We talked about a touchy issue.
4. We went to the city, ate at a restaurant, and then attended a concert.
5. My pet ran away this morning, and a citizen on the other end of town found her in a park near his business.
6. The student attends college, works in a restaurant, and plays an instrument in a band.
7. A college instructor has written a book about writing, according to the weekly newspaper.
8. The kid got into the car quickly and drove from the scene rapidly.

When writing paragraphs, use specific, concrete nouns early in each paragraph as antecedents for later pronoun references. Avoid vague nouns (a person, people) and pronouns (one, you, he, she, it, they). Also in your paragraphs, maintain consistency of verb tenses (present-past), person (first-third), and number (singular-plural).

PRACTICE 2K: Be Specific   Revise the following passage by making vague words and ideas SPECIFIC.

> I was taught to write when I was in kindergarten. In second grade, I wrote my first big story. Also in elementary school, I wrote a lot of poetry and even attended a poetry seminar and met an actual poet. As I entered junior high, we became more involved. The teachers expected our work to be more professional than what we wrote in elementary. I wrote many stories that I kept and still enjoy looking at them today to see how much I have changed as a writer.
>
> In high school, I took both literature and composition courses. We were expected to write a lot. They also kept us writing poetry, which I enjoyed. In college, I took a composition class. I never knew writing had so much to it. I learned a great deal, and I will use what I learned to reach my future goals.

PRACTICE 2L: Be Specific—ENTRY SLIP   Analyze the following Portfolio Entry Slip based on Project 2-1, Significant Place. Revise it so that it focuses on specific HOC (Higher Order Concerns) issues and avoids LOC (Lower Order Concerns) focus.

PORTFOLIO ENTRY SLIP 1

> I couldn't think of a place to write about. Then I thought about my back porch. It holds lots of good memories for me, so the essay wasn't hard to write. I had trouble, however, with the descriptive part. When the peer response day arrived, I felt nervous, but my group praised my essay, which built up my confidence. They also suggested I add more sense imagery.
>
> During the oral reading, I picked up on a lot of grammatical errors. The group also suggested quite a few things I could improve. For one, my introduction and conclusion were short. My group also suggested I get rid of weak verbs. I still need to work on my punctuation, but my editing is improving.
>
> From this writing, I learned how much sense imagery and figurative language can strengthen my writing by helping my readers see and feel my ideas. The opening paragraph gave me

the most trouble, so I went back to it after I finished the first draft. I was able to write a catchier opening since I knew what I had written throughout the paper. Overall, I feel proud of my first major paper because I found that if I write with heart, my personal voice comes through, and my writing is more interesting to read.

EXPANDED WRITING PROCESS—SHARING STAGE: PEER RESPONSE

An excellent means of improving writing and critical thinking is hearing and seeing other people respond and react to your words and ideas. Writing response groups offer this opportunity. Beginning with the first major project, you will expand your writing process to include sharing your writing with your classmates to get peer response. From this response, you will revise your essay and submit it to the instructor for response. Then, you will revise again and share the essay with classmates for proofing as you prepare it for your portfolio. Your writing will improve as you receive as much reaction and feedback as possible to your essays. Peer response offers one excellent means of getting this feedback. Instructors use various methods of peer response, some oral, some written, and some a combination of both. Your instructor will inform you of his or her preferred peer response procedure and the number of participants in each response group. You may have been involved in peer response groups in high school and feel comfortable sharing your writing with others. Many of you, on the other hand, will be sharing your writing for the first time and may feel some nervousness, but you will feel more comfortable in response groups as the course progresses.

PORTFOLIO IN PROGRESS

After your instructor returns your piece of writing, revise and edit it in preparation for placing it in your Demonstration Portfolio. Also, in your notebook or journal or on computer, designate an area for self-reflections of your essays and the writing process for each essay.

These self-reflections will help you assess your own writing progress and help you determine ways to improve your writing throughout your composition experience. Use the Entry Slip-Reflection ideas suggested below to help you reflect on your writing. Keep track of your self-reflections by dating them, labeling them, and saving them in a secure place (notebook, journal, computer) so that you can draw on these ideas as you write your portfolio entry slips.

~ ~ ~

*"Reflection is the act of seeing one's own work
and its relationship to the self and explaining it"* (156).
—Bonnie Sunstein

~ ~ ~

Self-Reflection Questions

The following series of questions may help you self-reflect on your individual pieces and on your writing progress:

(A) Why did you choose this topic?

(B) Did you take any risks in composing the piece or experiment with any strategic techniques (imagery, figurative language, dialogue, humor, satire, etc.) and WHY? Did they work?

(C) What changes (revisions) in content and/or organization did you make during your process? Why did you make these changes? What were the turning points or discoveries?

(D) How effectively did your peer group respond to and help in your processing of this piece? What did you change after peer response?

(E) Did you discuss your paper with anyone other than peer responders? What did you discuss? How did it affect your paper?

(F) Did your ideas about your topic change while you were processing the paper? If so, how?

(G) Why did you choose the title for the paper? Did you consider other titles? What were they, and why did you not use them?

(H) Identify a passage in your paper (maybe a single sentence or more, or a couple of paragraphs) that represents your best writing style. Then explain why you consider it your best.

(I) What was difficult or easy about this writing? Where did you get stuck? Where were you really cruising?

(J) In processing this paper, did you do anything different from what you've done before when writing papers? If so, what was it?

Why did you try this? What resulted?

(K) Identify the strengths of the piece at this point in your process.

(L) What revisions might still be implemented to improve this piece of writing?

(M) Do you see specific aspects of your writing or process or thinking that show improvement? Identify these and explain the change.

SAMPLE ENTRY SLIP—REFLECTION

The following sample shows Keri West's reflection on her descriptive essay *Forever Young*.

Forever Young
Entry Slip by Keri West

Mile number one: My cross-country race starts here with my descriptive essay, Forever Young. The ecstasy of this first mile of the run makes me feel as if I will remain "Forever Young." The memories embellished in my grandma's toy room made the title of this piece easy for me to choose. The calm in Bob Dylan's "Forever Young" seemed to parallel the serenity of the room. I used the title and the quotation from this song to place an image of happiness and tranquility in my piece so that my readers truly understand how the memories of this toy room continue to impact me. By describing various toys and the memories that accompany them, I tried to illustrate the significance of the title.

Through various forms of figurative language, I tried to make my story come to life. I wanted my readers to feel as if they were actually there. I compared the perfect placement of the cheese on the cracker to fitting pieces on a jigsaw puzzle because it reminded me of my obsessive-compulsive behaviors as a child. The paragraph demonstrating my encounter with the train passing recaps many childhood experiences since Grandma lived across the street from the train tracks in East Dubuque, Illinois.

Writing this piece helped me open my mind as I attempted to come up with different forms of figurative language to make my story more unique. The effort I put into describing the toy room from a stationary position makes me proud because I have never written a piece before from that limited point of view. It truly helped me describe the scene rather than tell a story. I know that practicing this kind of writing style will only help me develop as a writer just like practicing the first mile helped me as a long-distance runner.

~ ~ ~

*"Without reflection all we have is simply
a pile, or a large folder, a collection of
texts. For a writer to learn from the work
she or he has produced and collected,
reflection is necessary"* (119).
—Liz Hamp-Lyons

CHAPTER 3

"That's the glory of, that's the STORY of..."

~ ~ ~

*"I wish to live ever as to derive my satisfactions
and inspirations from the commonest events,
every-day phenomena, so that what my senses
hourly perceive, my daily walk, the conversation
of my neighbors, may inspire me, and I dream of
no heaven but that which lies about me"* (14).
—Henry David Thoreau

~ ~ ~

People love stories, and people love to tell stories about themselves. Storytelling allows writers to capture a moment or an event and keep it alive forever, to suspend time via their writing. In this chapter, you will focus on looking into your heart and mind to find a significant event in your life to write about. All stories, even fictional accounts, use similar elements—characters, plot, conflict or tension, setting, and point of view. These narrative elements can often be used to develop other kinds of essays, such as descriptive, expository, or persuasive.

Characters actively participate in the story's plot or actions. Often conflict between characters or a problem or tension acts as the focal point of the plot. The setting determines the where and when the story takes place, plus may help create the story's atmosphere. Your point of view establishes the narrative position from which you will relate your story. You might choose the first person narrator who participates in your story and relates your experiences. Or you might choose a third person perspective by narrating from a position outside the story and relating the action.

A powerful way of bringing a story, or any other piece of writing, to life is using dialogue—getting your characters to talk. Dialogue, the conversations between two or more of your characters, adds authenticity and feeling to your story. Dialogue also allows writers to show rather than tell as emphasized in the previous chapter on descriptive writing. But, as with most things, dialogue can be overused. So try to use dialogue as it comes naturally in your story rather than forcing it. Sometimes this unnatural force happens when writers try to have one character explain or tell too much. Let your event unfold naturally through all your characters' dialogue.

STRUT YOUR STUFF!

Writing Project 3-1: Your Significant Event   Think of a significant event in your life—maybe the most memorable, exciting, shocking, tragic, exhilarating, humorous, or educational. Your event may not have resulted in spectacular news coverage. Possibly no one except you realizes the significance of this event. For example, possibly you learned more from sitting on the bench than making the winning basket in the "big game" during high school.

Write a story about a significant event in your life that has impacted your life, either changing you in some way or teaching you an important lesson. Use vivid details (imagery, figurative language) and dialogue to help your readers see the event and its effect on you. You can think of the effects in different ways: ways that you think or behave differently now, ways that you perceive the incident now, things that you have learned from this experience. Most importantly, remember the focus of the essay: how have you been changed or affected by what happened? Above all, remember: **you've gotta have heart in your writing.**
Writing Checklist:

- ☐ 1. Does the essay focus on one significant event and show the significance of that event?
- ☐ 2. Does the essay stay consistent in tense (past or present)?
- ☐ 3. Is dialogue used effectively to help develop the characters? Are descriptive details (imagery, figurative language) effectively included?

☐ 4. Are scenes fully developed so readers can see what happens?
☐ 5. Do the title and opening grab readers' attention? Does the
conclusion provide adequate closure?
☐ 6. Is sentence variety in style and length evident? Are action
verbs used?

SAMPLE STUDENT WRITING

Significant Event
Brace Face
by Andrea Kedley

"Today is the day!" my mom says eagerly. I give her one of my evil looks, knowing she is talking about my orthodontist appointment that lands on this wonderful Wednesday. I glance over at the calendar, hoping the black chicken scratch stating "Ortho at 11:00" would disappear from the marker board hanging on the refrigerator.

"Don't forget to call the school and remind them that you are going to pick me up at 10:15," I tell my mom.

"Oh, don't think for a minute that I won't remember to call them on the one day you get braces!" she quickly remarks with a huge smile on her face.

Later in the day, sitting in my classroom, I hear the warning bell go off, knowing that a message is coming over the loud speaker. "Andrea Kedley, please report to the front desk window to sign out," says the school secretary. I cringe in my seat, knowing that just in a matter of minutes, so much metal will be put in my mouth it could cause me to pick up my own radio station. Picking my books off of the desk, I take my last walk down the hallway as a normal-looking teenager. As I come to the window, I pick up a pen and slowly sign my name, hoping to delay time. I walk around the corner, and sure enough, Mom waves frantically from her car waiting to pick me up.

"Are ya ready, Brace Face?" she asks.

"You know, we could just skip this whole thing, and who knows, maybe my teeth will work a miracle and fix themselves tomorrow!" I tell her as I glare.

"Oh, no way, we are so going to this appointment because my little girl is going to be so cute with train tracks in her mouth!"

"If you weren't my mom, I would hurt you so bad right now."

"Just remember, I love you!" she says with a smile and chuckles.

The car ride from Cascade to Dubuque usually takes thirty minutes, but today it feels like an eternity. Mom keeps making remarks about getting braces, hoping to get a rise from me. Thankfully I enjoy our relationship, or else I would hit her.

"Mom, I'm gonna look like a true nerd!" I say disappointedly.

"Why do you say that?"

"I already have glasses. Now that I am getting braces, there is no doubt that I'm going to be a nerd. When I smile now, people are going to freak out because they will see all the metal on my face and think I'm some kind of machine!"

"I think you are overreacting, but I can see why you don't want to do this." My mom loves giving me crap, but she knows when to stop.

After the long drive, she pulls into the parking lot leading to hell. I take a deep breath as I unbuckle my seatbelt. Turning toward Mom, I give her a fake smile and say, "This is my before picture for your memory. Hold on to it."

She laughs, "Come on, let's get this over with."

I open the door and see the secretary look up and give one of those evil smiles. She is probably thinking, "Oh, you poor child, you have no clue what we are going to do to you." Mom takes a seat and hands me a magazine.

"This will take your mind off of it for a bit," she says. Before I get the chance to even open the cover, the evil secretary calls my name to go back to the dungeon.

I follow her down the hall, and then she steps aside and points to the left. Looking into the room, I see a reclinable chair resembling the electric chair. I take my seat. A friendly assistant walks in and gets the doctor's tools out for operation. She places a bib around my neck, making me look like a toddler.

"What color of braces would you like?" she asks me, sounding so serious.

"Umm . . . I never really thought about it. Blue?" I say shyly.

I wait about ten minutes before Dr. Duehr enters the room. We greet each other, and he wastes no time getting to work. A lot of jerking and gagging on the tools shoved in my mouth happens during the procedure. The gritty, salty taste of the adhesive he uses to keep the actual braces on my teeth makes me want to puke. I keep trying not to swallow the dirty saliva, but I can't help it unless I want to drool all over myself.

Thank God for the little, pink bib because it's catching all of my slobber. Once the braces are cemented on, he tightens them to start the process of straightening my crooked teeth. I have never felt a more uncomfortable feeling than I do right now. I swear that my teeth literally move with every tug he makes.

"Does this hurt?" Dr. Duehr asks as he jams my mouth full of tools. I hate that. I hate that he is asking me questions when he knows that I can't answer them clearly.

"Yeah!" I somehow gurgle out of my mouth, really thinking I want to reach up and choke him because it feels as if he is pulling my teeth out one by one.

Finally, he finishes yanking at my poor teeth. I sit up in the chair and lean over the water fountain on my left. As I swish water around in my mouth, I just want to cry because I feel these chunks of metal hanging off my teeth. The assistant takes my bib off and helps me out of the chair. I feel ready to run out of the office because I am finally finished, but Dr. Duehr has different plans. He calls my mom back to the room. Mom peeks around the corner with a smirk on her face.

"Smile!" she says.

"Don't even start!" I tell her.

"She will probably have these on for one to two years," Dr. Duehr says.

I feel light-headed. One to two years! Is he smoking something? I can't help but ask myself what I did to deserve this. Mom and Dr. Duehr talk for about five minutes, but I can't pay attention because I keep thinking, "What are my friends going to say." I snap out of it.

"When you get home, you might want to take a few Tylenol because you will feel some pain, but that won't be for a while," he tells me as he pats me on the back. Mom chuckles and puts her arm around me as we leave the room. The secretary talks to Mom about making payments, and finally I open the door feeling freed from the gates of hell.

"Are you hungry?" Mom asks.

"Yeah, I'm starved because I missed lunch with the appointment and all."

We get into the car and drive to Burger King. Mom goes through the drive-thru to save time. I get my usual Whopper Jr. and fries with a lemonade. I rip open my food like a barbarian and start to stuff my face.

"Oh, my God, ouch!" I scream.

"What's wrong?" Mom says, sounding panicked.

I can't even eat because my teeth feel so sensitive. There goes that idea. Being a good mom, she swings by Wal-Mart and gets me pudding. I must lick the spoon because if my teeth even touch it, I will scream. Well, I guess this is going to take some getting used to, but at least my teeth will look good in a few years. For now, I'll dress in tin foil hoping to get a good song to come in.

Discussion Questions:

1. What event is the writer relating? What point of view is used and how effectively does it work?

2. What point or significance does the writer try to establish in the piece?

3. Evaluate the author's use of dialogue. How does it enhance or detract from the story?

4. Has the writer included details, such as sense imagery and figurative language? Do they enhance the writing? Why or why not?

5. Analyze the effectiveness of the title, introduction, and conclusion. How well do they support the topic?

6. Does the writer "have heart" in the essay? What specific aspects of the piece support your response?

7. Explain the strengths of this essay. What improvements for the piece would you suggest?

8. Evaluate the effectiveness of the piece holistically and provide rationale for your evaluation.

~ ~ ~

"One line of dialogue is worth paragraphs of description.
No matter what you say about a character, if he doesn't speak,
he hasn't truly come alive" (Murray, *Shoptalk* 151).
—Leslie Epstein

~ ~ ~

THE MECHANICS OF WRITING DIALOGUE

1. Begin a new paragraph and a new set of quotation marks each time a speaker changes.

My nephew lay tightly swathed in his mother Gretchen's arms. I finally held the little alien who, like a soccer player, had been kicking the inside of his mother's stomach. I gazed into his wrinkled, prune face and felt a rush of love swallow me like a tidal wave. "Hi, there, Buddy. I'm your Aunt Michie. You're so beautiful. Yes, you are. Oh, you're so sweet," I crooned.

When he came home from the hospital, I got my first opportunity to change a newborn baby's diaper. "He sure does poop a lot, doesn't he?" I asked.

"Not any more than any other newborn," Gretchen replied.

"You mean they all poop this much?" I gasped.

"Yep."

"You're kidding."

"Nope."

"Man, diapers must cost a fortune."

Gretchen just laughed at me and shook her head.

—Michie Sisler-Turner

2. **Begin a new quotation with a capital letter.**

"Get in the car—now!" commanded Dad.

Dad commanded, "Get in the car—now!"

NOTE: do not use quotation marks in an indirect quotation (not the speaker's exact words).

Dad commanded that we get into the car.

3. **Use new sets of quotation marks when a direct quotation is interrupted by "tags," explanatory words such as <u>he remarked</u> or <u>she explained</u>. Try to vary the tag words, if you even need them, rather than repeatedly writing "he said" or "she said."**

"Good prose," advises Somerset Maugham, "should resemble the conversation of a well-bred man."

NOTE: If the second part of an interrupted quotation begins a new sentence, it must begin with a capital letter.

"I never know when I start a draft where I will go and how I will get there," writes Donald Murray. "I hope you will be as fortunate as you find out that writing is rewriting" (*The Craft of Revision* 22).

Many times no "tag" is needed because the speaker is clearly recognizable and the action accurately reflects the intention of the speaker. For example,

Tom turned to Martha. "Are you taking composition this semester?"

"I can't wait to get started," she replied.

"Not me!"

"Why not?"

"I work 40 hours a week and take four other classes besides."
Martha lowered her eyes. "I feel sorry for you."

4. Use single quotation marks to enclose a quotation within a quotation.

Professor Bumpkin said, "I consider the advice of the *Hamlet* character Polonius, 'To thine own self be true,' to be applicable in any age."

5. Place other punctuation marks used with quotation marks as follows:

a. Place a comma or a period inside closing quotation marks.

"Good prose," suggests Somerset Maugham, "should resemble the conversation of a well-bred man."

b. Place a colon or semicolon outside closing quotation marks.

Professor Wright stated, "You have passed this course"; what he said after that I was too astonished to hear.

In the words of Professor Wright, the following writers have "exceeded my expectations": Norrie North, Samuel South, Erica East, and Walter West.

c. Place a question mark or exclamation point inside the closing quotation marks when it is part of the quotation.

"Are the peer response groups finished yet?" inquired the composition instructor.

d. Place a question mark or exclamation point outside the closing quotation marks when it is part of the entire sentence.

Have you read Frost's poem "The Road Not Taken"?

~ ~ ~

> *"In my view, stories and novels consist of three parts: narration, which moves the story from point A to point B and finally to point Z; description, which creates a sensory reality for the reader; and dialogue, which brings characters to life through their speech"* (163).
> —Stephen King

~ ~ ~

PRACTICE 3A: Dialogue   Punctuate the following groups of words by adding necessary capital letters, quotation marks, and any other needed punctuation.

1. I was late for class because my car wouldn't start explained

Tess.
2. Tess explained that she was late for class because her car would not start.
3. I was late for class Tess explained because my car wouldn't start.
4. Move back screamed the little girl's mother she needs room to breathe.
5. The revision of your last essay continued Professor Wright must be submitted at the beginning of the next class.
6. Why is he moaning is he hurt asked the nurse.
7. Ignore her suggested Bob she's just faking.
8. Effectively using dialogue added Derrick will help your story come to life.
9. The older of the two young men asked where Professor Hiccup's office was.
10. Getting that response group on track commented Phil could take a miracle they always seem to be distracted.
11. Why should our group be scheduled last complained Helen we got here first.
12. When the prof begins class whispered Allie we'll sneak out just be careful not to make any noise.
13. I'll write the story Martha replied if you give me some suggestions I always struggle with beginnings.
14. Yes I recognize the student who finished her portfolio said Ingrid but I can't find her editing partner.
15. Get out bellowed the editor you're wasting my time.

PRACTICE 3B: Dialogue   Indent and punctuate the following exchange of dialogue.

My ten-year-old son Jeremy takes his stance while holding the big, shiny, metal bat high. The pitch flies toward Jeremy at blazing speed. I hear a loud bang as bat meets ball and sends it flying into outer space. I get so excited that I stand up and scream way to go, Jeremy. I run from the stands to the field to congratulate Jeremy. I give him a big bear hug and exclaim you did it. Awesome hit, huh Mom? The greatest I have ever seen, I reply. It is the best feeling in the world! he states. I'm so proud of you, Jeremy. Thanks, Mom. My son made a memory that day, and I shared in his joy.—Bev Engler

DEVELOPING A STRONG STYLE
THROUGH ACTION VERBS

Strong Verbs Make Strong Writers

Strong, action-packed verbs invigorate, energize, and tighten writing style. Columnist Joan Beck calls verbs the vibrant heart of the sentence and says, "Verbs pump action into the message. They energize static nouns into motion and jab predicates into shape. Verbs tease, purr, shout, intrigue, hook, motivate" (Scott 57).

A writing style demonstrating strong, lively verbs will serve a number of purposes. Writing becomes more precise, exciting, and forceful. By allowing the writer to omit unnecessary words, verb strength also helps condense phrases and sentences, for as Robert Southey says, "Words are like sunbeams—the more they are condensed, the deeper they burn" (Perrine 450). In addition, writers broaden their vocabularies, which fosters a more interesting, specific style. Verb strength also forces writers beyond simple sentence structures into a variety of patterns, such as dependent clauses, phrases, and appositives.

When revising and editing, writers should identify weak, overused verbs which tend to deaden style and increase wordiness. Then they should substitute specific, action-packed verbs for the following at every opportunity:

- **DO:** do, doing, does, did, done
Walter does his studying at the kitchen table can be rewritten **Walter studies at the kitchen table.**
- **HAVE:** have, having, has, had
The rotten egg has a putrid smell can be rewritten **The rotten egg smells putrid.**
- **BE:** am, is, are, was, were, be, being, been
There are many examples to show that this team is great can be rewritten **Many examples show the greatness of this team.**

Note that forms of <u>do</u> (do, does, did, done), <u>have</u> (have, has, had), and <u>be</u> (am, is, are, was, were, be, been) might be used as helping verbs to form various tenses. The sentence, *"I have four rabbits,"* uses a weak verb <u>have</u> as the main verb while **"I have revised my writing for verb strength"** uses the helping verb <u>have</u> with the main verb <u>revised</u>. Writers may use forms of <u>do, have,</u> and <u>be</u> as helping (auxiliary) verbs but should try to avoid them as main (primary) verbs.

As writers use stronger, more specific verbs, they develop sentence structure variety which provides a livelier style. For example, *"Jay Gatsby is the protagonist of a novel in which he is deceitful and cunning in order to win back his first love, Daisy Buchanan"* can be revised by eliminating the weak verb <u>is</u> and by using an appositive: **"Jay Gatsby, the novel's cunning protagonist, uses deception to win back his first love, Daisy Buchanan."** This sentence could also be written using a dependent clause: **"When Jay Gatsby, the novel's protagonist, uses deception, he wins back his first love, Daisy Buchanan."**

As writers eliminate weak verbs, they sometimes replace the <u>be</u> forms with other unconvincing verb phrases. This practice also leads to wordiness and a sense of uncertainty in writing. Therefore, avoid replacing <u>be</u> forms with **seems, appears to be, exists as,** or **proves to be** or replacing <u>have/has</u> with **possesses.** These verbs only replace verb shallowness, enhance wordiness, and cause writing style to feel forced. For example, *"It seems to be snowing in Florida"* can be reduced to **"It is snowing in Florida."** *"Fred often possesses a smiling face"* can be revised to read **"Fred smiles often."**

Sentences beginning with *"There is (was), There are (were)"* or *"It is (was)"* will also force writers into using weak verbs. *"There are millions of Americans who love baseball"* can be revised to **"Millions of Americans love baseball."** *"It is necessary for writers to analyze their styles for vigorous verbs"* can be revised to **"Writers should analyze their styles for vigorous verbs."** In addition to adding a more forceful, energetic tone, eliminating *"There is (are)"* and *"It is (was)"* at the beginning of sentences helps develop a tighter, more economic writing style.

Writers can also enhance their verb strength by avoiding nominalization—adding suffixes such as -ion to verbs to form nouns. Whenever possible, rewrite sentences by transferring an

-ion ending noun into a verb. *"It is the company's intention to give the workers a raise,"* for example, uses the noun <u>intention</u> which becomes the verb <u>intends</u> in the following revision: **"This company intends to give the workers a raise."** The following example demonstrates the same idea. *"The administration made the decision to drop the athletic program"* might be revised to **"The administration decided to drop the athletic program."** Notice how the noun <u>decision</u> (ending in -ion) can form a more forceful verb <u>decided</u>. Besides <u>-ion</u>, "some other noun endings smother verbs: <u>-ance</u>, <u>-ment</u>, <u>-ancy</u>, <u>-ant</u>, <u>-ent</u>, <u>-able</u>" (Scott 57). Nouns ending in these suffixes can easily be converted to verbs like:

He has dominance over — he dominates
They are in agreement — they agree
They are in violation of — they violate
Her contention is — she contends that

Initially writers may find revising sentences for verb strength painful and time-consuming since they have relied on the same weak verbs for most of their writing lives. However, after a bit of practice, writers find revising with vigorous verbs both challenging and rewarding. In addition, a lively, economic writing style reinforces the value of this revision strategy.

~ ~ ~

"Colorful, vibrant verbs produce persuasive,
dynamic, specific writing. They energize and
uplift your writing. A strong verb evokes imagery
and movement. In contrast, a weak verb seems
vague and lethargic" (109).
—Elizabeth Danziger

~ ~ ~

PRACTICE 3C: Weak Verbs vs. Helping Verbs   On your paper, make two columns. Label the left column <u>helping verbs</u> and the right column <u>main verbs</u>. Write all helping verbs in the left column and the main verbs in the right column. Remember, a main verb may be preceded by one, two, or three helping verbs, or sometimes none at all. Also, main verbs may be separated from their helping verbs by adverbs, like <u>not</u>. See number 11 in the GLOSSARY of Editing FUNdamentals for a list of helping verbs.

Helping   Main

1. Wilmer had not yet finished his essay.

2. He must have been planning to complete it over the weekend.

3. He should have asked the instructor for help.

4. But he felt foolish, so he never approached the instructor.

5. Do you believe Wilmer's apprehension?

6. Our instructor would surely have understood.

7. He would probably even have extended the deadline for Wilmer.

8. Or would this instructor go that far?

9. We will never know.

PRACTICE 3D: Style—Verb Strength   Eliminate weak verbs to tighten and liven style by revising and/or combining the following examples.

1. My name is Robin Goodfellow. I was born on January 12, 1984, at Story County Hospital.

2. Gerald is my oldest child, and it was a cold Friday in November when he was born.

3. High school graduation is a milestone in many students' lives. It is not only the end of a long journey but also the beginning of adult life.

4. My parents' names are Herman and Hilda. They gave each of my brothers names that start with "H."

5. My sister is eleven, and she is in fourth grade at Romper Room Elementary School.

6. I am currently in the AA program. It is a big change from high school.

7. There were a lot of open fields and wild timber to explore.

8. When I was a little girl, I read a book called *Grimm's Fairy Tales.*

9. My parents are Mickey and Minnie Mouse. Until recently, they have lived in Disneyland.

10. I could be a writer with all the adventures I've had.

PRACTICE 3E: Style—Verb Strength   Tighten and liven style by eliminating weak verbs and combining sentences. Then count the number of words in your revised paragraphs.

I.   I have many memories from the past 18 years. There are plenty of years left to make more, but some of the greatest ones are in the past. I have a lot of accomplishments, but still have more to come. I am anxious for the new challenges of college life. Over the past years, when a problem would arise, there were familiar people to help me. Now it's a whole new world. (73 words)

II.   My high school was very small. It had about 110 kids in all four grades. My graduating class was about as big as my immediate family. However, even though it was small, it taught me the ropes of what future schooling would be like. Not only did I learn through the classes, but also through sports, as well. Basketball and baseball were the only two sports the school had to offer, and I was in love with both of them. (80 words)

PRACTICE 3F: Style—Verb Strength   Revise the following passage to improve the style by eliminating weak verbs and combining the sentences whenever possible. Edit carefully for awkward word choices, fragments and run-ons, usage, spelling, and punctuation. Count your words after you revise each paragraph to see how much you have tightened the style.

Pianists and Shortstops – Similar Players

There are many similarities between pianists and shortstops. Both talents are a combination of coordination, intelligence, and dedication. Playing piano is a talent that requires musicians to train their hands to hit the proper keys. Playing shortstop is a talent that demands athletes to develop their hand-eye coordination to handle opponents' batted balls and teammates' throws. (56 words)

Intelligence is also a requirement for both pianists and shortstops. Pianists do a lot of studying of musical theories and techniques in order to turn a musical score into a satisfactory performance. Shortstops also have to study baseball fundamentals and game situations in order to become successful athletes. Both playing piano and playing shortstop are skills that require focused dedication in spending hours upon hours of practice to improve. (69 words)

Good music teachers and good coaches are also essential for

pianists and shortstops to develop their skills. Both teachers and coaches are educators who must emphasize the fundamentals of both skills. Plus, it is important that teachers and coaches encourage their students to practice and progress throughout the learning process. Piano teachers have the responsibility to guide their students through learning stages from beginner to intermediate to advanced. Baseball coaches do the same for their shortstops as they direct their players through Little League to Pony League to Babe Ruth League. (90 words)

If they have talent, young pianists may be participants in high school bands, orchestras, or choirs. Similarly, shortstops may be members of high school junior varsity or varsity baseball teams. In these situations, pianists' or shortstops' talents, combined with those of their musical groups or baseball teams, may be a source of accomplishment and pride. In addition, gifted musicians or athletes may have the talent to progress to even higher levels of performance beyond the high school level. At these higher levels, pianists and shortstops can truly call themselves accomplished "players." (91 words)

(Total words = 306)

PRACTICE 3G: Style—Verb Strength   Revisit your essays and revise them for verb strength.

CONCISENESS / CUT THE DEADWOOD

Cut the Deadwood!

"Less is more." Good writers revise every sentence for conciseness until they are satisfied that every phrase cannot be rewritten more succinctly without sacrificing clarity. In their classic on writing, *The Elements of Style*, William Strunk, Jr., and E.B. White say:

> Vigorous writing is concise. A sentence should contain no unnecessary words, a paragraph no unnecessary sentences, for the same reason that drawing should have

no unnecessary lines and a machine no unnecessary parts. This requires not that writers make all their sentences short or that they avoid all detail and treat the subject only in outline, but that every word tells. (23)

Usually reduction for conciseness occurs during the revision or editing stages of the writing process. In his book *On Writing*, famous novelist Stephen King suggests the following formula for conciseness: "2nd draft =1st draft − 10%." So, revise for conciseness to develop a tighter, more readable writing style.

To avoid wordiness, implement the following suggestions:

1. **Use strong, action-packed verbs.**
    Jim is a composition teacher at NICC. (7)
    Jim teaches composition at NICC. (5)
    Writers have to revise for conciseness. (6)
    Writers must revise for conciseness. (5)
    Good writers do the job of revising for conciseness. (9)
    Good writers revise for conciseness. (5)

2. **Avoid repetition of the same word or idea.**
    In my opinion, I feel composition should be required of all college students. (13)
    I feel composition should be required of all college students. (10)
    Composition should be required of all college students. (8)
    It is obvious that our college's basketball record could dip down into the lower half of the conference standings. (19)
    Our college's basketball record could dip into the lower half of the conference standings. (14)

3. **Avoid wasted word groups like I believe, I think, I feel, In my opinion.**
    I think that the Cardinals should win the pennant this season. (11)
    The Cardinals should win the pennant this season. (8)

4. **Eliminate unnecessary adverbs, especially: definitely, just, quite, really, very.**
    The college student really enjoyed his composition class. (8)
    The college student loved his composition class. (7)
    The writer's creative work shows that he is very smart. (10)
    The writer's creative work shows his intelligence. (7)

5. **Eliminate fillers like The reason is... because or The thing that I am looking forward to is...**

The reason we are studying this concept is to eliminate wasted words in writing. (14)

We are studying this concept to eliminate writing wasted words. (11)

The thing that I am looking forward to is attending a Carrie Underwood concert next year. (16)

I am looking forward to attending a Carrie Underwood concert next year. (12)

6. **Cut who, which, that from your writing whenever possible.**

Mark Twain, who is a famous American writer, wrote *Tom Sawyer* in 1876. (12)

Mark Twain, a famous American writer, wrote *Tom Sawyer* in 1876. (10)

The letter that I gave you came from the Dean of Students. (12)

The letter I gave you came from the Dean of Students. (11)

MORE STRATEGIES FOR CONCISENESS

1. **Eliminate dummy subjects—There is (are), Here is (are), It is (was).**

There are seven ways I have found to reduce wordiness. (10)

I have found seven ways to reduce wordiness. (8)

It is apparent that William Shakespeare was a brilliant writer. (10)

William Shakespeare wrote brilliantly. (4)

2. **Write in active voice.**

The composition students were assigned a research paper by the instructor. (11)

The composition instructor assigned his students a research paper. (9)

A research paper will be written by the students in this course. (12)

Students in this course will write a research paper. (9)

3. **Combine sentences when the first word or reference of a second sentence repeats the last word of the previous sentence.**

For junior high, I went to Jefferson. Jefferson was a whole new experience for me. (15)

I attended Jefferson Junior High, which became a whole new experience for me. (13)

All the boys in the neighborhood were jealous of my new racing bike. The bike went faster and jumped farther than any other bike around. (25)

The neighborhood boys were jealous of my new racing bike,

which went faster and jumped higher than any other bike around. (21)

Last summer my parents moved to Buena Vista. Buena Vista is a small town located on the banks of the Mississippi River. (22)

Last summer my parents moved to Buena Vista, a small town located on the banks of the Mississippi. (18)

4.   Reduce clauses to phrases and phrases to single words.

Because we found no one in the instructor's office, we left a note. (13)

Finding no one in the instructor's office, we left a note. (11)

The students decided that they would start their research essays early. (11)

The students decided to start their research essays early.(9)

The tennis players who came from California were scheduled for the third day of the competition. (16)

The tennis players from California were scheduled for day three of the competition. (13)

Stephen King, who is a fine novelist, published another book this year. (12)

Stephen King, a fine novelist, published another book this year. (10)

The classes that were canceled will be rescheduled. (8)

Canceled classes will be rescheduled. (5)

Zelmo wrote all of his essays in a conscientious way. (10)

Zelmo wrote all his essays conscientiously. (6)

5.   Remove –ing words whenever possible.

The instructor was reading the class's essays for six hours. (10)

The instructor read the class's essays for six hours. (9)

PRACTICE 3H: Conciseness   Reduce wordiness in the following word groups taken from student essays.

1. due to the fact that	8. raised up	15. huddled together
2. at this point in time	9. be in agreement with	16. merge together
3. exact same spot	10. few in number	17. control over
4. sinks down	11. descend down	18. calmed myself down
5. finished up	12. gather up	19. ended up
6. passes by	13. replied back	20. return back
7. green in color	14. It is obvious that	21. smile on his face

PRACTICE 3I: Conciseness   Reduce the wordiness in the following examples.

1. We went and checked in.
2. I proceeded to start the car.
3. I very much feared…
4. I raced off in a sprint.
5. I completely told her everything.
6. I wondered to myself…
7. They pretty much became resentful of each other.
8. My brother replied by saying…
9. Three and four days passed us by.
10. It unites everyone together.
11. The inside of my truck is definitely not the neatest.
12. Cindy's parents decided to divorce. The divorce was a shock to everyone.
13. I also have some very strange luck.
14. I definitely ran down the stairs faster than I have ever moved in my entire life.
15. I quickly lost any momentary compassion I possessed toward the snake.
16. I didn't get much sleep that night.
17. We lined up in the cafeteria so that everyone could tell us congratulations.
18. Ima Writer went and sat down in front of her computer and proceeded to compose her first essay.
19. I was taught at a very young age to respect guns.
20. The reason for returning to school is because I want to make a better life for my family and me.

PRACTICE 3J: Conciseness   Reduce the wordiness in the following sentences.

1. It is evident that some students decided to hand in their essays early in order that they might receive bonus points. (21)
2. After the student had looked everywhere for a research article on dyslexia, he finally copied a section of information that he found in his psychology text. (26)
3. The vacation that we took to Seattle last year would have been perfect if it had not been for all the rain that fell each day we were there. (29)

4. Since we were sitting in seats right behind home plate in Wrigley Field, we were able to analyze and judge the accuracy of the home plate umpire's calls. (28)
5. The most common complaint that is made by students at this college is that all teachers choose the same day on which to give their exams. (26)

PRACTICE 3K: Conciseness   Revise the following paragraph for conciseness.

At this point in time in my college career, I am one of those students who think that the library should remain open during the week of final exams. It is obvious that students need a place that is very quiet and orderly in order for them to handle the pressures that go along with finals week. If the library is closed during this week of final exams, students will have to go to the cafeteria, which is very noisy, or to go to the conference center, which is definitely too far away from the main section of the college. Students of this college really have earned the right to have the library open during finals week. If things like this continue to happen, the morale of the student body could end up going down. (136 words)

UNNECESSARY SHIFTS IN TENSE, VOICE, PERSON

past tense   *present tense*
TENSE: I **wrote** four pages of my essay when my computer **starts** to malfunction.

            1ˢᵗ person   *2ⁿᵈ person*
PERSON: Anyone like **me** would feel frustrated after **you** wrote four
    1ˢᵗ person   *2ⁿᵈ person*
pages of **my** persuasive essay, and then **your** computer started to malfunction.

        active voice
VOICE: I **planned** to register for next semester's classes, but most of
        passive   voice
the sections **had** already **been filled** by sophomores.

The three examples above illustrate unnecessary shifts in tense, person, and voice. Writers must try to retain consistency in these three areas so they do not confuse or annoy readers. Consistency in tense, person, and voice requires conscientious revising and editing.

TENSE: Perhaps the most annoying shift to a reader involves tense (present, past, future) because the verb carries the main action and the sense of time. Shifting tenses illogically within a sentence or group of sentences can mislead or contradict the intended meaning of a passage. Obviously, verb tenses will need to change when they indicate obvious time changes.

PERSON: The English conjugation system uses three persons: first person (I, me, we, us) refers to the writer or speaker; second person (you) refers to the reader or listener; and third person (he, she, it, they) refers to people being written or spoken about. Most shifts occur when writers jump from first or third person to second person.

VOICE: Revise/edit carefully to avoid unnecessary shifts from active to passive voice. In the active voice, the subject of the verb acts. In the passive voice, the subject of the verb is acted upon. Many times a shift in voice causes a shift in subject matter. If you begin a sentence in the active voice, do not shift to passive voice, and vice versa.

PRACTICE 3L: Unnecessary Shifts Revise the following sentences to adjust inconsistencies in tense, person, or voice.

1. The professor reads a statement to the students but refused to respond to questions.
2. If first year college students expect to earn good grades, you need to organize your time and study habits consistently.
3. Students should not expect to rely on their parents for all their financial support because you need to support yourself as an adult.
4. When you feel the flu coming on, students should rest and drink plenty of fluids.
5. When we go to Florida for spring break, you visited the beach for sun and fun.
6. The wide receiver caught the pass and weaves his way through three defenders toward the end zone.
7. We leave for the library at 11 o'clock, and a sub-sandwich was eaten on the way at the snack bar.
8. If a person likes to see thrilling drama, you should watch Mel Gibson's portrayal of Hamlet.
9. The response group reads the first peer's essay, and the third essay is read forty-five minutes later.
10. The composition student read Chapter Five of the text, and then the essay was written.

PRACTICE 3M: Unnecessary Shifts   Rewrite the following passage to provide consistency in tense, person, and voice.

I learned better and succeeded in grade school because of my parents and teachers. I was forced by my parents to do my homework before anything else. That way you always have the assignments finished for the next day. The teachers also were always willing to help you, and then I started to like school. I was helped by teachers before and after school. Those teachers want students to learn, and they didn't let you get away with anything. You learned more and grow in knowledge because my parents and teachers guided you through your elementary school years.

PRACTICE 3N: Unnecessary Shifts   Revise the following paragraph for specific word choices and consistency of tense, person, and voice.

People annually gather with family and friends on the fourth Thursday of November to celebrate Thanksgiving. A feast is usually cooked by one of the family members. This get-together usually took place in the cook's home as well. When we arrive, the Macey's Parade on TV is watched by us. They really know how to put on a show in that parade. Then you sit down to a big meal of turkey, trimmings, and dessert. When we are stuffed, we sat in the living room and watched the NFL pro football game. When you finish that, they will start up a card game which always lasted a few hours. If a person likes parades, food, football, cards, and fun, they will enjoy Thanksgiving with our family.

PORTFOLIO IN PROGRESS

The Demonstration Portfolio, submitted near the end of the course, allows you to get responses, improve, and revise earlier pieces as the course progresses. In addition, you will continually self-reflect on your growth as a writer, determine ways to improve your writing, and prepare entry slips for your Demonstration Portfolio. The Entry Slip-Reflection ideas suggested in the "Portfolio in Progress" section at the end of Chapter 2 may help you reflect on your writing. Keep track of your self-reflections by dating them, labeling them, and saving them in a secure place (notebook, journal, computer) so you can draw on these ideas as you prepare your portfolio entry slips.

PORTFOLIO INTRODUCTION

Process a preliminary introduction for your portfolio. Let it introduce you and your writings and the organizational theme you will use. The excerpts below are taken from longer pieces. They are intended to show how other students have introduced their portfolios. Choose a style and format for your introduction that fits you and helps you feel comfortable inviting readers into your portfolio.

*****

I invite you to uncover the many fine treasures hidden within my treasure chest. When you open my treasure chest, you will discover the rich, sparkling, fine jewels that I have carefully selected and polished before adding them to my collection. Each jewel within my treasure chest reflects on a special event, a special person, or a memorable past experience. I encourage you to sit back, relax, and enjoy the many treasures I have collected throughout Composition I.

In jewel one, "I'm Not Sure Which Path to Take," I invite you to feel the uncertainty I felt when I decided to further my education...

—Luetta Bockenstedt

*****

Hi! Are you ready for an adventure? You are invited to ride with me through the jungle of my life. The jungle holds some scary things, but I assure you that you won't get hurt. Make sure you come prepared. For this safari, you will need an open mind, a sense of humor, and a desire to learn about different things. Oh! I almost forgot. You will also need a safari hat.

The safari consists of nine parts. In the first section of the jungle, I will try to show you a little about myself and the events that have shaped me. In the second section...

—Kara Pickel Schroeder

*****

Welcome to the forest of my young adult life. In this forest, you will find that life can be rewarding and challenging...So I invite you to sit back and enjoy the journey through my forest.

Upon entering the forest, you will spot a majestic eagle, "The Inspirer," perched high on a tall, oak branch. His regal appearance will inspire you to continue your journey to discover what other mysteries lie within my forest. Just like my high school teacher, Mr. Lynn Hoernke, the eagle serves as a symbol of inspiration and comfort...

As you wander deeper into the forest, you will come upon a dense fog. You can see the sun shining above you, but the fog brings on another feeling making it "A Joyful, Sorrowful Day." This piece of writing brings to life my memories of the day I lost my best friend, a significant event in my life...

—Amanda Mathe

*****

Welcome to Gina's Cinema Center #1. The latest viewings include: *Opposites Attract, Field of Dreams, I Hate Everything About You, Letter to Maggie Burger, Writer's Profile*, and *Abandon All Hope, You Who Enter Here*. All are rated A. The popcorn is freshly made here, and the Coca-Cola stays chilled. The crowds are packing in. You, the viewer, must hurry to find a seat.

Which would you like to view first? I will make it a bit easier for you by offering you a sneak preview. The first viewing, *Opposites Attract*, is written comically and realistically. It tells the story of one couple's finally realizing the differences between them...

—Regina Shafer

GLAD, BAD, SAD, OR MAD

The following sentences are taken from student writings. Note how the misuse of language or failure to edit affects meaning. Evaluate the sentences by rating each one as GLAD (witty), BAD (accidental error), SAD (misuse of language), or MAD (a little off center).

1. The pain in my chest was so great I could do nothing but wine.
2. The lady said, "Ladies and Gentile men, we have five minutes before we begin.
3. I side with relief, "Yes, I'm fine."
4. Mr. Max not only gave us testes but also made us demonstrate our understanding of the subject.
5. My opponent is starting to feel more powerful, and I am briefly weekend.
6. Police help drug attics to seek help.

CHAPTER 4

Hey, Expert, Explain Yourself!

~ ~ ~

*"Good writers work hard to make sense and to
avoid confusion and to write with grace as well as clarity"* (6).
—Richard Marius

~ ~ ~

Many of the pieces you write for college or in the job market will ask you to explain something to "make sense and avoid confusion." For example, in an essay exam in history, you might need to explain the causes of the Civil War while in biology, you might explain the language of bees. This type of writing will focus on conveying information; therefore, you will need to focus on the subject more than on yourself.

For this type of writing, you will explain to a novice reader a concept, activity, or hobby about which you feel like an expert. Focus your readers' attention on a part of the concept, activity, or hobby if your topic seems too broad. Much of your success with this piece of writing depends on your ability to see natural breaks or divisions in an activity and to select part of that activity. Rather than trying to explain an entire baseball pitcher's motion, you might select only the wind-up or only the delivery. It would be unrealistic to try to explain how to be a parent. But you might select some aspect of parenting, like motivating your daughter to do her homework. It would be equally impossible to teach a beginner how to play football or a golfer how to use all the clubs. But you could explain tackling or putting.

Use writing strategies you've developed in the preceding chapters—such as sense imagery, figurative language, dialogue—to help explain your topic. Humor may also serve as an effective strategy for this essay.

STRUT YOUR STUFF!

Writing Project 4-1: You're the Expert Think of some interesting aspect of your life in which you consider yourself an expert. Assume that you, the expert, are introducing a novice (beginner) to this concept, activity, or hobby. Single out a process within your topic (like attending school full-time and parenting, or getting up out of the water in water skiing, or hitting a serve in tennis). Explain the concept, the activity, or the hobby to a novice. Write creatively rather than letting your explanation sound like a list of steps in a cookbook or assembly kit. Keep a personal focus by narrating from first (I, me, we, us) or third person (he, she, it, they), instead of second person (you) or using imperative sentences (you implied subject). Provide concrete examples and details to help the readers see your explanation come to life. Above all, remember: **you've gotta have heart in your writing.**

Writing Checklist:

- [ ] 1. Have you clearly explained the concept, activity, or hobby by using concrete examples and details? Do you come across as an expert?
- [ ] 2. Is the explanation geared to a novice's level of understanding?
- [ ] 3. Does your personal voice come through the writing?
- [ ] 4. Do the title, introduction, and conclusion effectively serve the topic and explanation?
- [ ] 5. Do you stay consistent in narration (first or third person) and tense (present or past)?

SAMPLE STUDENT WRITING
You're the Expert

A Hard Act to Follow
By Jennifer Basten

"Oh, Honey, what time is supper tonight?" I hear this question over and over, again at least thirty times or more, each night I work at the Galena Stauss Hospital Assisted Living. Caring for people with dementia poses many challenges for families and caregivers. I happen to be an expert in dealing with the most common form of dementia,

Alzheimer's. People with Alzheimer's experience many emotions, and I, the caregiver, must remain alert to how the Alzheimer's patient may react in any given situation such as episodes of patients' inability to remember things; difficulty in thinking clearly; a lack of communication skills; and an increased challenge in caring for themselves, mood swings, and changes in personalities and behaviors.

Good communication skills enhance my ability to handle the difficult behavior I may encounter when dealing with Alzheimer's patients. I start work at three-thirty in the afternoon and get off around eleven at night. During this time frame, I spend a great majority of my time with Alzheimer's patients. I hear the same questions over and over again. My favorites include, "What time is supper tonight?" "Do I live here?" "What is your name again?" The solution to this sort of repeated question remains in the care-giver's hands. First, I always act in a positive manner because my attitude and body language communicate feelings stronger than words. I respond, "Supper is at five o'clock." "Yes, you do live here, in apartment 205." "My name is Jennifer."

Many Alzheimer's patients seem to experience states of confusion and forgetfulness. I must remain calm and patient when these situations arise, and speaking in a soft, subtle voice using short, simple sentences helps. Sometimes, it seems as if I am speaking to a group of preschoolers instead of a group of elderly men and women. I recall a case when I used my voice as a tool in calming or reassuring an Alzheimer's patient. An elderly lady with Alzheimer's came up to me and asked if I could tell her husband something for her. I knew her husband died years ago, but she believed he still lived with her. When this situation occurs, I never argue or fight with the patient. The best approach involves slowly bringing the patient back to reality. Our conversation went like this:

"I was wondering if you could tell my husband something for me."

"OK, what would you like me to tell him?"

"I want him to walk Julie to school tomorrow because I will be busy."

"Oh, OK, I will be sure to tell him."

After this conversation, I walked her back to her room. I then explained to her that her husband died several years ago. She then told me that he lived with her and slept on the bed with her. I followed her to her bed, and she showed me a photograph of him. Then in a calm and subtle voice, I explained to her that her husband died and that the picture could not talk. She then came back to reality and told me she had gone crazy. I responded by saying, "You are far from crazy."

She giggled and said, "I know. You are the crazy one, but I still adore you."

One situation that required me to act in a different manner involved an agitated Alzheimer's patient. This type of behavior involved displays of irritability and verbal or physical aggression. Alzheimer's or dementia patients become agitated by a variety of things. The most common reason involves a change. People with this type of disease may respond in a violent manner when they encounter a change. For example, I just got a haircut an hour before going to work. My hair looked different; my hair was not pulled back in a ponytail. It remained straight down with bangs hanging over my eyes. A patient of mine approached me yelling absurd things to me about my hair. She even yanked on my hair saying that I looked like a slob. I liked my haircut, but I forgot the change might stir up some negative emotions with my patients.

If an Alzheimer's patient becomes violent about a particular topic, I change the topic. I simply distract or redirect the patient. Some things I do include changing the subject by asking him or her to go for a walk or to play a game. Another good technique in calming a patient involves humor. I tell jokes because people with dementia, or Alzheimer's, tend to retain their social skills and are delighted to laugh with or at me. I enjoy using humor with my patients because it brings out the best in them. They even tell some wild and funny jokes.

Another major problem with the disease Alzheimer's involves memory loss. I encounter a wide variety of memory loss problems. The number one problem occurs at meal times. Many of my patients forget eating supper five minutes after supper has ended. An example of a situation involved an elderly Alzheimer's patient who stepped into my office after supper. She approached me and said she never ate dinner. I knew she ate because I served her the meal. She became upset with me, and we discussed the fact that she ate. Our conversation went as follows:

"Excuse me, but I never got to eat supper. I think I am feeling hungry."

"Oh, Honey, you just ate supper."

"I did. Well, can you tell me what I ate?"

"Yes, we served chicken, mashed potatoes with gravy, and corn."

"Did I drink some coffee?"

"Yes, you did."

"Oh, maybe that explains why I have a coffee stain on my blouse."

This situation seems to be the most popular memory loss episode I experience. They all must want to make sure I fill their tummies and feed them properly. The funniest thing I experienced involved the same patient asking me several times if she ate. I simply repeated the previous story, and we repeated the same conversation over and over again in ten to twenty minute intervals.

In my job, I must often work under pressure. I enjoy working with people with Alzheimer's because I get to be a problem solver. It feels great being able to be a part of someone's solution to a problem. This job has led me to encounter many experiences I never dreamed possible. I also find it amazing how I have made an impact on my patients' lives. Many of my patients like to treat me as a member of their family. Most of them classify me as their long-lost granddaughter because of my age and being the youngest employee. It feels wonderful to make people happy by just spending time talking to them and making them laugh. Each day I experience different and unpredictable behaviors, and I react to them in an appropriate manner. Working with Alzheimer's patients has made me a better person, and I have learned to realize that someday I might find myself in their shoes. If I ever suffer from the Alzheimer's Disease, I hope others will care for me as I care for my patients. But for the time being, I enjoy practicing my skills with Alzheimer's patients.

Discussion Questions:

1. What is the writer trying to explain, and how well does she explain it? Does the writer seem like an expert? How can you tell?

2. Do the title, introduction, and conclusion effectively serve the topic? Explain your response.

3. Identify any descriptive (figurative language, sense imagery) or narrative (dialogue) strategies that the writer uses and evaluate how effectively they are used.

4. Identify the strengths of the essay. What ideas do you suggest for improvement?

5. Does the piece of writing "have heart"? Cite specific areas of the essay that support your response.

6. Evaluate the essay holistically and provide rationale for your evaluation.

Writing Project 4-2: Study Advice   Compose an article for the college newspaper in which you explain to an incoming first-year student how to study for college exams. Draw on your own personal experiences to support your advice. Write creatively rather than letting your advice sound like a list of steps in a cookbook or assembly kit. Provide concrete examples and details to help your readers see your advice in action.

Keep a personal focus by narrating from first (I, me, we, us) or third person (he, she, it, they), instead of second person (you). Above all, remember: **you've gotta have heart in your writing.**

Writing Project 4-3: Ritual or Ceremony   Choose some ritual or ceremony that you are involved in or know a lot about. Compose an essay in which you explain to a novice reader the ritual or ceremony's procedure and the significance of the procedures. Write creatively rather than letting your advice sound like a list of steps in a cookbook or assembly kit. Provide concrete examples and details to help your readers see your ritual or ceremony in action. Keep a personal focus by narrating from first (I, me, we, us) or third person (he, she, it, they), instead of second person (you). Above all, remember: **you've gotta have heart in your writing.**

Writing Project 4-4: Marvel at Yourself

~ ~ ~

"People gape at mountain peaks, at the boundless tides of the sea, the broad sweep of rivers, the encircling ocean and the motions of the stars; and yet they leave themselves unnoticed; they do not marvel at themselves."
—Saint Augustine

~ ~ ~

Look into your heart, and write a piece that describes and explains your uniqueness as a person. What talents, abilities, gifts, attitudes are you blessed with that speak to your uniqueness. Provide concrete examples and use descriptive details, such as imagery and figurative language, plus narrative strategies to illustrate your ideas and make your writing interesting and readable. Above all, remember: **you've gotta have heart in your writing.**

HOT TIPS FOR WRITING SENTENCES
1. Less is more. The "lean" style is in!
2. Connect each sentence to the one before it and the one after it for smooth flow and continuity.
3. Use a variety of long and short sentences.
4. Vary sentence beginnings.
5. Avoid beginning sentences with dummy subjects—There, Here, It.

6. Write sentences with nouns and verbs. Keep adjectives to a minimum, and use adverbs sparingly.
7. Use participle phrase openers sparingly.
8. Don't write more than one dependent clause in a sentence, and don't put a dependent clause in every sentence.

FRACTURED FRAGMENTS

Sentence fragments, incomplete sentences, can confuse your readers and cause them to consider you a careless writer. So, edit carefully to insure that all sentences are complete, unless you write a fragment for a particular purpose.

Analyze the following types of fragments, grammatically incomplete sentences:

1. When the prof finished reading the essay.
2. Hunting for his glasses.
3. Who talks in someone else's sleep.
4. The composition instructor on fourth floor.
5. At the top of the stairs to the left.

1. Number one, a dependent (subordinate) clause fragment, might be revised into sentences like,
   The prof finished reading the essays.
   When the prof finished reading the essays, she was delighted with the improvement in clarity.
2. Number two, a verbal (gerund) fragment, might be revised into a sentence like,
   The professor's research work consisted of hunting for his glasses.
3. Number three, a relative clause fragment, might be revised into a sentence like,
   At times, professors talk in someone else's sleep.
4. Number four, a phrase fragment, might be revised into a sentence like,
   The composition instructor on the fourth floor has mastered the art of responding to students' writing.
5. Number five, a prepositional phrase fragment, might be revised into a sentence like,
   You will find your composition instructor at the top of the stairs and to the left.

THREE WAYS TO FIX FRAGMENTS:

1. *Add* **words:**

Frag: More gas in Glen than in his car.

Sentence: Glen stores more gas in his stomach than in his car.

2. *Delete* **words:**

Frag: When Frank finished revising his essay.

Sentence: Frank finished revising his essay.

3. *Hook* **the fragment to a nearby sentence:**

Frag: After I hit my head on the sidewalk. The cement cracked.

Sentence: After I hit my head on the sidewalk, the cement cracked.

Sentence: The cement cracked after I hit my head on the sidewalk.

NOTE: If the fragmented element comes before the sentence, a comma is needed after the fragmented element. However, usually no comma is required if the sentence precedes the fragmented element.

PRACTICE 4A: Fix the Fragments   Eliminate the fragments from the following word groups.

1. Also the inner peace of knowing I can reach any goal I set my mind to.
2. Since class was scheduled to begin in less than a month.
3. Looking back on my days at Watertown High School.
4. I hope my children learn valuable lessons. Lessons that will stick with them throughout their lives.
5. When I moved into an apartment by myself. Everything changed.
6. Having already received five speeding tickets.
7. Zelmo sat at his computer for more than two hours. Writing the apology.
8. After collecting the winnings from the lottery, Mr. Richman opened a hardware store. And became a successful merchant.
9. Buying a house, what a huge accomplishment, especially at age 21.
10. My mother was always the nurturing type. Focused on her children.
11. I was born in Dubuque, Iowa. On the third of May in 1983.
12. Although I did lots of volunteer work at the hospitals and nursing homes.

PRACTICE 4B: Editing Fragments   Locate fragments and revise them into correct sentences. Edit your punctuation carefully.

Geoffrey Chaucer

Geoffrey Chaucer was born in London. Sometime around 1340. Since Chaucer's father made his living as a well-to-do vintner. Who had royal connections to King Edward III's butler. Young Geoffrey was given an excellent education. When he was ten-years-old. Geoffrey became a page to the King's son, Prince Lionel. During this time as a page. Chaucer was required to attend the royal school. Where he learned Latin and French. And to write verse.

Chaucer served in the English army and was captured by the French. And later ransomed. Chaucer became a royal English diplomat. In 1373, he was sent to Italy on the King's business. Learned to love Italian literature. Especially Boccaccio and Dante. Around 1374. Chaucer began to write his famous *Canterbury Tales*. A realistic look at the people of England from all economic and social classes.

Chaucer received many royal appointments. The most important coming in 1386. When he became a Knight of the Shire. Along with the renowned *Canterbury Tales*, he wrote other narratives such as *Troilus and Criseyde*, *The Book of the Duchess*, and the *Legend of Good Women*. Geoffrey Chaucer died October 25, 1400. After he was buried in Westminster Abbey. His grave became the first in what has become known as "The Poet's Corner."

RUPTURED RUN-ONS

A run-on contains two or more sentences punctuated as one sentence. Like fragments, run-ons can confuse readers and leave the impression of careless editing. Two kinds of run-ons are the fused sentence with no punctuation between sentences or the comma splice with only a comma between two sentences.

> **Fused:** Wendy lost her temper she screamed at her roommate.
> **Comma Splice:** Wendy lost her temper, she screamed at her roommate.
> ~*OR*~
> Wendy lost her temper, therefore, she screamed at her roommate.

FIVE WAYS TO FIX RUN-ONS:

1. **Compound Sentence:** *add a comma and coordinating conjunction (For, And, Nor, But, Or, Yet, So = **FANBOYS**).*
   Wendy lost her temper, and she screamed at her roommate.
2. **Compound Sentence:** *separate sentences with a semicolon.*
   Wendy lost her temper; she screamed at her roommate.
   Wendy lost her temper; consequently, she screamed at her roommate.
3. **Complex Sentence:** *turn one into a dependent clause.*
   When Wendy lost her temper, she screamed at her roommate.
   Wendy screamed at her roommate after she lost her temper.
4. **Simple Sentence:** *use a double verb.*
   Wendy lost her temper and screamed at her roommate.
5. **Simple Sentences:** *separate sentences with a period.*
   Wendy lost her temper. She then screamed at her roommate.

PRACTICE 4C: Repairing Run-ons   Eliminate the run-on errors in the following items.

1. People's personalities change with time, self-esteem plays a prominent role in the change.
2. I would like to thrill you with my exciting childhood, however it was not very exciting.
3. I actually graduated from high school I couldn't believe it after all the struggling and doubt I actually made it.
4. I advise all high school students to try hard for four years as long as they try they will succeed.
5. It worked like a charm, I have done well on my tests since I started using the flash card review method.
6. Life is like a box of chocolates, we never know what we will get until we try it.
7. In my job, I walk a lot to check on locked doors, plus I do a lot of bending and lifting.
8. I know I can do it, I have confidence in myself.
9. Tyler was born at 9:32 p.m. he weighed seven pounds, eight ounces.
10. I went to the downtown learning center and studied hard it paid off I passed the biology exam.
11. I registered for a computer class, then I signed up for medical terminology.

12. I never miss a day of running. In my mind, I can never become the best runner, I can only get better.

PRACTICE 4D: Editing run-ons   Locate and correct run-ons in the passage below.

Jonathan Swift

Jonathan Swift was born in Dublin, Ireland, on November 30, 1667. He became one of the world's most famous literary satirists. Swift's father died prior to Jonathan's birth his mother couldn't support her family. Swift's relatives donated money for his education at Kilkenny Grammar School, he later graduated from Trinity College in Dublin in 1686.

Because of the religious upheaval in Ireland, he left for England in 1689 he became secretary to politician and man of letters, Sir William Temple, for five years. After a disagreement with Temple, Swift left to become an Anglican priest, he served as pastor of a parish in Belfast. In 1713, Swift was appointed to the Deanship of St. Patrick's Cathedral in Dublin, he married Hester Johnson in 1716.

Because Swift was incensed by the British lack of empathy for the starving Irish, he wrote a savage essay of bitterness and irony, "A Modest Proposal," in 1729, in the proposal, Swift suggests that in order to reduce starvation, the Irish should raise children until age one and then eat them. Swift wrote his masterpiece, *Gulliver's Travel*s, in 1726, this four-journey travel book contains one of the bitterest attacks on humankind ever written.

Toward the end of his life, Swift was victimized by a degeneration of the middle ear, this caused him horrendous pain for long periods of time. Jonathan Swift died on October 19, 1745, at age 78, at the wishes of his wife Hester, he was buried in St. Patrick's Cathedral.

PRACTICE 4E: Editing Fragments and Run-ons   Eliminate fragments and run-ons from the following passage.

William Shakespeare

William Shakespeare was born in 1564 in Stratford, England, his father was a successful businessman. Who served as a town official for a time. Until age 13, Will attended the local grammar school. But then withdrew to become a tradesman's apprentice. In 1582, Shakespeare married Anne Hathaway. Nine years older than he. They became parents of three children—Susanna and twins, Judith and Hamnet. Who died at age 11.

For unknown reasons, Shakespeare moved to London in 1590. And became an actor and playwright. He became a member of the leading acting company, the King's Men he also became a wealthy co-shareholder of the Globe Theater. Where his plays were staged until 1613. At that point, Shakespeare retired to Stratford, he lived on one of the largest estates called New Place. Shakespeare wrote 154 sonnets and 37 plays, and is heralded the world's greatest dramatist.

PARALLELISM

~ ~ ~

"Parallelism enables you to harness one of the most powerful needs in the human mind: the need to find patterns" (92).
—Elizabeth Danziger

~ ~ ~

Parallel structure in writing means using the same grammatical forms when writing pairs or a series (list of three or more items). Words are paired with words, phrases with phrases, and clauses with clauses. Parallel structure can add rhythm, style, grace, and power to your writing. Parallel structure may help you clearly express ideas of equal importance, highlight a comparison, or emphasize important ideas. Lack of parallel structure, on the other hand, makes writing sound choppy and disconnected. For example, note how two great craftsmen of literature use parallelism for emphasis and smooth flow. Charles Dickens begins *A Tale of Two Cities*, "It was the best of time, it was the worst of times, it was the age of wisdom, it was the age of foolishness..." William Shakespeare's Hamlet rhythmically states, "To die, to sleep. To sleep, perchance to dream" (3.1.55-56).

Note the breakdown of parallel structure in the following examples:
1. Alfred looks like a <u>miser</u>, an <u>egotist</u>, and <u>not married to a wife</u>.
   (noun)   *(noun)*   *(verb phrase)*
2. Hilda looks <u>healthy</u>, <u>wealthy</u>, and an <u>athlete</u>.
   (adj.)   *(adj.)*   *(noun)*
3. Old beliefs about witches have been rejected as <u>superstitions</u>
   (noun)
   and <u>detrimental</u> to society.
   (adj.)

4. Irma was known as a <u>mother</u>, <u>married</u>, and <u>sewed</u> clothes.
            (noun) *(adj.)* *(verb phrase)*
5. I love writing <u>for personal enlightenment</u> and <u>to develop</u>
          (prep. phrase)   *(infinitive*
   <u>mental creativity.</u>
    phrase)
6. Mildred <u>not only</u> returned Homer's engagement ring, <u>but also</u> his
     (correlative conj.)   *(correlative conj.)*
   love letters were burned by her.

Balance sentence structure, meaning, and rhythm by using the following suggestions for parallel structure:

A. Use similar grammatical forms for items in pairs or in a series.
- Mary plays guitar well, a good voice, and lots of stage presence.
   > Mary plays guitar well, sings beautifully, and shows good stage presence.
- The sky looks pleasant and with no clouds in it.
   > The sky looks pleasant and clear.

B. Insert only the first preposition or <u>all</u> prepositions in a series of prepositional or verbal phrases.
- To celebrate Thanksgiving, my family came from Chicago, Detroit, and from Seattle.
   > To celebrate Thanksgiving, my family came from Chicago, Detroit, and Seattle.   OR
   > To celebrate Thanksgiving, my family came from Chicago, from Detroit, and from Seattle.
- Abigail likes to sing, dance, and to eat.
   > Abigail likes to sing, dance, and eat.   OR
   > Abigail like to sing, to dance, and to eat.

C. Use similar grammatical forms in comparisons.
- I like croquet better than to play indoors.
   > I like croquet better than indoor games.

D. Use the same grammatical forms for subject and predicate nominative.
- To see is believing.
   > Seeing is believing. *OR* To see is to believe.

E. Use the same grammatical form and positioning for sentence

parts joined by correlative conjunctions.

not only...but also...	both...and...
either...or...	neither...nor...
	whether...or...

- Although the bar was closed, she ordered not only a martini, but she also asked for two beers.

    Although the bar was closed, she ordered not only a martini but also two beers.

~ ~ ~

"Parallelism not only holds sentences together,
it adds emphasis, provides flow, expresses thoughts
more clearly, makes reading more pleasurable,
takes up less space, and makes
what we say easy to remember" (74).
—Richard Andersen

~ ~ ~

PRACTICE 4F: Parallelism   Revise the following sentences to improve the parallel structure.

1. Knowing the rules of grammar and to follow them make a piece of writing more orderly and with more clarity.
2. Wilbur likes to dance more than singing in the choir.
3. Waldo either will attend NICC or he will enroll at UNI.
4. To issue a response would be magnifying the problem.
5. A grade alert went out to Francis Flunk, Missy Work, and to Dorothy Dropped.
6. The fast pace of contemporary society threatens the development and growing of children's personalities.
7. Both the coach and those who assist her were awarded conference honors last season.
8. Since writing is controlled by purpose, the writer's purpose determines selection and how he organizes the content.

PRACTICE 4G: Parallelism   Add a smoother flow to the style of the sentences listed below by adding parallel structure after the double bars (//).

1. While walking in the woods today, I saw // three French hens, two turtle doves, and...
2. He // not only looks energetic but...
3. As we were leaving the airport, the weather forecast warned of

    // gale-force winds, pea-sized hail, and...
4. Madeline gave a lecture // about her trip to Ireland and ...
5. // To the non-sports enthusiast, golf on TV may seem boring, but...
6. The Dean of Students displayed // a stoic expression, a monotone voice, and ...
7. Her family members were // not only proud but...// by her success.
8. The class members were annoyed not so much // by the course requirements as ...
9. The instructor insisted // that all essays be handed in promptly and ...
10. Most students come with // both a positive attitude...

MANGLED MEANING:
Misplaced, Dangling, Squinting Modifiers

Misplaced Modifiers: place words, phrases, clauses as closely as possible to the words they modify.

> **For Sale: Beautiful Yamaha piano by professor with attractive oak legs.** Who has the oak legs?

> **President Barack Obama to visit Burma** (BBC, Nov. 8, 2012) **Fresh from his election win, Barack Obama will become the first US president to visit Burma this month, the White House says.** How many U.S. Presidents have visited Burma this month? How many U.S. Presidents are serving concurrently this month?

> From newspaper headline: **"High school honors student charged with killing family members, friend"** Why is this student being honored for killing?

PRACTICE 4H: Misplaced Modifiers　　　Reword the following examples to add clarity by eliminating misplaced modifiers.

1. Two college dorms were reported ransacked by the Peosta police.
2. In Illinois, a calf was born to a farmer with two heads.
3. The college's cafeteria serves beverages to students in little cans.
4. A new computer was donated to the English Department, which has caused a lot of trouble.
5. Her godfather Elmo gave little Marissa a new doll for Christmas called "Little Cuddles."
6. Working on her essay, the dog distracted Gladys.

7. The fawn was missed by the swerving semi, which was standing in the middle of the highway.
8. Professor Wright bought a composition book for his library that costs $12.50.

Dangling Modifiers

A dangling modifier falsely modifies a sentence's subject. To correct dangling modifiers, add a word (person) that the phrase can sensibly modify, or change the phrase into a clause (contains a subject & verb).

Smoking a cigar, the bear stood on its hind legs.
Does the bear smoke cigars?
Following the scent, the lost skiers were located.
Are the skiers following the scent?

PRACTICE 4I: Dangling Modifiers   Revise the following sentences to clarify the dangling modifiers.

1. Lying on the hammock for three hours, the sun's rays grew hotter and hotter.
2. After pulling my three teeth, my gums felt sore.
3. At the age of four, my mother gave birth to my younger brother.
4. In preparing this essay, a detailed free-write will be required.
5. Coming up the front walk, the mailbox was located near the front door.
6. After spending all night in the library, exhaustion overcame me.
7. At the age of ten, my family took a vacation to the Grand Teton Mountain.
8. While visiting with friends recently, the topic of graduate school came up.

Squinting Modifiers

Squinting modifiers are placed in such a way that they could modify two words. Move the modifier from the middle of the sentence to the beginning or end of the sentence to clarify meaning.

Waldo said on his way home he would stop to buy snacks.
Did Waldo say it on his way home, or will he stop on his way home?
Judith only has composition on Monday evenings.
Is Judith the only composition student; does she only have composition; or does the class meet only on Monday evenings?

PRACTICE 4J: Squinting Modifiers   Reword the following sentences for clarity by adjusting squinting modifiers.

1. I only told the police officer what I had seen.
2. I almost ate the whole pie.
3. Hilda said during class the professor belched three times.
4. My daughter was advised frequently to submit her tax forms.
5. Jack was told the next day to register for next semester's classes.

PRACTICE 4K: Mangled Meaning   Reword the following sentences for clarity by adjusting misplaced, dangling, or squinting modifiers.

1. The student was referred to the Writing Center with misplaced modifier problems.
2. Tom will make plans tomorrow to publish his writing.
3. At four-years-old, my mother took me to swimming lessons.
4. While dressing for the winter formal, the doorbell rang.
5. Zelmo was told often to practice the guitar.
6. Cy Young soaked his arm he strained in ice.
7. Driving down the winding road, the duck and her ducklings halted traffic for five minutes.
8. Tom saw the swans swimming in the lake on the way to class.
9. Watching the evening news, Liz's pet hamster escaped from its cage.
10. Grabbing hold of the juicy burger, my mouth begins to water.
11. A dying plant catches my eye, sitting on a table at the far end of the tiny room.
12. Looking past the window into our backyard, the world is drenched in a chilly rainfall.

DEMONSTRATION PORTFOLIO

METACOGNITIVE ESSAY

Assess your performance in this course in a minimum seven-paragraph essay. Don't evaluate the course, but rather assess how you performed. Reflect on your growth as a writer, learner, and thinker during this course. Refer to the course outcomes as a means of reflection. Although you may need to mention some weakness or strength of the course, focus on how you reacted to that weakness or strength. **What do you know now that you didn't know before? What can you do now that you couldn't do before?** If you've made gains, list the kinds— gains in writing skill, confidence, study habits, organizational skills... Or if you've gained little, list the reasons why—lack of time, lack of interest, getting off to a bad start. (No entry slip)

SAMPLE STUDENT WRITING
Portfolio Metacognitive Essay
by Leah Jane Meiers

My tour of the Dubuque Arboretum of essays is coming to an end as is this composition course. Because I excelled in writing classes in high school, I confidently entered this semester's composition class thinking I knew a lot about writing. I enjoy creating ideas and expressing myself through writing, so I approached this course with an open mind and willingness to learn even more. But little did I realize how much I would learn. I am amazed at how many writing skills I had not heard of before this class and how much they helped my writing improve.

After receiving the syllabus on the first day of class, I felt overwhelmed. Then I received my diagnostic essay back, and I was pleasantly surprised by the grade, which reduced some of my stress. I also saw specific areas of writing that I needed to focus on to improve. One of the major areas of improvement was implementing a full writing process. In high school, I never used a pre-write, and most of the time, I simply wrote one draft, edited it, and handed it in for grading. Through this course, I discovered the advantages of using a complete process. After experimenting with the scratch outline and formal outline, I finally settled on the cluster pre-write, which helps me unlock my brain to lots of ideas in the shortest amount of time. I also found that revision, a stage I rarely used previously, allows me to upgrade my ideas and organization.

I also found the peer response sessions to be a major stage in helping each essay improve. I had been required to do peer editing in high school, but our high school groups only focused on editing our papers. In this composition class, my peers identified specific content and organizational strengths in my writing, which boosted my confidence, and offered pointed suggestions for improvement of my ideas and organization as well as helping me edit my essays. Also, analyzing my peers' writings helped me improve my own revision and editing skills for my papers. I also like using the track changes feature of Word because I can actually see the revisions and editing changes I make from one draft to the next.

In addition to my improved use of the writing process, I also now use some composition strategies that I had not tried before. My use of sense imagery, figurative language, and dialogue adds more creativity and life to my writing. My peer responders often complimented me on how much those improvements in my writing helped draw them, the readers, into my essays. Along with those improvements in HOC issues, I saw improvement in my style when I use stronger verbs. I did not realize how many weak verbs I was using, but when I revise to add more action verbs, my writing seems to come alive on the page.

In this course, I also recognized frequent shifting of my point of view. I did not realize how often I was writing in first or third person when suddenly, I would shift to "you," second person, which tended to distract my readers. I found it difficult many times not to refer to my audience as "you." I tend to write the way I talk, which uses "you" a lot. By remedying that issue, my essays seemed more unified and easier to follow. I also learned things to watch for in editing; such as misplaced and dangling modifiers, parallel structure, and adjective-adverb usage; which will help my writing in other courses and in the job market after I graduate.

The major change I have noticed, however, which takes my writing to a higher level, is putting my "heart into my writing." I did not realize how often I was writing for various classes just to complete the assignments. I was not putting "my heart" into my writing. Once I started to focus on "heart" in my writing, I found that my personality and personal voice came through in a much stronger, sincere way. My writing now seems more convincing and unique. It doesn't just look and sound like every other student's writing.

I cannot believe how much my writing has improved this semester. I entered this course as a good writer, but I have improved more than I would ever have predicted. I can see huge improvements in my papers, and I have begun to apply the skills I have learned in this class in my other classes as well. Most of all, I have become much more confident in my writing abilities. I now recognize problem areas in my writing, and I have learned ways to fix those problems. This will help me in the future, especially when I tackle Composition II next semester.

CHAPTER 5

Be Convincing

~ ~ ~

"If you are temperate and measured and reasoned,
and if you think of your reader as a friend to persuade
rather than a foe to slay, you will have a far better chance
of carrying your point than if you dip your pen in fire and
write to burn" (46).
—Richard Marius

~ ~ ~

Many times your purpose as a writer may call for you to convince your readers to accept some issue you care about. This does not mean you engage in a semantic "fight to the finish" argument with your readers. Rather you attempt to convince your readers to do something about the issue or to at least consider your position on the issue. In other words, you take a stand on an issue. To be convincing, your writing will require a clear explanation of the issue and a convincing, persuasive position stated in a thesis claim (your opinion or proposition) supported by logical reasoning and evidence.

You will need to project a positive, confident, knowledgeable, reasonable attitude toward your issue and your position. Try to develop a responsible, respectful, sincere tone as a concerned person interested in improving people's lives. A respectful, sincere tone will carry your argument much further than name-calling or put-downs (argumentum ad hominem), such as "Senator Smithson is nothing but a liberal windbag. How can he stay in Congress any longer?" Naturally, some readers will agree with your position, but others will need to be convinced of your opinion or position. Therefore, you will need to take the opponents' views into account so you can refute their arguments or at least arrive at some common ground on the issue. Recognizing the other side of the issue can also help strengthen your own argumentative position and help you alter the oppositions' position.

In working toward convincing your reader, you must organize your paper clearly and logically. The title must grab readers' attention by identifying your topic and suggesting your position on that topic. The introduction must sustain the readers' interest and present your position statement or thesis claim. Also, you need to take the oppositions' views into account and may find it necessary to anticipate opponents' objections by presenting counter arguments to offset these objections. A summary of the opponents' position usually works well when it appears early in the essay, although concessions may appear at various places in an essay.

While acknowledging concessions to the opponents' views, try to build a common ground between you and readers who initially disagree with your position. Then supply evidence for your position by citing premises and supporting those premises. Valid support or evidence might come in the form of facts, examples, and/or reasons. While you organize your essay to convince your readers, consider what format will work to your best advantage—weakest support to strongest or strongest support to weakest. Finally, bring closure to your essay with a strong concluding paragraph that frames the essay by relating to the introduction and/or thesis.

STRUT YOUR STUFF!

Writing Project 5-1: Letter for Change   Compile a list of changes, large and small, that you would like to see implemented in the place where you live, in the neighborhood where you live, in the community where you live, or in the place where you work. Then identify those items that might be subject to change. Write a letter to a designated audience in which you set forth the need for the change, the ways the change will occur, and the advantages of the change. Naturally your letter will try to persuade your audience to change something; therefore, let the clarity of your proposal convince your audience to institute the change. Above all, remember: **you've gotta have heart in your writing.**

Writing Checklist:

☐   1. Are the change itself, the need for the change, the ways it will occur, and the advantages of the change clearly presented?

☐   2. Are concrete examples of the situation and results of the change clearly presented?

☐   3. Is the piece written in letter format? Is it written in a firm and respectful tone?

☐   4. Does the letter present a title and an opening that grab attention, plus a clear thesis and a strong conclusion?

☐   5. Is the letter edited to support its message?

SAMPLE STUDENT WRITING
Convince Your Readers

Letter for Change

The Destructive Invasion
by Elias Langlois

Dear Mr. Dale Garner:

I was looking through the *Hunting and Trapping Regulations*, and I noticed that you manage the program for the DNR to control the deer population in Iowa. As I write this letter, I am looking out my family's picture window at several deer happily munching on my mother's prize tulips and crocuses. My mother is frazzled and upset about this invasion of deer in our yard. As the old saying goes, "If Mama ain't happy, ain't no one happy." In order to restore happiness to our home, I have taken it upon myself to find a solution. I hope that you will read my letter and seriously consider some of the suggestions I provide.

Deer belong in the country where they can run wild and free. The habitat that deer prefer consists of woods, valleys, and open areas. The city contains many such valleys and ridges covered in trees and thick vegetation that ideally suits their needs. Bunker Hill, a 200-acre golf course in Dubuque, boasts of a great deer habitat and holds many of the deer in our city. Many deer also reside in and around the perimeter of Eagle Point Park. At night, they eat many of the flowers and shrubs planted throughout the park.

A deer's appetite is driven by its desire to survive. A deer's diet consists of alfalfa, grass, corn, soybeans, bark, tree leaves, flowers, and shrubs. Every year thousands of young trees, flowers, and shrubs are planted in Dubuque's parks and along its roadways. The deer do not care how much these cost. As winter approaches, the deer will start eating a lot more, trying to store up fat for the winter. Bark from newly planted trees tastes best to them at this time of year. Their appetites never wane, and they seem to eat constantly.

Why does it seem that sometimes more deer live in the city than in the country? Well, for a deer, many advantages come with living in an urban area. Little hunting is allowed in Dubuque; only a few bow hunters are authorized to hunt every year. So, why shouldn't deer live in the city if hardly anybody hunts them? To make matters worse, many people feed the deer unintentionally, some even in my own neighborhood. If a person throws out mashed corn and grain every day or even once a week for the birds and squirrels, the deer will get the idea that food abounds in this area. Out of habit, they continue to come back to our yards year after year. We sit back helplessly watching them eat away like uninvited guests.

The damage deer cause does not stop with the plants and shrubs they eat. Deer cross streets and highways in Dubuque all the time. Every time a deer crosses a street, it could potentially cause an accident which may result in injury or even death to people. Last year alone, two accidents caused by deer occurred on my street. The insurance claims on deer-related accidents in our city must run in the hundreds of thousands of dollars. It surprises me that the insurance companies do not put more pressure on the DNR to try harder to get rid of the deer in the city as well as in the country.

Obviously, the DNR needs to change the way it controls the deer population, but how can this be accomplished? Every year a few selected bow hunters get to hunt deer within Dubuque's city limits. They must pass a special safety course and hit three out of five arrows in a paper plate at twenty-five yards. After qualifying, they become eligible to harvest as many does as they want during the regular season. In order to shoot a buck, the city bow hunters' names are put in a lottery, and whose name is drawn gets to hunt a buck that year. Instead of allowing the bow hunters to hunt as many does as they want, they should also be allowed to hunt as many bucks as they want. Far fewer bucks than does reside in Dubuque. If we could eliminate all the bucks, the deer population will eventually decline, and the problem will take care of itself.

Another successful plan in other towns is bringing in an animal control expert who specializes in harvesting deer. If the DNR allows a highly trained professional to use a rifle in Dubuque, our deer problems will quickly be solved. A classic setup would be placing bait in a park. The sharp-shooter would sit in his car on the side of the road and wait until the deer come out to eat the bait. His rifle would be equipped with a silencer that would muffle the shot, thus allowing him to harvest a large number of deer at one time. The deer wouldn't hear the shots and thus wouldn't be alarmed and scatter.

Not wanting to be wasteful, I have come up with yet another idea to handle the deer meat. Hunters could dispose of the meat in many ways, but the best way is donating the meat to a local food pantry. When a hunter brings in a deer, the food pantry charges a nominal fee of twenty-five dollars. This fee allows the food pantry to process the meat and give it to the hungry and needy in our community. If the city paid the fee to donate the deer to the pantry, many of the extra deer would be donated instead of being dumped in the landfill.

Mr. Garner, I know you must keep extremely busy at the Department of Natural Resources. I also know that you must get many letters like mine each year. Undoubtedly, you have heard about Dubuque's deer problems many times. Hopefully you can see the importance of fixing this problem as soon as possible. If we can reduce the deer population in Dubuque, driving will become safer and less stressful. Also, insurance claims will decrease because of fewer deer/auto collisions taking place on our streets, and also our trees and flowers will be able to grow freely without deer damaging them. In addition, happiness will be restored to my home, and my mother can enjoy her flowers once again.

Sincerely,

Elias Langlois

Discussion Questions:
1. Identify the issue and the need for change the writer proposes. What ways does the writer suggest to bring about the change? What advantages of the change does the writer present?
2. Are concrete examples of the situation and possible changes presented? If so, identify these.
3. Analyze the tone of the piece. Does it seem appropriate for the purpose of the essay? Why or why not?
4. Does the essay provide a title and opening that attract attention, a clear thesis, and a strong conclusion. Support your answer.

5. Does the writer "have heart" in the essay? What specific aspects of the piece support your response?
6. Cite the major strengths of the essay. What ideas do you suggest for improvement?
7. Evaluate the essay holistically and provide rationale for your evaluation.

Writing Project 5-2: Letter to the Editor   Identify an issue that you care about (family, job, college, community…). Write an extended letter to the editor of a newspaper or magazine in which you argue your position on the issue and offer reasons and supporting evidence for your claim (thesis). Remember, this is not a research paper but rather a persuasive letter to convince your readers to do something about your issue or at least to consider your issue. Above all, remember: **you've gotta have heart in your writing.**

Writing Checklist:
- 1. Does your personal voice come through the writing?
- 2. Is the thesis (claim) statement effectively written?
- 3. Are the reasons and supporting evidence written clearly and orderly?
- 4. Do the introduction and conclusion effectively frame the essay?
- 5. Are the sentences written in a lively, tight style? Is the text cleanly edited?

SAMPLE STUDENT WRITING
Letter to the Editor

Peosta, Iowa 52068
March 1, 2017

Editor
Glamour Magazine
P.O. Box 37690
Boone, IA 50037

Dear Editor:

I am appalled at the way your magazine objectifies and falsely represents women. If your magazine truly cares about women, you wouldn't give readers the idea that women's worth is measured by their looks and their ability to attract a member of the opposite sex. As a twenty-year-old woman, I fall into your target audience, so I feel compelled to address this issue on behalf of all women in this country who feel the same.

While browsing through your magazine, I am amazed at most of your ads and articles. Your magazine is insulting and damaging. I understand that your focus is pop culture and fashion, and I am not condemning you for writing about these things. Rather, I disagree with the way you deal with fashion and women's issues, and I find it offensive. In your magazine, women are most often shown in the same way—rail thin and in demeaning positions. These images are presented because they are profitable, not because they are right or true. Women deserve to be represented respectfully and with the diversity found in real life.

While women have earned more respect than ever before, they are still prisoners of magazines like yours. Millions of women spend their time and money focusing on dieting and on getting a body closer to the ones thought to be ideals in magazines and on television. The quest to be thin controls women and keeps them from pursuing more meaningful things.

Are women like me so terrible in their natural form that we must be plucked, waxed, shaved, hair-dried, eyes-painted, starved, breasts-lifted and padded, tummy tucked, and wrinkles-smoothed? We are fed such contradicting ideals by magazines like yours that tell us to be strong and achieve our dreams, on one hand, but look "pretty," manipulate men, and change our behavior so we will be liked, on the other. You run articles promoting self-esteem and then completely contradict that message with other articles and images.

It's not just the articles that promote the feminine illusion, but the images spread throughout your magazine, as well. Models used in fashion ads are not larger than a size six. Few women fit the height and weight requirements to be models. Furthermore, pictures in magazines like yours have been fixed with lighting and by professional make-up artists. Even after the pictures are taken, the images are most often airbrushed before they are ready to appear in the magazine. No human being could achieve the perfect looks models display in their photos. If women never see bodies like their own being portrayed, they will always assume they are far too large. If women and girls can learn to recognize that these ads are placed in magazines like yours to make money, maybe they will see them in a less threatening way.

Women continue to buy creams to make them look younger, implants to make their breasts look larger, and expensive diets to make them look thinner. They continue to buy magazines because they believe they need guidance on how to live, how to appear right for men, and how to become the right sort of person. This fuels the entire magazine industry. I realize that women enjoy adorning themselves with fashionable clothes and makeup. However, they should not be told that they must do so in order to look just right and feel feminine.

Your magazine makes women and girls think that beauty is the most important part of womanhood, which makes them susceptible to whatever standards the mass beauty culture can throw at them. Fifty to seventy-five per cent of females are dissatisfied with their bodies. This vulnerability becomes a key issue as girls enter adolescence. Just as girls notice their bodies developing curves, they also are bombarded by media images of underweight, and often degraded, women.

Since girls feel so much pressure regarding weight and beauty, the pressure on young girls to maintain a socially acceptable appearance seems to be the most important thing in life. The idea that no woman can be too thin has caused even underweight women to consider themselves overweight. Psychologists agree that negative body image is directly related to self-esteem. Though we are led to believe otherwise, there is no relationship between beauty and goodness, between thinness and sexuality, between flawlessness and femininity. For most women to fit into your magazine's definition of beauty would require starvation and surgical alteration of the body. In fact, no one can achieve the ideal you propose. Not even models look as good as their pictures.

I will not buy your magazine or the products in it until I see some change. You need to know that the ideas and pictures you provide are unacceptable to millions of women. You should feature serious articles on real feminine role models whose professions are not appearance-based, and you should reflect the reality that clothes and makeup are not the center of every woman's life.

Sincerely,
Becky Kuhl

Discussion Questions:
1. Identify the change and the need for change the writer proposes. What ways does the writer suggest to bring about this change? What advantages of the change does the writer present?
2. Are concrete examples of the situation and possible changes presented? If so, identify these.

3. Analyze the tone of the piece. Does it seem appropriate for the purpose of the essay? Explain.
4. Does the writer "have heart" in the essay? What specific aspects of the piece support your response?
5. Cite the major strengths of the essay. What ideas do you suggest for improvement?
6. Evaluate the essay holistically and provide rationale for your evaluation.

Writing Project 5-3: Letter to Legislator   Compose a persuasive, formal letter to an Iowa legislator in which you try to convince him or her to grant Iowa community colleges and their students the financial support they deserve. Try to approach this request by drawing on your personal and financial situation and how this lack of support affects you, your education, your future plans and dreams, and your family. State your position clearly and in a respectful, convincing tone. Above all, remember: **you've gotta have heart in your writing.**

Writing Project 5-4: Problem-Solution   Everywhere we look in our world, we see problems needing solutions. Identify a current and newsworthy global, national, state, local, or personal problem. Then write an essay in which you identify the problem, the extent of the problem, the causes of the problem, the effects of the problem, and the solutions for the problem. Above all, remember: **you've gotta have heart in your writing.**

Writing Project 5-5: War   General Douglas MacArthur said, "I know war as few other men now living know it, and nothing to me is more revolting. I have long advocated its complete abolition, as its very destructiveness on both friend and foe has rendered it useless as a method of settling international disputes" (http:www.wisdomquotes. com). In a persuasive essay, convince readers of your agreement or disagreement with General MacArthur's statement. Provide an effective thesis plus logical reasoning and evidence to support your position. Above all, remember: **you've gotta have heart in your writing.**

USING MODIFIERS CORRECTLY

	Modify:	Answer the questions:
ADJECTIVES	nouns	what kind? how much?
	pronouns	which one? how many?
ADVERBS	verbs	how? how much?
	adjectives	where? how often?
	adverbs	when?

ADJECTIVE	ADVERB
The **efficient** student	The student works **efficiently**.
The **new** computer	The computer **never** works **well**.
My boss is **honest**.	Her boss seems **completely** honest.

MODIFIER IDENTIFICATION: Underline and identify each adjective and adverb in the following sentence. Draw an arrow to the word it modifies.

The very appreciative instructor generously gave the eager students a really high grade for their dedicated efforts toward writing improvement.

Points of Emphasis:

1. Most, not all, adverbs end in **-ly**, but adverbs such as **almost, much, never, not, often, quite, seldom, there, too, very** do not end in **-ly**.

Mary <u>often</u> speaks <u>cheerfully</u> in the morning.

2. Adjectives are often used after linking verbs (predicate adjectives). The most common linking verbs are: **act, appear, be (am, is, are, was, were, be, been), become, feel, grow, look, remain, seem, smell, sound, stay, taste.**

The composition student is <u>late</u>.

My instructor feels <u>better</u>.

The ice cream tastes <u>good</u>.

PRACTICE 5A: Modifiers   Choose the correct form:

1. Theodore Roosevelt said, "Speak (soft, softly) and carry a big stick."
2. Babe Ruth was (real, really) lucky to reach second base.
3. After Waldo gave up onions, his breath improved (immense, immensely).
4. My instructor smiled (hearty, heartily) after I learned to use adverbs (correct, correctly).

5. The trainer grabbed the alligator's neck (quick, quickly).
6. The violin and piano sound (wonderful, wonderfully) together.
7. The pie smelled (delicious, deliciously) but tasted (horrible, horribly).
8. When the instructor arrived, the class became (silent, silently) and remained (still, stilly).
9. Jim's after-shave smells (sweet, sweetly).
10. The board of directors met (recent, recently).

PRACTICE 5B: Modifiers   Edit the following for correct adjective/ adverb usage.

1. The bride's father seemed happy as he looked happy at his new son-in-law.
2. The students tried to talk soft, but their voices seemed loud to the instructor.
3. Come quick to your place and sit quiet in your seat.
4. Drive slow near school playgrounds.
5. When the four-thirty bell rang loud, we quick scurried from the classroom.
6. The golfer's coach commented correct about her swing which looked smoothly.
7. Something in the yard smelled oddly; then, the skunk appeared sudden.
8. Juliet crept to the balcony cautious and seemed calmly.
9. As Hamlet appeared unexpected in his mother's chamber, Polonius hid real quiet behind the curtain.
10. The weather outside looks frightfully, but the fire is so delightfully.

CONFUSING ADJECTIVES / ADVERBS

Good—Well

Good—an adjective which precedes a noun or follows a linking verb.

He displays **good** skill at the keyboard.

He is **good** at writing.

The rain felt **good** on my burning skin.

Well—

1. Adverb – indicating how action is performed

The professor teaches **well**.

Waldo supervises the staff **well**.

2. Adjective – indicating physical health

She feels **well** after her visit to her internist.

Hilda looks **well**. (She no longer looks sick.)

"Doctor, I don't feel **well**," said Homer.

3. To be satisfactory

Shakespeare writes, "All's **well** that ends **well**."

Real (adjective) Really (adverb) / Sure (adjective) Surely (adverb)

This classroom runs **really** smoothly.

The instructor was **surely** right about those nasty adverbs.

PRACTICE 5C: Modifiers   Edit modifier usage in the following sentences:

1. She seemed to be in a real good mood while typing the essay.
2. The new computers sure cost a lot less than the old models.
3. The copy machine in the office works real good.
4. The professor was not prepared very good for the composition class.
5. Previous class records can be found easy in the updated files.
6. Dale felt he played center good, but he was also real good as a forward.
7. The ceiling in the office is deteriorating slow but sure.
8. Peer response often gives writers good feedback on whether their writing works good or not.

COMPARISONS OF ADJECTIVES AND ADVERBS

POSITIVE (1)	COMPARATIVE (2)	SUPERLATIVE (3 or more)
fast	faster	fastest
slow	slower	slowest
fine	finer	finest
happy	happier	happiest
careful	more (less) careful	most (least) careful
beautiful	more (less) beautiful	most (least) beautiful
POSITIVE (1)	**COMPARATIVE (2)**	**SUPERLATIVE (3 or more)**
good, well	better	best
little	less	least
much, many	more	most
bad	worse	worst

PRACTICE 5D: Degrees   Choose the correct modifier form.

1. Jane is the (smarter, smartest) of the twins.
2. Jane is also the (faster, fastest) typist in the class.

3. He spoke (more, most) calmly to his students than Tad did.
4. Of all the replies, his was the (more, most) prompt.

PRACTICE 5E: Modifiers   Correct any modifier errors in the following sentences.

1. The elderly patient looks good today.
2. The instructor will respond to our writing real quick.
3. The professor responded real good to the last question.
4. The new tax form looked good to the accountant.
5. The concrete building was sure built sturdy.
6. The concrete building appears real sturdy.
7. The noon flight to North Buenie was late.
8. Report all valid results quick to the supervisor.
9. You look sharp in that new suit.
10. You should look sharp to the left and right before you turn the corner.

PRACTICE 5F: Modifiers   Correct any modifier errors in the following sentences.

1. Mary heard an unusual loud noise in the break room.
2. The professor looked odd at the questioning students.
   The professor looked odd to the questioning students.
3. Gomer read the sign real slow.
4. Of my triplet relatives, Dandy Dan is the better swimmer; Tenacious Tim is the better drummer, and Cute Kate is the best looking.
5. With my sinus passage cleared, I now smell well.
6. The dandelion wine sure smells well.
7. Business is progressing as good as can be expected.
8. Kay certainly drives more careful since her fender bender.
9. Of all the coats I have tried on today, this one feels better.
10. My dad talked loud and clear when he wanted to make his point.
11. Our barn smells well.

~ ~ ~

"Writing without errors doesn't make you
anything, but writing with errors—if you
give it to other people—makes you a hick,
a boob, a bumpkin" (Power 167).
—Peter Elbow

~ ~ ~

CASE OUT THE PRONOUNS

CASES OF PRONOUNS

	Nominative	Possessive	Objective
Singular:	I	my, mine	me
	you	your, yours	you
	she, he, it	her, hers, his, its	her, him, it
Plural:	we	our, ours	us
	you	your, yours	you
	they	their, theirs	them

Nominative Case—subject or predicate nominative
***Editor's Trick: try each pronoun separately with its verb.

Incorrect Pronoun Usage

1. Him and me were assigned to the project.
2. Mary and him came to the meeting together.
3. Have you and her had a vacation?
4. Usually David and me work together.

Predicate Nominative—**a noun or pronoun that follows a linking verb** (am, is, are, was, were, be, been). **The predicate nominative refers back to the subject; therefore, if it is a pronoun, it requires the nominative case.**

Correct Pronoun Usage

1. The caller was I. I was the caller. (I = caller).
2. Was the chairman he? He was the chairman. (he = chairman)
3. The receptionist who took the message was she. She was the receptionist who took the message. (she = receptionist)
4. The new students are she and I. She and I are the new students. (she and I = students)
5. The graduates were they. They were the graduates. (they = graduates)
6. The judges should have been we. We should have been the judges. (we = judges)

PRACTICE 5G: Nominative Case: Choose the correct pronoun.

1. Mr. Wright and (she, her) worked late at the office.
2. After Julia and (she, her) left, the class was cancelled.
3. What are you and (he, him) going to do about the missing assignment?

4. The winner of the award was (he, him).
5. The person who called for the appointment was (she, her).
6. Kate and (I, me) attended the writing seminar.
7. On the other hand, (he, him) and Brett did not attend.
8. I don't know if it was (he, him).
9. For our benefit, Michael and (he, him) will explain the new policy.
10. (She and I) (Her and me) took the new student to the Writing Center.
11. Are you and (they, them) writing the essay together?
12. Could it have been (he, him)?
13. It was probably (I, me) who made the error.
14. How are you and (he, him) getting to the meeting?
15. Did Jim and (she, her) leave early?

Objective Case—direct object, indirect object, object of preposition
***Editor's Trick: try each pronoun separately.
1. She hastily called Tom and (I, me). Called whom?
2. I thanked (she, her) and (he, him). Thanked whom?
3. Maureen invited her sister and (we, us). Invited whom?
4. Walter gave the essay to his sister and (he, him). To whom?

PRACTICE 5H: Objective Case   Choose the correct pronoun.
1. Call the receptionist and (I, me) when you find time.
2. Did you ask the doctor and (she, her) to give you a report?
3. You should remember (he and she, him and her) from last semester's class.
4. Matt will drive Paula and (she, her) to the meeting.
5. The company will call Betsy and (she, her) for an interview.
6. Tell Maxwell Smart and (he, him) about the new course.
7. Do you know Ellen and (she, her) through your business?
8. The Dean required Homer and (I, me) to prepare an agenda.
9. Dr. Slice sent Harry and (she, her) the X-ray report.
10. We will see Hilda and (they, them) at the board meeting.
11. He stood between you and (I, me).
12. Ron worked for Mr. Handy and (he, him) for ten years.
13. Between you and (I, me), we can finish this essay easily by tomorrow.
14. Tell the boss about the secretary and (he, him).
15. Have you told the instructor and (he, him) about your essay yet?

Possessive Case—ownership

***Possessive nouns use apostrophes. However, possessive pronouns never use apostrophes.

John's report	His report
The workers' lunch hour	Their lunch hour

Incorrect Use of Possessive Case:

This brick building is our's.

The dog chewed on it's bone.

Are these people friends of your's?

***Possessive case pronouns or nouns are used in front of a **gerund**, a verbal used as a noun. Gerunds end in **-ing**.

His playing of the violin has improved.

The dentist objected to **my** eating candy.

Your speaking to the instructor aroused suspicion.

Her arriving late to class became a problem.

Additional Pronoun Issues

***When using **than** or **as** in a comparison, complete the sentence in your mind to determine which pronoun to use.

The captain played better than **he**. (than he played)

Are you as smart as **she**? (as she is)

He is nicer to Matt than **me**. (than he is to me)

He is nicer to Matt than **I**. (than I am)

***When a pronoun is written next to the noun it refers to in **apposition**, omit the noun to decide the correct pronoun. (The **appositive** renames a noun or pronoun).

(We, Us) mechanics service our own vehicles.

The instructor greeted (we, us) new students.

Give the bonus to (we, us) hard-working students.

***Avoid using reflexive pronouns (**myself, himself, yourself, etc.**) if another pronoun form (**without -self**) is suitable.

Samson gave the best grades to my friend and (me, myself).

My boss, my assistant, and (I, me, myself) will go to the seminar.

NOTE: Never use "hisself" or "theirselves"; they are considered substandard English words even though you may sometimes hear them spoken.

PRACTICE 5I: Pronoun Usage   Correct any pronoun errors in the following sentences.

1. Mail the report to him and I.
2. She and I will be late for class.

3. The secretary asked them and she for the letters.
4. Him and the nurse filled in the patient's chart.
5. The receptionist showed the speaker and she to the main office.
6. He types better than she.
7. Us accountants registered early for the seminar.
8. The new building renovation pleased we employees.
9. She gave instructions to my colleague and myself.
10. He accidentally hit hisself with a hammer.

WHO / WHOM / WHOSE USAGE

Cases: Nominative = **who**   Objective = **whom**   Possessive = **whose**
To determine the correct form:

1. Isolate the who-whom clause.
2. Use **who** if: (a) no other subject is found, **or** (b) the verb is linking.
3. Use **whom** if: (a) another subject is present in the clause, **and** (b) the verb is action, not linking.

Examples:
The new instructor, (who, whom) has taken Mr. Wright's position, came from Texas.
The new instructor, (who, whom) I met today, came from Texas.
Does anyone know (who, whom) the new teacher is?

PRACTICE 5J: Who / Whom   Select the proper form.

1. (Who, Whom) came first?
2. The paper machine operator is (who, whom)?
3. (Who, Whom) shall I send to control the flow of materials into the print center office?
4. (Who, Whom) do you think will operate the computer in our office?
5. Everybody (who, whom) received an invitation will attend the school picnic.
6. The writers (who, whom) I most admire are those who take the time to revise and edit.
7. If we had known (who, whom) the student was, we would have explained the assignment more carefully.
8. The union officers will be (whoever, whomever) the committee nominates.
9. Send the job application to (whoever, whomever) applies first.
10. (Who, Whom) do you want to win the World Series?

PRACTICE 5K: All Pronoun Usage   Correct any pronoun errors.

1. She is the person whom, I believe, should be promoted.
2. Kathy and me qualified for a big raise.
3. It was them.
4. The class policy regarding absenteeism was written by the instructor and he.
5. Us students will help the custodian clean out the basement.
6. Did you leave Hortense and her in the library?
7. Mr. Wright will give you and she another chance to do the exam.
8. The new student is whom?
9. Ruth and her are trying to coordinate their rides to campus.
10. Neither Ed nor them can complete their portfolios until next summer.
11. A dispute arose between their pastor and they.
12. To whom did you and her give the keys to my office?

PRACTICE 5L: All Pronoun Usage   Correct any pronoun errors.

1. Us students can write essays in our sleep.
2. Them and their assistants keep the office running smoothly.
3. Are us students invited to the professors' banquet?
4. Show Carol and me the new computer system.
5. Working in the tax division usually relaxes Doyle and I.
6. I do not appreciate him messing with my computer.
7. Waldo knows whom the boss really is.
8. Mr. Smith, who hired me today, is the new branch manager.
9. It couldn't have been them.
10. The secretaries and myself will go out for lunch.
11. Somebody, either Waldo or him, answered the phone.
12. Have you seen Bridget or she yet?

PORTFOLIO IN PROGRESS

TABLE OF CONTENTS

Prepare your annotated table of contents for your portfolio. List each entry and annotation (a short explanation or commentary) plus the page number in the order it will appear in your portfolio. Try to create an annotated table of contents that fits you and your writings. A partial example is provided.

TABLE OF CONTENTS

PAGE

INTRODUCTION   2

FOUR MAJOR PROJECTS

A) SIGNIFICANT EVENT—MY CHOICE PIECE   4

I've chosen my significant event, "A Hot Time on the Boat," to be evaluated by the instructor because I enjoyed writing this piece the most and I like the lively dialogue. I've also included its full process, pre-writes through revisions to final draft.

B) SIGNIFICANT PLACE   32

My significant place project, "A Day in Hell," describes my view of my former job in a foundry.

C) YOU'RE THE EXPERT   37

I explain how to shoot free-throws because as an eighth-grader, I won the Dubuque County free throw contest, an accomplishment I'm extremely proud of.

D) CONVINCE YOUR READER   43

Telemarketers who call me at home drive me crazy. I am trying to convince legislators to come up with a law to control the frenzy.

FIRST WRITING

"A Long, Long Trail A-winding"   49

My autobiography, along with its process, gives a short summary of my life and provides a sample of my writing at the beginning of the semester. The revision and entry slip show and explain my writing improvements throughout this course.

FOUR PERSONAL INCLUSIONS

1) "Tribute to Dad"   61
This piece pays tribute to the most influential person in my life. He died in 1991, and I miss him a great deal.

2) "Golfing: Stresser or Stress Reliever?"   65
This short essay explains my passion for golf, sometimes too much so.

3) "They Call Me Grandpa"   68
In this piece, I share the love and joy my grandchildren have brought to my family.

4) "Desdemona—Foxy Fraud"   70
This essay, written for my World Literature class, analyzes the character of Desdemona in Shakespeare's *Othello*.

METACOGNITIVE CONCLUSION   73
This final essay evaluates my performance over the course of this semester.

GLAD, BAD, SAD, OR MAD?

The following sentences are taken from student writings. Note how the misuse of language or failure to edit affects meaning. Evaluate the sentences by rating each one as GLAD (witty), BAD (accidental error), SAD (misuse of language), or MAD (a little off center).

1. We existed the bus one by one.
2. My editing partner pointed out a few punctuation eras.
3. It seems some students take learning for granite.
4. The wedding party put lace strands through the pillars which come pairs with a car going through traffic on a busy day in New York.
5. We know the import ants of family.
6. I added dialogue to create a pitcher for my readers.

CHAPTER 6

"Comparatively-Contrasting"

~ ~ ~

"By comparing one thing with another, you may see them both more clearly. But not every comparison is illuminating. Any two things can be compared, but the comparison helps only if it is significant" (35).
—Richard Marius

~ ~ ~

Comparison–contrast writing offers a basic method of looking at things closely, that is, explaining similarities and/or differences in two or more objects, people, or ideas. Many times writers use comparisons or contrasts to convey information to readers in expressive, explanatory, or persuasive writing. Comparisons and/or contrasts help especially in discussing two or more subjects with marked similarities and differences to show superiority and preference.

Analysis through comparison-contrast is part of everyone's life. Which type of car–Model A or Model B–should you buy? Which computer seems to be a better buy–Brand X or Brand Y? Of two sections of college courses taught by different instructors, which will you select? Many instructors, in fact, like to assign comparison-contrast assignments or exams in order to challenge students to know specific details of two or more topics and the relationships between or among these topics.

In this type of writing, you must establish a reason–a why, a so what–for comparing or contrasting two subjects, presented logically and clearly to your readers. You must establish a significance for your comparison or contrast. Simply comparing your mother or father, for example, will not suffice. You must establish some purpose in doing so. The comparison-contrast must prove or illustrate a point: for example, how despite their different attitudes and habits, they have remained happily married; or how their different personalities affected their children. Remember, the comparison-contrast essay must make a point, a so what. The thesis statement of your comparison-contrast essay should inform the readers of not only the subjects you plan to compare and contrast but also the point (so what) you will make about them. The thesis should also tell whether you will focus on similarities or differences or a combination of the two and also the order main points will appear in the essay.

Often the so what or significance of a comparison-contrast essay establishes a preference of one subject over another. In this case, state your preference clearly in your thesis, and support and develop that thesis preference throughout the comparison and contrast points in your essay. The examples and word choices you use to compare and contrast your subjects will help illuminate your preference.

In organizing the comparison-contrast essay, you must consider balance. Make sure that all points cited in a section analyzing X are also brought up in the section devoted to Y and are also presented in the same order. Plus, you will need clear transitions, links between ideas or sections of your text, to provide smooth flow between parts. You might use transitional devices like the following to alert readers to connections or differences in your text:

TO COMPARE: also, as well, similarly, like, likewise, in like manner, in like fashion, in the same way

TO CONTRAST: although, but, conversely, despite, even though, however, still, nevertheless, in contrast, on the contrary, on the other hand, otherwise, unlike, yet

METHODS OF COMPARISON-CONTRAST

Three methods are commonly used to develop comparisons and contrasts. These patterns offer some overall organization into which you can fit each point or aspect you choose to write about. Usually it works best to present points in increasing order of importance, saving the "kicker" (the most important point) for last. This leaves the reader with a strong impression of your explanation or position. You may choose to organize your essay in one or a combination of the following three ways:

I. Point-by-Point	II. Block	III. Similarities-Differences
Point A of Subject 1	Subject 1	Similarities between Subjects 1 & 2
Point A of Subject 2	Point A	Point A
	Point B	Point B
Point B of Subject 1	Point C	Point C
Point B of Subject 2	Subject 2	Differences between Subjects 1 & 2
Point C of Subject 1	Point A	Point A
	Point B	Point B
Point C of Subject 2	Point C	Point C

NOTE: The diagram above assumes two subjects are being compared/contrasted on three points, but obviously any number of points and any number of subjects may be included.

STRUT YOUR STUFF!

Writing Project 6-1: Compare/Contrast   Compose a piece of writing developed by means of comparison-contrast of at least two objects, ideas, or people. Establish a persuasive preference of one subject over the other(s) stated in your thesis. Include specific details and examples to support your thesis. In this type of writing, you must establish <u>a reason—a why</u> for comparing two subjects, presented logically and clearly to the readers. Above all, remember: **you've gotta have heart in your writing.**

Writing Checklist:

- ☐ 1. Are the comparison-contrast items and your preference stated clearly in the thesis?
- ☐ 2. Is the essay organized by the point method, the block method, or the similarities/differences method?
- ☐ 3. Does the essay include specific details and examples?
- ☐ 4. Does the essay provide a point, a "so what"?
- ☐ 5. Does the essay provide smooth transitional words and phrases?

☐ 6. Does the piece open with an effective introduction and close with an effective conclusion?

☐ 7. Has the piece been revised and edited for clarity, conciseness, and correctness?

SAMPLE STUDENT WRITING
Compare-Contrast

Four-Year or Two-year Nursing Degree:
Two-year Works For Me
by Jayne Reymer

Throughout my life, my parents stressed the importance of a college education. So I always knew that I would attend college, but the decision of which college did not start until my senior year at Cascade High School. As a high school junior and senior, I worked 20 hours each week as a CNA (Certified Nursing Assistant) at River Bend Retirement Community in Cascade, a job I loved. This experience in providing health care motivated me to want to pursue a career in nursing. In addition, my strongest and most interesting subjects in high school were science and math, which helped steer me to a career in a science field like nursing. So during my senior year at Cascade High School, I began exploring two colleges, University of Iowa (Iowa) and Northeast Iowa Community College (NICC), that could provide me the education I needed to reach my goal of becoming a nurse. After studying the pros and cons of each institution, I chose to attend NICC because of its two-year program, smaller class sizes, closer proximity of clinical locations, solid reputation, and cheaper cost.

After exploring six four-year schools and three two-year colleges, I narrowed my search to the University of Iowa and Northeast Iowa Community College for a number of reasons. First, both of my parents graduated from the University of Iowa and met there as students in the 1980's. My dad majored in accounting at Iowa and graduated in 1983 while my mother graduated in 1984 with a nursing degree. My older sister Marcie also graduated from Iowa two years ago with an elementary education major. So Iowa Hawkeye blood ran through my veins. Second, I did not want to move a long way away from my family and friends. Since both colleges are relatively close to my home of Cascade, with Iowa about 70 miles away and Peosta 15 miles away, the distance factor was reduced. Third, since I am a resident of the State of Iowa, tuition costs could be held in check rather than spending extra money to attend an out-of-state college.

As I analyzed the nursing program at the University of Iowa, I learned that it required four years of schooling. The first year consists of general education courses and some preliminary, pre-requisite courses required for admission into the nursing program. Acceptance into the Iowa Nursing program is extremely competitive. Each fall the Iowa Nursing program accepts only 75 new applicants. That means if a student applies but is not accepted, he or she must take other classes to retain full-time student status and wait another year to reapply. Northeast Iowa Community College, on the other hand, offers a two-year nursing degree, so I would be able to earn my RN degree in half the time. I would take my general education courses the first year and move into my nursing major the second year. NICC also has a waiting list for nursing students, but usually about 40 students are accepted into the nursing program each semester throughout the academic year rather than waiting for the fall semester acceptance that Iowa requires.

Another factor in my decision was based on the overall size of the two colleges and their individual class sizes. I learn best in a small environment where I can actively participate in class presentations and discussions and gain easy access to my instructors. When I visited both campuses, I was given a tour by a student tour-guide who took me into classes that I would probably take during my first semester. At Iowa, I visited two large, lecture classes, World Cultures and Introduction to Psychology, of 400 students each. The professors lectured from a huge stage, and students sat quietly and took notes. I did not see any questions or discussion take place in either class, and I felt uncomfortable with the size. At NICC, my tour guide took me to a World History course of 18 students and an Introduction to Psychology class of 22 students. In both classes, the instructors were able to ask numerous questions and get responses. Plus, the Psychology class also spent about twenty minutes in group discussion of three students per group. After experiencing both situations, I felt I would feel more comfortable and be able to learn better at NICC because of its smaller-sized classes.

In addition to the two versus four-year time frame and class sizes, I was also struck by the difference in the proximity of clinical component locations. Both Iowa and NICC would require me to travel to a clinical location in any one of numerous towns in eastern Iowa to complete my clinical requirements. This travel could range from assignments in small towns to the west of Iowa City or possibly to larger medical facilities in Cedar Rapids and may even require residence near those clinical sites. Although NICC's nursing clinicals may require some traveling to sites in outlying areas, I would most likely be able to train at Mercy and Finley Hospitals in Dubuque, both of which are reasonably located within a half hour of my home. That factor would reduce the stress of arranging transportation and maintaining traveling costs.

Both Iowa and NICC can boast about their excellent reputations in nursing education. The University offers nurses the opportunity to train in the renowned University Hospital setting, learning from some of the best researchers and nursing professors in the country. Although NICC is not involved in medical research like Iowa, the NICC nursing faculty, like the Iowa faculty, consists of experienced nursing professionals who have come to teaching after successful careers in the nursing field. The quality of the NICC faculty is reflected in the results of the State of Iowa Nursing Board Exam. Each year NICC nursing students rank among the top colleges, either two-year or four-year, in successful passage of the State Board Exam.

Another important consideration in my decision was overall cost. I considered commuting to Iowa City each day, but the cost of car maintenance and the high cost of gas, in addition to time lost on the road, easily negated a commuting decision. Therefore, my next option would be to live in the University's dorms. That would add a large financial burden in paying for room and board as well as tuition, books, and fees; not to mention incidental costs of transportation, recreation, and other necessities. By choosing NICC, I am able to live with my parents and pay a minimal amount of rent each month. Plus, the short distance from my home to the NICC campus saves huge amounts of time and money. And as a bonus, I am able to keep my part-time job at River Bend Retirement Community so that I earn a consistent income and gain experience in nursing care at the same time.

After weighing my options two years ago, I am pleased with the decision I made to attend Northeast Iowa Community College and major in nursing. The learning environment fits my needs perfectly. I am enrolled in small classes and can get extra help when I need it. I saved lots of time and money by getting a two-year RN degree rather than a four-year BSN degree, which I can always pursue in the future, if I choose. I know I made the right decision because I stayed on schedule and will receive my RN degree in four months. And, to top it off, I have already been offered a full-time nursing position at River Bend.

Discussion Questions:

1. Is a clear, specific thesis statement provided? Does the writer clearly establish a preference in the thesis statement?
2. Analyze and explain the organization the writer has chosen for this essay.
3. What specific details and examples does the writer use?
4. Does the essay grow to a point, a significance, a so what? What is it?
5. Evaluate the title, introduction, and conclusion. How effective are they? Explain your responses.
6. Identify any writing strategies (figurative language, sense imagery, dialogue, humor, satire, etc.) that the writer uses, and evaluate their effectiveness.
7. Point out the strengths of this essay. What suggestions or improvements for the piece would you suggest?
8. Does the writer "have heart" in the essay? What specific aspects of the piece support your response?
9. Evaluate the effectiveness of the piece holistically and provide rationale for your evaluation.

Writing Project 6-2: College vs. High School   Compose an essay for an incoming, first-year college student in which you compare and contrast the differences in expectations and challenges between college courses and high school courses. Provide concrete examples and details to help your readers understand the similarities and differences in high school and college courses and focus on a so what, the point or significance of your comparison-contrast essay. Above all, remember: **you've gotta have heart in your writing.**

Writing Project 6-3: School Days   A 1906 song, "School Days," by Will Cobb and Gus Edwards says, "School days, school days, Dear old, golden rule days." Interview your parents or grandparents about their school experiences of previous decades. Then write a comparison-contrast essay that explains the differences in schooling experiences in their era compared to your present era. Provide concrete examples and details to help your readers understand the similarities and differences in schooling and focus on a so what, the point or significance of your comparison-contrast essay. Above all, remember: **you've gotta have heart in your writing.**

Writing Project 6-4: You've Changed? Compose an essay in which you explain how you've changed as a student and/or a person since you've attended college. Provide concrete examples and details to help your readers understand how you've changed and focus on a so what, the point or significance of your comparison-contrast essay. Above all, remember: **you've gotta have heart in your writing.**

WRITING THESIS STATEMENTS

Your thesis establishes your main idea or position, opinion, or claim about the topic or issue you are trying to inform or convince your readers to consider. The thesis is usually placed at the end of the introductory paragraph, but this placement serves as a guideline, not a hard and fast rule. Write the thesis as a statement (not a question) of your controlling idea along with the main points of your evidence in the order those main points will appear. This gives readers an organizational "roadmap" for the remainder of the essay. Also, note that your thesis may need revision and change as your essay develops. Therefore, always revisit and revise your thesis after you complete your paper to ensure that it accurately and clearly establishes your main point or position and the organization of your paper.

In persuasive writing, you might formulate a clear position on an issue by asking yourself, "What should be done about it?" Your thesis might fit the following WHO, WHAT, WHY formula:

WHO		WHAT		WHY
A	should (not) do	**B**	because	**1, 2, 3, 4, 5**.

Examples of Thesis Statements:

❖ **Expository:**

The writing process consists of many stages which occur in a recursive manner.

Prewriting strategies help writers unlock their brains and focus clearly on their topics.

Pianists and baseball players share many similar talents such as hand-eye coordination, focused concentration, and the ability to perform under pressure.

❖ **Persuasive:**
Governments around the world need to combat global warming in order to deal with possible increases in violent storms, infectious diseases, deadly heat waves, and rising sea levels.

In order to develop better personal discipline, social skills, and team work, all high school students should be required to take music courses.

The United States Government should create ways to save the Social Security system rather than force citizens to plan for their own retirements.

Consider the following guidelines for thesis development. The thesis should:

1. **NOT be written as an announcement.**
   YUK! – The following essay will tell the reader how to behave during a job interview.

   YES! – A job seeker must become aware of proper interviewing skills in order to land a dream job.

2. **Present something arguable or in need of explanation, rather than a statement of fact or opinion.**
   YUK! – Drunk drivers are a menace.

   YES! – To make roads safer for everyone, authorities should suspend the driver's license of anyone convicted of drunk driving.

3. **Present a manageable topic; it should not take on too much.**
   YUK! – The American system of education needs a complete overhaul.

   YES! – In order to improve the quality of education, United States math teachers should spend more time teaching basic facts—addition, subtraction, and multiplication—in the primary grades.

4. **Be written in specific language; avoid using vague words such as "nice," "interesting," "good," "bad," or "great."**

YUK! – Playing high school football was a great experience.

YES! – Playing high school football taught me self-confidence and the importance of teamwork.

5. **Be written in a positive rather than negative language.**

YUK! – Smoking should not be allowed in eating places.

YES! – Smoking should be prohibited in restaurants.

PRACTICE: 6A: Analyze the following thesis statements to determine their effectiveness. If the thesis works well, write OK on your paper. If it seems deficient, explain why, and write an effective thesis statement.

1. Composition students have too much homework.

2. In this paper, I will tell you the characteristics of a model college student.

3. Guided missiles, advanced combat aircraft, and nuclear war plants should be removed in all countries to prevent the horrors of another world war.

4. Why is it that females still face discrimination in the job market?

5. A good college instructor must display knowledge of the subject matter, a commitment to excellence, the ability to communicate, and a sense of humor.

6. Because of the danger posed by passing traffic, no toddler playgrounds should be placed within 50 yards of a through street.

7. Colleges and universities should not require physical education classes because they delay students' progress and contribute little to students' education.

8. Statistics show that Asian Americans are one of the fastest growing ethnic groups in the United States.

9. The following essay will explain why all college students should take a composition course.

10. The St. Louis Cardinals are a better baseball team than the Chicago Cubs.

PRACTICE 6B: Create an effective thesis statement for each of the following college-related topics:

1. fees for computer use
2. smoking on campus
3. required foreign language
4. fraternities/sororities
5. national competency testing

6. prayer in classrooms
7. published teacher evaluations
8. state aid to community colleges
9. paid varsity athletes
10. child care for student-parents

VOICE: ACTIVE & PASSIVE

~ ~ ~

"It's a little slimy for a writer to hide behind the passive voice. Relying too heavily on the passive voice eventually undermines your readers' trust" (89).
—Elizabeth Danziger

~ ~ ~

Generally, writers prefer active voice over passive voice because active voice is more vigorous, emphatic, forceful, direct, and concise. The passive voice requires two more words than the active voice. In an active voice sentence, the subject does the action; in the passive voice, something is done to the subject. The passive voice can be recognized by TO BE form helping verbs plus a past participle. In addition, most passive sentences end in a by _____ (prepositional phrase). Note the difference in voice in the following examples:

PASSIVE: The essay was written by Sharon.
ACTIVE: Sharon wrote the essay.

Occasionally, the passive voice may be favored, such as (1) when the doer of the action is unknown, (2) to place the focus on the receiver of the action.
Examples:
1) My computer was stolen last night.
2) An error in judgment has been made by the registrar in the calculations of the student's grades.

Remember:

Use active voice whenever possible for a stronger, more concise writing style.

Using three steps, writers can easily change passive voice verbs into active voice.

1. **Flip the sentence.** Make the object of the preposition <u>by</u> the subject of the sentence. The passive voice subject then becomes the object of the sentence.

2. **Eliminate TO BE verb forms** (am, is, are, was, were, be, been) used as helping verbs.

3. **Keep helping verbs <u>has-have</u>, <u>had</u>, <u>will</u>,** which form the perfect and future tenses. This preserves tense consistency.

Examples:

PASSIVE: The gerbils have been fed by my roommate. (present perfect tense)

ACTIVE: My roommate has fed the gerbils.

PASSIVE: A new computer was bought by my writing partner. (past tense)

ACTIVE: My writing partner bought a new computer.

PASSIVE: A Writing Center conference is needed by Clarence. (present tense)

ACTIVE: Clarence needs a Writing Center conference.

NOTE: The helping verbs <u>am</u>, <u>is</u>, <u>are</u> signal present tense.

~ ~ ~

"If you are blessed with confidence, whether it be innate or earned as a result of knowing you've mastered your subject, you'll almost instinctively employ the active voice, since it will be natural for you to assert what you know, and to assert it in bold terms. If, however, you are fundamentally insecure about your thesis, you'll almost instinctively turn to the passive voice as a refuge" (64).

—John R. Trimble

~ ~ ~

PRACTICE 6C: Active Voice   Revise the following sentences by changing passive voice verbs to active voice verbs.

1. The expectations explained in the course syllabus must be met by all composition students.
2. Narrative essays have been processed by each student, and they will be shared at the next peer response session.
3. Ankle-supported basketball shoes were used by many college basketball players over the years.
4. Flu shots had been given to the majority of the first year class by the college's medical staff.
5. Active voice sentences are preferred over passive voice sentences by most good writers.

PRACTICE 6D: Active Voice   Revise the following passage by changing passive voice sentences to active voice.

Robert Frost

Born in San Francisco in 1874, poet Robert Frost was raised by his mother in New England after his father died. Dartmouth and Harvard were both attended by Frost, but he did not graduate from college. Farming and rural New England life were loved by Frost, and these subjects were addressed prominently in his poetry. Frost was married to Elinor White, and he, along with his wife and children, moved to England in 1912 to farm and write. In 1913, Frost's first book, *A Boy's Will*, was published by Englishman David Nutt. Two years later the Frost family returned to New England, and for the rest of his life, Frost was heralded as a major American poet. The Pulitzer Prize was awarded to Frost four times. In 1961, Frost was invited by President John F. Kennedy to read the poem "The Gift Outright" at the Presidential Inauguration. Robert Frost died in 1963 in Boston, but his poetry lives prominently in American literature.

~ ~ ~

"Verbs in the passive voice are dressed for
a funeral; they have about them a tone of
stiff formality which, perhaps, accounts
for their irresistibility to those who...speak
in a cemetery voice" (44).
—Irving Younger

~ ~ ~

PORTFOLIO IN PROGRESS

The Demonstration Portfolio, submitted near the end of the course, allows you to get responses, improve, and revise earlier pieces as the course progresses. In addition, you will continually self-reflect on your growth as a writer, determine ways to improve your writing, and prepare entry slips for your Demonstration Portfolio. The Entry Slip-Reflection ideas suggested in the "Portfolio in Progress" section at the end of Chapter 2 may help you reflect on your writing. Keep track of your self-reflections by dating them, labeling them, and saving them in a secure place (notebook, journal, computer) so you can draw on these ideas as you prepare your portfolio entry slips.

SAMPLE ENTRY SLIP—Compare-Contrast Project

The following entry slip, written by Kristen Runde, preceded her compare-contrast essay in her portfolio.

The Customer Is Always Right
Entry Slip by Kristen Runde

As I walk through the garden of flowers, I instantly notice a Hawaiian flower. This Hawaiian flower seems to be what most customers buy in hopes of finding the most beautiful flower. They notice this flower first because it shows off its bright colors on a sunny day. My first bright-colored flower is my first major assignment for Composition II. I chose to write about the similarities and differences between Wal-Mart and Target. I chose to compare and contrast these because I shop at these stores so frequently. When people visit Dubuque, they notice the shopping centers. Tourists tend to think about what activities seem to be of interest before they travel. Likewise, when someone visits a garden, he or she thinks of what kind of beauty the garden and its flowers can bring.

When I wrote my compare and contrast paper about Target and Wal-Mart, I noticed aspects of both stores that I hadn't paid attention to before. As I traveled to both stores, I realized how differently both stores present themselves, which became the focus of my paper. My peer group praised my writing and organization and suggested some important improvements. They suggested I use figurative language; like similes, metaphors, and personification; to bring the stores' descriptions to life. This improvement added much more specific, focused imagery to my paper and helped readers visualize both stores.

A difficult part of the essay process was deciding which I preferred. So I also took the paper to the NICC Writing Center. Writing Center Director Larry Kruse complimented me on my choice of topic, but he indicated that my paper lacked a "so what" because I had not taken a forceful enough position on my preference for one store over the other. After I revised the paper with a more persuasive preference for Wal-Mart, the paper seemed to have more purpose and more power. Adding my peer response group's and Larry's suggestions improved the paper and helped put me on the road to writing success. My revisions helped my paper immensely. I am anxious to see what else I will find on my way through this marvelous writing garden.

PRACTICE 6E: Be Secific—Entry Slip   Analyze the following Portfolio Entry Slip based on Project 6-1, Compare-Contrast. Revise it so that it focuses on specific HOC (Higher Order Concerns) issues and avoids LOC (Lower Order Concerns) focus.

Entry Slip 6-1

I chose a topic that I thought would interest me and be easy to compare and contrast. Many people do not see the differences between high school and college. I had some HOC issues to deal with to improve my paper. I focused on one side of the topic more than the other, so my paper was not balanced. I also did not have a so what in the paper.

When I first started writing the paper, I had trouble coming up with ideas. The opening paragraph gave me the most trouble. My peer group helped a lot in revising my paper. The suggestions they gave helped me develop the paper. My group also suggested I get rid of weak verbs. I still need to work on my punctuation, but my editing is improving. I then took the paper to Larry in the Writing Center, who helped me polish the paper.

Overall, my first major paper went well. My personal voice comes through, and my writing is more interesting to read.

GLAD, BAD, SAD, OR MAD?

The following sentences are taken from student writings. Note how the misuse of language or failure to edit affects meaning. Evaluate the sentences by rating each one as GLAD (witty), BAD (accidental error), SAD (misuse of language), or MAD (a little off center).

1. Comas always present an editing challenge for me.
2. Once we finish the main meal, it's on to the desert, which consists of Better Than Sex Cake.
3. This intern makes US troops victims of cross fire from Iraqi violence.
4. Anyone can say shooting free throws requires talent, but 90% is mental and only 50% physical.
5. One way I could handle slow speed would be to have more patients.
6. Freshman year was pretty tough, but I pasted with good grades.
7. The window is covered with an old, tie-dye sheet that gives a collide scope of color when the sun shines through.

CHAPTER 7

Cement an Abstract Term in Concrete

Extended Definition

~ ~ ~

"Writing is magic, as much the water of life as any other creative art. The water is free. So drink. Drink and be filled" (270).
—Stephen King

~ ~ ~

The extended definition, a common academic topic, goes into greater detail by describing and explaining key characteristics about a subject. The extended definition tries to provide enough information so that the audience can gain a thorough understanding of the term. You will need to define an abstract term, an idea or a concept, versus a concrete term, a tangible object. Define the abstract term in such a way that the term becomes concrete for the audience. That means provide numerous examples and descriptions of the term. Try not to constrict the meaning of the word but rather "open it up" for your audience. To do this, you will need to go beyond the denotation, the literal, dictionary definition without any additional, subjective meanings attached to the term. You will need to focus on the connotation, which refers to various meanings that the term evokes or implies. While the term "mother" denotes "female parent," the term "mother" connotes a loving, caring, warm, sensitive, protective, tender, self-sacrificing woman.

When writing an extended definition, avoid two common fallacies that weaken the definition. First, avoid the circular definition—using a form of the word—in the definition, such as "happiness is the state of being happy." Second, avoid expressions like "is when" or "is where" in your definition. For example, "peer pressure is when certain members of society pressure their peers to believe or do as they wish."

Simply defining the term will not suffice. The extended definition focuses on a detailed explanation of one term and grows to a point, a why or so what. Why are you defining the abstract term you've chosen? What point are you trying to make by defining the term you have chosen? In other words, explain the importance or significance of the term you have chosen to define. To extend your definition, you might use other possible patterns of development to move beyond simple denotation, such as: (a) origin of the term, (b) necessary conditions for the term, (c) description of how the term might look, (d) explanation of the uses of the term, (e) division of the term into parts, if applicable, (f) examples, illustrations, anecdotes of the term, (g) causes and effects of the term, (h) comparisons and contrasts of the term (use simile and metaphor), (i) negation, what the term is not, (j) any other pertinent information.

Cement abstract ideas in concrete!

STRUT YOUR STUFF!

Writing Project 7-1: Make an Abstract Concrete   Write an essay in which you define an abstract term or phrase that significantly applies to you. By using a variety of methods, make the abstract term concrete so that your audience completely understands the meaning of the term and its significance to you. Above all, remember: **you've gotta have heart in your writing.**

Writing Checklist:

- ☐ 1. Have you chosen an abstract term?
- ☐ 2. Does the introductory paragraph grab readers' attention and state the thesis and the term's significance?
- ☐ 3. Have you used a variety of methods to make the abstract

☐   term concrete and to help your readers understand the term?
        4. Does the essay focus on a <u>so what</u>—the significance of the
        term to you?

☐   5. Does the point of view stay consistently in first or third
        person and avoid unnecessary shifts to second person (you)?

☐   6. Does the conclusion bring effective closure to the essay?

☐   7. Has the piece been edited for clarity, conciseness, and
        correctness?

SAMPLE STUDENT WRITING
Definition

The Fruit of Friendship
By Elliott Zelinskas

I love the company of others. In today's fast-moving society, people interact and communicate with each other daily. This social outlet lets people gain a sense of importance and a bonding relation with others. Staying social lets people live healthy, normal lives. The friendships I create help each day to flow smoothly into the next.

When I reflect on friendship, emotions and memories flood my brain. Everyone has experienced lasting, wonderful friendships; therefore, everyone knows how a good friendship feels. I define friendship as companionship through thick and thin, comradeship for life, the loving and affectionate alliance between two people. Sallust, a Roman historian, once said, "To like and dislike the same things, that is indeed true friendship." Liking and disliking the same things may keep a friendship, but liking and disliking opposite things, yet keeping the friendship alive will show true friendship.

Creating friendships will always be accepted in any society. As each day passes, I encounter hundreds of new people who could potentially become my best friend. Friendships are not limited, the more the better. They affect my daily life and make me feel special and individual. Friendships build my self-esteem, and without that bond, I would feel empty and alone.

One night, my friend, Zack, threw a party; another friend, Justin, picked me up to go together. I wasn't drinking, but Justin was drinking. The police came, and all of my friends ran. Because I didn't drink, I didn't run. However, Justin did. I waited 45 minutes before Justin called my cell phone. Justin's keys were buried in his pocket, which left me stranded at Zack's house. At 4:30 a.m., I needed someone to pick me up. I called my friend Jordan and told him my situation. Without hesitation, he told me to stay at Zack's house and wait for him. I felt relieved that he was coming to get me. Jordan arrived in 15 minutes; and I knew if he would wake up at 4:30, get dressed, and pick me up, Jordan would help me with anything. That night, Jordan showed me what true friendship means.

Last summer, I worked as a skateboard instructor at Lake Owen Skateboard Camp in Cable, Wisconsin. A boy from Chicago named Drew Rose car-pooled with me. Because we both worked at camp the same two weeks, we decided to drive together. After spending time with each other, we instantly became best friends. Neither of us wanted to go home, so we each convinced the camp director to let us stay for an additional five weeks.

After camp, I lived with Drew in Chicago for a month. I ate his food, used his car, and stayed in his house. Drew showed me the in's and out's of Chicago, and I now love the city. Drew is more welcoming and generous than anyone I ever met; he lives by the saying, "What's mine is yours." After I stayed with Drew for a month, we ventured on another skateboard trip together. We drove from Chicago to Kentucky to Ohio and then to Wisconsin and back to Chicago. As a result of frequently visiting Drew in Chicago, I became acquainted with DePaul University, where I will transfer for my fall semester. I still visit Drew at least once a month. He takes me to new skate parks and introduces me to new people. Together, we help each other grow, and we have become best friends.

For me, friendship does not require material items. The beautiful and prestigious store, Bloomingdales, located in Chicago, does not carry "friendship." FAO Schwartz, Ralph Lauren, and Gucci may all carry infinitely wonderful items. However, none of these own a shipment of "friendship." I cannot purchase friendship, yet if I could, I don't think I would want to.

Friendship comes from a true pal or buddy who actually cares, feels, and empathizes with the other friend. Friendships help two people grow and become stronger. They guide a person to make the right decisions, to never look back, and to leave no regrets. Trust, patience, and unconditional love follow a true friendship closely. These simple yet meaningful conditions set genuine friends apart from two strangers.

Friendship is universally experienced and knows no national boundaries. Everyone has the power to become friends with someone because friendship requires no rules or money. Two summers ago, I met a French kid named Axel at the Lake Owen Skateboard Camp. Axel fluently spoke English, but wanted to learn American slang. I taught him English slang each day, and he taught me a new French word each day.

Friendship can tie two people together like string, hold two people together like a hanger, and keep two people close like a paperclip. Friendship is helpful like a flashlight in a dark cave, is useful like shelter during a thunderstorm, and is needed like food for a famished stomach. A friendship blossoms like a summer's sunflower, becomes ripe like a raspberry, and grows like a weeping willow tree. John Lennon once said in a song that "he gets by with a little help from his friends"; however, I get by with a lot of help from my friends. My personal and unique friendships help support my life. I value them more than a school grade, cherish them more than a first-place trophy, and treasure them more than a rare ruby. I make a conscious effort to show that I respect, enjoy, and celebrate my friendships every day.

Discussion Questions:

1. What abstract term has the writer chosen to define? Identify the writer's thesis. Is the thesis effective?
2. List the methods the writer uses to define the term. How effectively does the writer use these methods?
3. Identify the point, the so what–the significance of the essay.
4. Do you as a reader understand the term better after reading this piece? Why or why not?
5. Analyze the effectiveness of the title, the introduction, and the conclusion.
6. Explain the strengths of the essay. What aspects might improve the essay?
7. Does the writer "have heart" in the essay? What specific aspects of the piece support your response?
8. Evaluate the essay holistically and explain your rationale for that evaluation.

Writing Project 7-2: Connotation   The list below contains pairs of terms closely related in meaning but different in connotation. Select one pair; then write an essay in which you define the terms by elaborating on the distinctions between the words in that pair. Include such considerations as when, where, why, how, and by whom each word might be used, and provide concrete examples to bring the terms to life. Use comparison-contrast organizational methods developed in the previous writing project and descriptive, narrative, and expository strategies to develop your definitions of these terms.

Job...Profession   Lady...Woman

Recreation...Play   Religion...Spirituality

Terrorist...Revolutionary

(Advanced Placement Language-Composition Exam. Educational Testing Service, 1986).

Writing Project 7-3: Fool   In William Shakespeare's *A Midsummer Night's Dream*, the character Puck says, "Lord, what fools these mortals be!" Define what the term "fool" means to you in both its positive and negative connotations. Include such considerations as when, where, why, how, and by whom the word might be used, and provide concrete examples to bring the term "fool" to life. Use strategies developed in previous writing projects (descriptive, narrative, and expository) to develop your definition of the word "fool." Above all, remember: **you've gotta have heart in your writing.**

Writing Project 7-4: Pride   In his *Anatomy of Melancholy*, English clergyman Robert Burton (1577-1640) writes, "They are proud in humility, proud in that they are not proud." Define what the term "pride" means to you in both its positive and negative connotations. Include such considerations as when, where, why, how, and by whom the word might be used, and provide concrete examples to bring the term "pride" to life. Use strategies developed in previous writing projects (descriptive, narrative, and expository) to develop your definition of the word "pride." Above all, remember: **you've gotta have heart in your writing.**

Writing Project 7-5: Hero/Heroine   In *The Sketch Book*, Washington Irving writes, "The idol of today pushes the hero of yesterday out of our recollection; and will, in turn, be supplanted by his successor." Define the term hero/heroine from your experiences. Use strategies developed in previous writing projects (descriptive, narrative, and expository) to develop your definition of the word hero/heroine. Above all, remember: **you've gotta have heart in your writing.**

MAY WE COME TO AGREEMENT?

SUBJECT-VERB AGREEMENT

1. **The subject and verb of a sentence must agree in number (singular or plural) and gender.**

   Singular: The composition student writes the essays.
   Plural: The composition students write the essays.
   Singular: She goes to class at 8 a.m.
   Plural: They go to class at 8 a.m.
   Singular: The office closes at 5 p.m.
   Plural: The offices close at 5 p.m.

   NOTE: A verb in the third person singular, present tense, ends in -s and requires a singular subject. The ending -s on a subject, however, usually signals plural and requires a plural verb, not ending in -s. Note the following exceptions, however:

   Mumps is a bad disease.
   Economics has given me lots of trouble.
   Mathematics is much harder than English.
   My boss treats me fairly.
   Physics has to be taught well.
   The waitress was hired for the lunch rush.

2. **A company or corporation, even consisting of many names, is considered a single body requiring a singular verb.**

   Fuerste, Carew, Coyle, Juergens, & Sudmeier is a law firm in Dubuque.
   Honkamp Krueger & Co., P.C. is a large company featuring certified public accountants and business consultants.

3. **A collective noun, referring to a group, uses a singular verb.**

   The writing committee is meeting today.
   The basketball team has been practicing for two weeks.
   The news about the economy is shocking.
   The Peosta City Council meets on Mondays.

4. **The subject of a sentence cannot be located in a prepositional phrase.**

   The performance (of the secretaries) was excellent.
   The decision (of the personnel managers) is final.
   The supervisor (as well as the managers) was upset about the report.
   The instructor (together with the students) does his best.
   The Dean of Students (along with six professors) is flying to Chicago.

5. **Compound Subjects:**
   (a) If the compound subject parts are joined by **and**, make the verb plural.
   (b) If the compound subject parts are joined by **or** or **nor,** make the verb agree with the nearer(est) subject to the verb.
   A new computer **and** printer were placed in every office.
   Tom, Dick, **and** Mary are taking English Composition.
   Tom, Dick, **and** Harry want to participate in the writing seminar.
   Either a new computer **or** a new printer was placed in every office.
   Either Dick **or** Harry wants to participate in the seminar.

6. **Indefinite Pronouns:**
   (a) Singular: **each, either, neither, one, every, anyone, everyone, someone, anybody, everybody, somebody**
   Everybody who can is encouraged to attend the writing seminar.
   Everyone has his or her own ideas about social security.
   Each of the students is given a course syllabus.
   Neither of the computers works well.
   (b) Plural: **several, few, both, many**
   Several of the participants are late.
   Few of my friends have taken their spring vacations.
   Many are cocky; few are confident.
   (c) Singular or Plural depending on the meaning of the sentence:
   all, any, none, some, most, half, part
   All of the computer looks clean.
   All of the computers look clean.
   Most of the essay was lost.
   Most of the essays were lost.

7. **Inversion: When a sentence begins with *Here, There, Where, Which,* or *What,* the subject will follow the verb.**
   There are many writing guidelines to follow.
   There is a vacant seat in the 10:30 a.m. composition class.
   Here are the supplies the instructor ordered.
   Where are the surveys and reports?
   What are our options in this matter?

8. **Book titles (*The Three Musketeers*), courses (economics), diseases (measles), or other words singular in meaning require a singular verb. Quantities such as miles, dollars, or years require a singular verb when the amount is considered a collective unit.**

Two Gentlemen of Verona was chosen as the next school production.

Physics is a tough class for Wanda.

The mumps usually lasts three days.

The Tenants by Bernard Malamud is an interesting novel.

Two hundred pounds is too heavy for a jockey.

Ten miles to the gallon was all I could get.

Eighty-one to nothing was the final score.

- **The number of** requires a **singular** verb. **A number of** requires a **plural** verb.

  The number of students in the writing seminar is surprising.

  A number of students have signed up for the writing seminar.

- For graduates or former students of a school or college: **alumna** = singular female, **alumnae** = plural females; **alumnus** = singular male, **alumni** = plural males or both genders.

  My wife Kay is an **alumna** of Clarke College.

  My husband Jim is an **alumnus** of Loras College.

  Mark and Mary are **alumni** of the University of Dubuque.

PRACTICE 7A: Agreement   Underline the subject of each of the following sentences and choose the verb that agrees with the subject.

1. Mathematics (is, are) difficult for many people.
2. The boss (rides, ride) his bike to work each day.
3. The participants (is, are) ready to begin the seminar.
4. The Weber Paper Company (was, were) to call back by three o'clock today.
5. The construction of the new offices (was, were) begun last week in downtown Dubuque.
6. Measles (is, are) a contagious disease.
7. The printer, in addition to the two computers, (needs, need) to be repaired.
8. *Snow White and the Seven Dwarfs* (is, are) a Disney film.
9. There (is, are) six students sleeping throughout this class.
10. The writing in these classes (is, are) improving rapidly.
11. Each of the secretaries (types, type) 120 words per hour.
12. Waldo, Ralph, and Fritz (has, have) started a new consulting business.
13. Either the instructor or the students (is, are) misinformed about the policy.

14. Eighty-five dollars (is, are) too much to pay for a composition book.
15. Here (is, are) six copies of the essay for the peer response session.
16. Which (is, are) your favorite type of writing assignments?
17. Neither Monday nor Tuesday (seems, seem) to fit into our schedules.
18. The number of horses in the parade (is, are) staggering.
19. Every one of my essays (is, are) too long.
20. The alumni (has, have) been contributing generously.
21. The choir of professors (sings, sing) at each Christmas party.
22. Some of the phones (needs, need) to be replaced.
23. One of the accountants (flies, fly) to Las Vegas each Thursday.

PRACTICE 7B: Agreement   Edit the following sentences for subject-verb agreement.

1. Neither of the computer operators have transferred the data correctly.
2. The members of our staff is on the alert throughout the weekend.
3. Somebody in our offices is assigned to refill the printers.
4. Where's the classes you described?
5. A few of the maintenance staff stay behind to clean up the classrooms.
6. Statistics 212 were a tough course for any writing major.
7. Here's three options you can choose from.
8. One of the night watchmen were injured during the office Christmas party.
9. Neither her classmates nor Lila is going to work overtime on Thursday.
10. The Dean's responses to our letter changes our strategy.
11. A police officer or an official from the parking commission are planning to address the students about improper parking.
12. Do either of the positions being advertised require special skills?
13. Several of the instructors and tutors were given the day off.
14. Somebody with a set of keys lock the door from the outside.
15. Either Henry or the two students is getting lunch for the professor.

PRACTICE 7C: Agreement   Write sentences demonstrating correct subject-verb agreement for the following formulas:

1. Write a sentence in the present tense with a singular subject.
2. Write a sentence in the present tense with a plural verb.

3. Write a sentence in the present tense whose subject and verb are separated by a prepositional phrase.
4. Write a sentence in the present tense using a singular indefinite pronoun as subject.
5. Write a sentence in the present tense using a plural indefinite pronoun as subject.
6. Write a sentence in the present tense with a compound subject joined by **and**.
7. Write a sentence in the present tense with a compound subject joined by **or**.
8. Write a sentence in the present tense with compound subjects joined by **either...or**.
9. Write a sentence in the present tense with a compound subject joined by **neither...nor**.
10. Write a sentence in the present tense beginning with the word **There, Here, Where, Which,** or **What.**

PRONOUN-ANTECEDENT AGREEMENT

(The antecedent is the word to which the pronoun refers.)

1. **A pronoun and its antecedent must agree in number (singular and plural) and gender.**

   The writer should clean off **her** desk. (singular)
   The writers should clean off **their** desks. (plural)

2. **Use a plural pronoun to refer to a compound antecedent joined by <u>and</u>.**

   Martha **and** her friend bought **their** plane tickets to Cancun.

3. **When a compound antecedent is joined by <u>or</u> or <u>nor</u>, the pronoun agrees with the word closer(est) to the pronoun.**

   Neither Miss Morton **nor** her classmates have written **their** essays well.

   Either her classmates **or** Miss Morton will write **her** essay again.

4. **Indefinite Pronouns:**

   (a) Singular: **each, either, neither, one, every, anyone, everyone, someone, anybody, everybody, somebody**

   Every student is working at **his or her** desk.

   Each of the students turned in **her or his** essay.

   **NOTE: Use a plural antecedent to add smoother flow to sentences. Varying gender reference can become cumbersome.

All students are working at their desks.
All students turned in their essays.
(b) Plural: **several, few, both, many**
Both of the writers brought **their** own essays.
Few of the complaints have reached **their** targets.
(c) Singular or Plural depending on the meaning of the sentence: **all, any, none, some, most, half, part**
All of the equipment was returned to **its** place.
All of the instructors like **their** new computers.
Half of the printers remained in **their** boxes.

PRACTICE 7D: Agreement   Select the correct pronoun to agree with its antecedent.

1. All of the secretaries wish (she, they) could type as fast as Hilda.
2. The receptionist is good at (her, their) job.
3. Neither Frank nor Homer received (his, their) Christmas bonus.
4. Either the boss or the employees will take (his, their) vacations early.
5. All students looked happy when (he or she, they) picked up their grades.
6. Some of the letters need (its, their) envelopes retyped.
7. Either the ledger or the account book lost (its, their) cover.
8. Employees should monitor (his, their) own work.
9. The No-Doz Company likes (its, their) employees to stay awake.
10. Both the professors and the instructors earned (his or her, their) raises.

PRACTICE 7E: Agreement   Edit the following sentences for pronoun-antecedent agreement.

1. Every writer should recognize their own special talents.
2. None of the essays were in its original folder.
3. All writers should revise their own essays for clarity.
4. Does anyone want their job to be interesting?
5. Either the accountant or the bookkeepers left his calculator in the lobby.
6. Few employees can give his or her explanation of the deficit.
7. Everyone created their own set of grades.
8. Neither the debit nor the credit was posted in their proper column.
9. None of the appreciation was relayed to its recipient.
10. All students were told to turn in his or her parking permits at the gate.

PRACTICE 7F: Agreement   Complete the following using a pronoun to refer to the subject provided.

1. Everyone in the class

2. All of the students

3. Neither the instructor nor the students

4. Each of the receptionists

5. Few of the instructors

6. Every student in the class

7. Both of the professors

8. Either the custodian or the night watchman

PRACTICE 7G: Agreement   Correct the subject-verb and pronoun antecedent problems in the passage below.

Two sports, basketball and track, displays many similarities. They both require well-trained, dedicated athletes and knowledgeable coaches. Basketball focuses on the team concept while track focuses on the individual athlete. Both sports offer their participants many physical and mental rewards. Each athlete must choose which sport they prefer to participate in.

In basketball, more of a team sport, every player must be actively involved with their teammates at all times. They must never give up, or the other team may score a run of points. Defense makes basketball a physical sport. When a player plays defense, they are applying as much pressure on the ball as possible, which can cause physical contact and sometimes results in injury.

Track, on the other hand, does not require physical contact, but it does require consistent concentration. The athlete must mentally prepare themselves before each event. At times, the runner may want to give up because they are tired and experiencing pain. But with concentrated mental focus, they learn to forget these physical pains and focus on winning their event.

Whether a person enjoys watching or prefers competing, they can find a sport to match their interests. Basketball and track illustrates a different emphasis on the team or the individual. An athlete's skill, in addition to their preference, determines whether they choose basketball or track. No matter what sport, if every athlete perform their required role, their basketball or track team will achieve success.

PORTFOLIO IN PROGRESS

Self-Reflection

The Demonstration Portfolio, submitted near the end of the course, allows you to get responses, improve, and revise earlier pieces as the course progresses. In addition, you will continually self-reflect on your growth as a writer, determine ways to improve your writing, and prepare entry slips for your Demonstration Portfolio. The Entry Slip-Reflection ideas suggested in the "Portfolio in Progress" section at the end of Chapter 2 may help you reflect on your writing. Keep track of your self-reflections by dating them, labeling them, and saving them in a secure place (notebook, journal, computer) so you can draw on these ideas as you prepare your portfolio entry slips.

GLAD, BAD, SAD, OR MAD?

The following sentences are taken from student writings. Note how the misuse of language or failure to edit affects meaning. Evaluate the sentences by rating each one as GLAD (witty), BAD (accidental error), SAD (misuse of language), or MAD (a little off center).

1. We had been studing quietly for the quiz.
2. If I dint learn this stuff, I would fail the course.
3. When I am in my special place, all other fascist of life just don't matter.
4. Jason, the Valid Victorian of the senior class, delivered his speech at the final assembly.
5. They placed his body in a black bag and wheeled him up to the Hearst.
6. Life is too short to waist.
7. After I thought about where my expertise lye, my thoughts flowed onto the paper.

CHAPTER 8

Let's Get Critical, Critical

~ ~ ~

"Getting responses from others helps
writers see how their writing is
experienced by readers, where it is
and where it is not working, and how
it might be made to work better" (3).
—Richard Straub

~ ~ ~

Critical essays involve writing about writing. Critical writing demands higher order thinking skills of analysis, evaluation, and synthesis. Analysis means dissecting a piece of writing into its parts and examining their relationship to the whole. Evaluation involves judging the quality of these parts. And synthesis involves combining this analysis and evaluation into a unified piece of reasoned response, which offers writers broader perspectives on their writing.

Obviously, you will need to understand the piece of writing you are analyzing. This implies that you will need to read the piece of writing multiple times to analyze it effectively. A cursory reading or skimming the essay will not work. Your initial readings should allow you to become acquainted with the content and the writer's style. You will find that writing notes and responses on the text will help stimulate your depth of analysis and help you get a handle on the writer's thinking process.

You will need to focus on higher order concerns in your analysis. React to the strengths and weaknesses of the writer's purpose, content/ideas, personal voice, tone. Does the piece of writing "have heart"? Evaluate if and how well the writer supports ideas with strategies like sense imagery, figurative language, dialogue, wit, humor, satire, irony, etc. Analyze the effectiveness of the essay's organization—the title, opening, middle paragraphs, and closing. After you praise the strengths of the higher order concerns, point out sections or ideas that seem unclear or confusing and identify ways that the essay might be improved in these areas.

Then re-analyze the essay and focus on lower order concerns, such as sentence development and variety (syntax), conciseness, usage, word choices (diction), and mechanics (spelling and punctuation). Evaluate the strengths of these lower order concerns and their effectiveness in supporting the content of the essay. Next, reread the essay and suggest ways the writer might improve the style and editing of the piece. Be as specific as possible.

Then, compose a critical essay in which you synthesize your points of analysis and evaluation. Write the piece in a positive, sincere, respectful tone. You are trying to offer constructive criticism to help the writer improve the piece, not tear down the writing or the writer. Try to reinforce good ideas and good writing and encourage improvement of weak areas. Try to strike a balance between reinforcing good writing strategies and suggesting constructive ideas for improvement.

In composing your critical response, write in the present tense and use quotations from the text to direct your readers to specific passages and to provide evidence of the validity of your analysis. As you quote from the writer's essay, blend quotations into the flow of your writing by using leads or embedding quotations into the syntax of your sentences. For example, note how Jamie Byremis blends Brenda Jasper's words into her critical analysis in the following two examples. Jamie writes:

> (1) I especially like the contrast in the sentence that closes paragraph three, "Some people die for love; others never taste love's sweetness." (introductory lead taken from the middle of paragraph 9)
>
> (2) You also carry this Biblical passage nicely into the final paragraph, where you capture positive qualities like "love is patient and kind, always ready to forgive." (embedded quotation taken from the end of paragraph 3)

Write leads in present tense and connect quotations to your leads to form grammatically correct sentences written with tense consistency, proper punctuation, agreement, and usage.

STRUT YOUR STUFF!

Writing Project 8-1: Critical Writing   Compose a critical essay in letter format in which you demonstrate your use of higher order thinking skills—analysis, evaluation, synthesis—to assess a piece of prose writing. Reread the essay as many times as needed to gain material and evidence to compose your letter. Focus on a PQSP (Praise, Question, Suggestion, Polish) strategy. Praise the strengths and Question confusing or unclear sections or ideas. Suggest ways to improve the content and organization. Then reread and analyze for editing (Polishing) issues. Mark up the student's paper liberally with your responses.

Compose your letter using a positive, sincere, constructive tone that will reinforce good writing and encourage writing improvement. Your letter should reflect your expertise in composing and editing skills and your attitude as a concerned college student. Write the letter in the present tense and provide at least four textual references (quoted passages) taken from the writer's essay that support and develop your analysis. Write in your personal voice and, above all, **write from your heart**.

Writing Checklist:
- [ ] 1. Have you pointed out specific strengths and suggested areas of improvement regarding higher order concerns—the writer's purpose, content/ideas, personal voice, tone?
- [ ] 2. Have you pointed out specific strengths and areas of improvement regarding lower order concerns—sentence development and variety (syntax), conciseness, usage, word choices (diction), and mechanics (spelling and punctuation)?
- [ ] 3. Is your letter written in present tense, and do you include at least four pieces of textual support (quoted passages)?
- [ ] 4. Does your personal voice come through in a positive, sincere, constructive tone? Does your letter "have heart"?
- [ ] 5. Do your opening and closing paragraphs effectively serve your purpose and audience?
- [ ] 6. Have you edited for clarity, conciseness, and correctness?

SAMPLE STUDENT WRITING

Definition of Love
by Brenda Jasper

Webster's Collegiate Dictionary defines love as a "fond or tender feeling, warm liking; affection; attachment; or a strong, passionate feeling for a person of the opposite sex." An abstract word used more than any other in the English language. The meaning of love often misunderstood and misinterpreted by many people. No two people seem to agree on a single, definitive definition of love. But yet the word love appears in more songs and poems and is the theme of more books than any other concept or word.

Love is a word that is used in songs like "Love Makes the World Go Round" and "All You Need is Love." And famous poems like Elizabeth Barret Browning's "How Do I Love Thee, Let Me Count the Ways" or Shakespeare's "Shall I Compare Thee to a Summer's Day." And, of course, we have books about love like *Love Story* and *Lady Chatterly's Lover.*

It is interesting to note that the word love has both positive and negative connotations. Love can make some people totally and completely ecstatic while it is miserable for others. Some people search for love while other people are afraid to risk love for fear of being crushed. Some people die for love, others never taste love's sweetness.

The word love can be used in many different ways. You have all heard such phrases as lovebirds, love charms, and love ins. Love is even a term used in tennis as a score of zero. Some people apply love to a liking for something like a sport, a craft, or food. Some people love baseball or golf, knitting or crocheting, pizza or ice cream. But real love is not one of these "things."

Some people confuse infatuation or one-sided love with real, true, sincere, genuine love. Infatuation is the "love at first sight" look of attraction from "across a crowded room." Infatuation is the "teeny bopper" type of love that causes a fast beating heart and a loss of breath. Infatuation is more of a what's-in-it-for-me type of love than a what-can-I-do for the betterment of another. Infatuation is physical attraction, it is not real love.

Love is not a liking for steak or tennis. Love is not blind as in infatuation. Love is not jealous or conceited or proud. Love is not ill-mannered or selfish or irritable. Love does not put on airs. Love does not keep a record of wrongs. Love is not like a drug that causes euphoria or lightheadedness.

Love is a concept that is more in-depth. Love puts another's well-being above one's own. Love is patient and kind, always ready to forgive. Love gives and does not look for returns. And ironically, the more you give love away, the more it boomerangs back to you. Those who have found love have found a treasure worth more than wealth, power, or fame. Love conquers all.

SAMPLE STUDENT WRITING

Critical Writing Response to <u>Definition Of Love</u>
by Jamie Byremis

To: Brenda Jasper
From: Jamie Byremis
Title: Definition of Love

I like your definition and interpretation of love. Your topic works well because everyone at one time or another has experienced some type of love. I agree with your premise that people "often misunderstand and misinterpret love." That may occur because no one seems to be able to capture the definitive meaning of the term. Defining love can present as difficult a challenge as finding true love in our sometimes hate-filled world.

Your excellent references to songs and poems and books about love helped me to contemplate the vast meaning of the term. Although I have read only *Love Story*, the other titles are intriguing, and I may try to read some of those you mention. Plus, your mention of Browning and Shakespeare puts the concept of love in the realm of some of the greatest writers of all time. You also clearly and firmly stress an important point: love does not involve objects, like hobbies or foods. Rather, love involves people and the most powerful of human emotions.

I am also impressed by your use of negation in defining love. You go into extended detail in trying to show what love is not, and you present a strong case for readers not to confuse infatuation with love. You effectively use a Biblical allusion (Corinthians, I believe) to show negation, "Love is not jealous or conceited or proud. Love is not ill-mannered or selfish or irritable. Love does not put on airs." Most people who have attended a Christian wedding have heard that passage. You also carry this Biblical passage nicely into the final paragraph, where you capture positive qualities like "love is patient and kind, always ready to forgive."

Although your essay shows many strong ideas and references, some areas seem underdeveloped and confusing. First, the title seems more like the assignment rather than a captivating title for a topic of the magnitude of love. Can you create a catchy title that shows your feelings about love? Along with the title, I don't feel that your opening hooks readers very well. Referring to a dictionary seems like an over-used and bland way to begin a paper. Possibly you could use a line from one of the songs you refer to in the second paragraph, or possibly you might consult *Bartlett's Familiar Quotations*, or a similar library reference, to find a catchy opening quotation about love that will grab readers' interest.

I am confused on the direction of your paper. I can't seem to find your main point about love. Are you trying to capture the various types of love, such as "brotherly" love versus romantic love? Your references in the second and fifth paragraphs imply romantic love, but the focus shifts to a "brotherly" connotation in your last two paragraphs. Defining an abstract term calls for making the abstract term concrete and growing to a significance, a main point, which frankly I cannot find in this piece.

The content of your paper seems to deal with your interpretations of love in the abstract. I urge you to use lots of concrete examples of love in action so that we readers can see your specific interpretation of the term. In other words, try to bring the concept of love to life through examples rather than simply trying to define or interpret the term. You might show examples of brotherly love by sharing times when you helped neighbors or friends or a friend helped you. Maybe you cut grass or shoveled snow for a neighbor. Maybe you took a meal to a sick relative. Maybe a friend called you on the phone at just the needed time. Try to provide as many concrete examples as possible so that readers can see and feel love in action.

If you are aiming at a romantic definition, possibly you might share your experiences in love relationships. Or maybe you might be willing to share times in your life where you were crushed by a rejection of love. This type of sharing of personal examples may require courage and risk on your part, however. If you feel uncomfortable being that intimate, you may be able to draw on examples from books or movies that you know. I am suggesting that you try to provide as many concrete examples of love to help the reader visualize the love you are trying to define.

The order of your paragraphs might flow better if you place the fourth paragraph ahead of the third. Your fourth paragraph deals with objects and seems to fit better after your references to things like songs and books in paragraph two. The topic of your present paragraph three focuses on people and will lead nicely into your third last paragraph beginning "Some people..." This adjustment will organize your paper into two unified sections, the first dealing with things and the second with people, the true focus of love.

I see numerous strengths in your writing style. I'm impressed by your clear vocabulary and easy-to-read style. You seem to be in control of your sentence and paragraph development without trying to overdo or overwrite your style. I especially like the contrast in the sentence that closes paragraph three, "Some people die for love; others never taste love's sweetness." That sentence shows beautiful structural balance (five words on each side of the break) and the power of love to take people to the ultimate sacrifice-death. Note, however, the sentence needs a semicolon to correct the comma splice (run-on).

I also love the force and strength of the last pair of sentences in your concluding paragraph, "Those who have found love have found a treasure worth more than wealth, power, or fame. Love conquers all." That reinforces the power of love; it can overwhelm hate, money, fame, or fortune. True love continues to grow with time. And "the more you give love away, the more it boomerangs back to you" seems to be a conscious allusion on your part to the famous "Prayer of St. Francis," a poem on love which many readers will recognize without your needing to identifying the source.

Some of your sentences are not fully developed. For example, in paragraph one, your second and third fragments need to be revised into complete sentences. You might consider something like, "The word love is used more often than any other word in the English language." Your third sentence is missing the helping verb "is," which may be a simple oversight. Plus, you could revise that sentence into the active voice by rewording it, "Many people misunderstand and misinterpret the meaning of love." Your second paragraph also includes a fragment. See if you can detect and correct it.

Another adjustment you might consider is maintaining consistency in the point of view you use to narrate the essay. You write primarily in the third person; however, in a couple of places, you shift to second person—you. In the second sentence of paragraph four, "You have all heard such phrases as..." could be rewritten, "People talk of love birds, love charms, and love ins." The third last sentence of the essay also shifts from third to second person. You might consider, "the more people give love away, the more it boomerangs back to them."

I might also suggest some places where you could cut wordiness. The second sentence in paragraph two states, "Love can make some people totally and completely ecstatic while it is miserable for others." You might consider tightening that sentence by writing, "Love can make some people ecstatic and others miserable." That revision saves nine unnecessary words. In your fourth paragraph, you can again reduce the third sentence to read, "Love is used in tennis as a score of zero," a reduction of four unneeded words.

I appreciate the opportunity to read your thought-provoking topic. Focusing on a significant point and adding concrete examples will improve your essay immensely. Your paper shows excellent potential but needs revision, as do all of my essays, as well. I hope my responses give you some ideas to help improve your paper. I would love to see your finished product as you continue to develop this interesting topic.

Good luck,
Jamie

Discussion Questions:

1. Identify where the writer has pointed out specific strengths and suggested improvements regarding higher order concerns—the writer's purpose, content/ideas, personal voice, tone.

2. Identify where the writer has pointed out specific strengths and suggested improvements regarding lower order concerns—sentence development and variety (syntax), conciseness, usage, word choices (diction), and mechanics (spelling and punctuation).

3. What higher order concerns, which the writer did not mention, would you commend or suggest for improvement?

4. What lower order concerns, which the writer did not mention, would you commend or suggest for improvement?

5. Is the analysis written in present tense, and does it include at least four pieces of textual support (quoted passages)? How well does the writer blend quotations into the text?

6. Does the writer's personal voice come through in a positive, sincere, constructive tone? Does this critical letter of response "have heart"? Support your response.

7. Evaluate how effectively the opening and closing paragraphs serve the writer's purpose and audience?
8. Evaluate the essay holistically and explain your rationale for that evaluation.

PRACTICE 8A: Using Leads in Critical Analysis   Analyze the definition essay below. Locate the following: (1) at least two HOC strengths, (2) at least two HOC suggestions, (3) at least two LOC strengths, (4) at least two LOC suggestions. Using your findings, write four leads with textual references (quotations from the text) in present tense that focus on the required sections of the Critical Analysis essay.

Success
by Danny Schlemme

Oh the sweet taste of success! The soul feeling of success lies within our values in life. People search for their own in many different ways. Everyone wants to gain success whether on the field, the job, or in the classroom. People try becoming successful in many ways, but what is success? Is success the feeling of pride after a job well done? Is it the pat on the back when crossing the goal line? Living through another day on earth defines success for some people. Success holds numerous different meanings to all people. Everyone tries to become successful, but why? What true sensation does success hold and what does it mean to us as human beings?

When talking about the term success with my family, I found interesting definitions. My father believes working hard for what one wants in life shows great success. On the other hand, my brother believes gaining knowledge and wealth to bring happiness resembles success. My mother thinks success comes with the feeling of happiness and joy. Success means something different to each member of our family and I thought families were similar to one another? If my family differs this much, imagine how differently everyone in the world defines success. Success lays different paths, and everyone travels their own to find it.

Success defined as a positive outcome, doing what one desires, and an attempt to gain wealth; achieving ultimate happiness and enjoyment in life; improving one's status based on hard work; reaching goals. The thesaurus states success as achievement, accomplishment, advance, benefit, fame, fortune, good luck, good time, happiness, progress, reward, successfulness, and victory.

Success serves many important functions in life, bringing self-confidence and self-worth when reached. Setting goals and achieving them with success gives a sense of pride, feeling as if all of the hard work and dedication paid off. Success breeds more success. When someone experiences success, it pushes them to exceed in other areas, keeping people going and wanting to achieve more in life. Success brings a feeling of pride nothing else in our lives could bring; the feeling of victory after setting a goal and seeing it all the way through.

Success brings many positive attributes to our lives; feelings of victory, triumph, joy, achievement, and much more. The ability for one to succeed is an amazing event because it means this person overcame the hardship of the task at hand. Moving this person onto the level champions compete at. Success can come within the career, the home, competitive activities, or anywhere that drives your motivation to succeed. The level of success can be achieved is strictly dependent upon the level of interest the successor withholds.

People create their own ideas toward what they feel is successful in life. Some think success comes with money or power. Others feel success is associated with standards and moral values within their lives. Success can also come with happiness or freedom. It can come with any type of goal or task someone hopes to accomplish. Success creates the feeling of hard work and motivation finally paying off after all the hard work. Success is the place at the top of the podium where champions stand and what the losers work to accomplish for next year.

Writing a Critical Essay About Literature

~ ~ ~

*"People write about literature in order
to clarify and to account for their responses
to works that interest or excite or frustrate them.
The last word is never said about complex thoughts
and feelings, but when we write, we hope to make
at least a little progress in the difficult but
rewarding job of talking about our responses"* (2).
—Sylvan Barnet

~ ~ ~

Undoubtedly your college experience will entail taking at least one literature course in which you will write critical essays. The literary critical essay demands higher order thinking—analysis, evaluation, and synthesis. Writing a critical literary analysis helps you expand your understanding of the literature by asking you to read more deeply than merely "getting the story." The literary critical essay may involve an analysis of fiction or drama, which deal with five common elements: plot, character, setting, point of view, and theme. A third genre, poetry, may require you to analyze poetic devices, meter, or form to see how they affect the meaning of the poem you analyze. Writers should consult a literature handbook for explanations of these literary terms.

One of the difficult challenges of writing about literature is choosing an insightful topic of significance and depth. A plot summary alone will not suffice. You are looking for a "fresh take" on the literature rather than writing about an obvious topic or one that has been over-analyzed by other students or critics. Finding that fresh, analytical topic will not happen with one reading. Similar to analyzing prose non-fiction, you will need to read the literature multiple times to analyze it effectively. A cursory reading or skimming of the literature will not work. Your initial readings should allow you to become acquainted with the subject of the piece, the author's style, and elements of fiction, or poetic devices. You will find that writing notes and responses on the text will help stimulate your depth of analysis, help you get a handle on the writer's thinking process, and possibly lead to a fresh insight on the literature. Make a list of ideas that might work in a literary analysis paper; then, analyze your list to see if some ideas might connect and could be formulated into a single topic.

Next, formulate a thesis statement—one sentence that will clearly express your interpretation. Make your thesis specific and direct with a "what" and a "so what." For example, *"The Great Gatsby* uses excellent symbolism" offers a vague interpretation of that novel. However, "The symbols of Doctor T.J. Eckelberg's eyes, the valley of ashes, and the green light on Daisy's dock help to illuminate the theme of illusion versus reality in F. Scott Fitzgerald's *The Great Gatsby*" offers a pointed thesis with both a <u>what</u> and a <u>so what</u>.

Like any other essay, the title of your critical essay should grab readers' attention. The opening should then hook readers to keep them interested. The author's name and title of the literature you are analyzing should appear early in your paper. Also remember: *titles of novels and plays* are italicized while "titles of poems" use quotation marks. You should write your literary analysis paper in present tense. Write your essay in a firm, convincing tone. Don't let your paper become a "wimpy dumping ground" of waste like "I think (feel) that," "in my opinion," "definitely," "really," "very." Write clearly and confidently as you convince your reader of the validity of your analysis.

To do this, you will need to provide textual support, verbatim quotations from the literary work you are analyzing. Your quotations will direct your readers to specific passages and provide evidence of the validity of your analysis. Blend quotations into the flow of your writing by using leads or embedding quotations into the syntax of your sentences. Write leads in present tense and connect quotations to your leads to form grammatically correct sentences written with tense consistency, proper punctuation, agreement, and usage. Then in parentheses at the end of the quotation, place the page or line source of the quotation. For novels or plays without numbered acts, scenes, lines, use the following format: "........." (68). For plays with acts, scenes, lines, use the following format: "........." (3.1.12-15). For lines of poetry, use the following format: "........." (ll. 8-11).

Generally, quoted passages of four lines or fewer of your writing should be blended into your text. Passages of five or more lines (which should be used sparingly) should follow a colon and appear in double-indented, block form. Quotation marks are not used with block quotations. Short quotations work best. Textual references should be used for support and evidence, not simply "because a literary paper needs quotations" or "to take up space." An analytical paper should present your ideas with occasional textual support rather than present a series of pasted together quotations with your ideas interjected occasionally.

The conclusion of your literary analysis should "glance back" at your thesis and other assertions. But, simply restating your thesis or summarizing your paper will not work. Do not write, "In conclusion" or "Let me conclude by saying." A good conclusion closes the issue while enriching it. The conclusion draws an inference from your analysis that has not been previously expressed; it sees your material in a fresh perspective. Like a good joke or the last scene of a play, the conclusion adds a final punch to your literary analysis. Finally, provide an MLA works cited reference for your quotations, which includes author, title, publisher, city and state, and year of publication.

STRUT YOUR STUFF!

Writing Project 8-2: Critical Writing-Literary Analysis   Compose a critical literary essay on a fresh, insightful analytical topic of your choosing which could appear in a book of critical essays. Your essay must demonstrate a significant depth of analytical thinking beyond mere plot summary. Support your analysis with parenthetically documented, textual references (quotations). Above all, remember: **you've gotta have heart in your writing.**

Writing Checklist:
- [ ] 1. Have you chosen a "fresh," literary topic of significant analytical and critical depth?
- [ ] 2. Does your thesis statement contain a "what" and a "so what," a significance?
- [ ] 3. Do you support your analysis with properly cited, textual evidence (quotations), but not so many as to detract from your own writing and personal voice? Have you added the source in MLA format at the end of the essay?
- [ ] 4. Do your opening and closing paragraphs, along with your title, effectively serve your topic and purpose?
- [ ] 5. Is your critical literary essay written in present tense?
- [ ] 6. Have you edited for clarity, conciseness, and correctness?

SAMPLE STUDENT WRITING
Critical Literary Analysis

Flaubert's Treatment of Women in Madame Bovary
By Rebecca Stroschein

Gustave Flaubert, author of *Madame Bovary*, is called the father of "realism." Uncharacteristic to popular trends in his time, Flaubert's formula for literature includes as many pathetic, despicable characters in it as possible. He even makes his main character, Emma Bovary, extremely flawed; her very misdeeds propel the plot along to its end. Had Flaubert been *avant garde* enough to allow the bad women command their destiny and given them a frightening persona, this would have been a good book. Instead, his flawed female characters are harmless, pesky gnats that I feel like swatting. Although Flaubert's book represents a change from the conventional, his book proves no more *real* than the preceding books of the time, and I find it tiresome. His work faithfully portrays women as weak underlings influencing men only through sex, guilt trips, and temper tantrums. If a woman is written as a villain, she should at least pose a formidable threat to the other characters in the story.

Emma Bovary is written as a weak, stupid child, so selfish she cannot see beyond her daydreams and fantasies. If I could rewrite Flaubert's book, Emma's character would utilize her brain as well as her looks in the novel. My Emma would find a way to either ride away from the financial mess she made, or she would con Msr. Lheareaux and flee with his money. The way Flaubert writes the book, Emma leads herself into a predicament and commits suicide to free herself from trouble. This ending lacks originality. Fable-like, this story teaches a lesson to all would-be Emmas and young women of the time; they must be good, or no one will rescue them. Msr. Flaubert takes liberties with writing about female characters, reveals their flaws, and makes them all too shallow to show anything but two dimensional personalities. When in trouble or displeased, the women of the book consistently whine and throw fits, and when faced with insurmountable problems, they die, commit suicide, or run away.

Mother Bovary, for example, controls Charles's life for the first part of the book. Does this make her a strong female character? No. After Charles meets Emma, his mother is left on the sidelines. Apparently she fails to invent plans to sabotage Emma's character in Charles's eyes except to whine openly to Charles about how rotten Emma is. A *real* manipulative and controlling mother-in-law could approach the problem of Emma subtly with intent to disparage Emma's character. She could set inventive and elaborate traps Emma could not get herself out of and win her son Charles back easily in the process. The older Madame Bovary Flaubert describes does not use the most obvious weapon against Emma any *real* mother-in-law would use in a second, namely Charles and Emma's daughter Berthe. Convincing Charles of Emma's ineptness in motherhood would prove so much easier than throwing a hissy fit and whining.

The story shows inconsistency in depicting Mother Bovary's character when it says, "To gain her ends Madame Bovary had to get rid of all the rivals, and her outwitting of one of them, a butcher whose candidacy was favored by the local clergy, was nothing short of masterly" (13). If Older Madame Bovary possessed the capacity to manipulate Charles's first marriage pick, why is she unable to rid herself and Charles of Emma? Unfortunately, the main females in Flaubert's novel seem only capable of singing endless laments. Madame Bovary could not even interject herself into Charles and Emma's wedding plans. This hardly seems consistent to the controlling woman Flaubert tries to paint her as being earlier in the book.

Nearly every woman in Flaubert's novel is openly flawed in one way or another. The older Madame Bovary is described as "...touchy, nagging and nervous, like stale wine turning to vinegar" (7). This shows the result of Charles's father's inattentions and indiscretions. She then turns all her affections onto her son and "...kept him tied to her apron strings" (8). Her crushed dreams are channeled into hopes for her son's future, and she lives vicariously through his accomplishments. Mother Bovary's ambitions end in the utter control of Charles's life. Charles's mother chooses his career, his house, the location of his first job, and even his first wife, Hortense.

The author describes Hortense as "ugly...thin as a lath, with a face as spotted as a meadow in springtime" (13). Hortense exceeds Charles's age by about 20 years, and she "opened his mail, watched his every move, and listened through the thinness of the wall when there were women in his office"(13). Charles's mother sets Hortense in the place of his wife to rule Charles by proxy. Poor Charles, readers are forced to pity him.

Msr. Flaubert does a wonderful job of making readers feel sorry for Charles because of all the rotten women in his life. Hortense is supposed to be a pathetic hypochondriac. Hortense complains "incessantly about her nerves, of pains in her chest, of depressions and faintness" (13). She dies coughing up blood. Maybe her health complaints are real. Marrying a doctor, it turns out, does not guarantee quality healthcare.

After delivering Berthe, Emma leaves her child in the care of Madame Rollet. Rollet's abode is described as a ramshackle hut in severe disrepair. Flaubert uses the word, "squalor" (105) to describe the cottage. The condition of Madame Rollet's house reflects poorly on both the wet nurse and Madame Bovary for leaving her infant in such unsanitary conditions so early in her life. Children left in Rollet's care are wretchedly neglected and dirty. Madame Rollet is also seen trying to score some brandy for her drunkard husband.

While Madame Lefrancois's character is less developed in the story than the other characters, she is written as a vicious gossip. She runs the Lion d'Or Hotel and comments about the Café Français, "We're not afraid of fly-by-nights like Tellier" (85). Of the few times she speaks in the story, she seizes opportunities to spread dirt about the townspeople. Homais, the town pharmacist, learns of Tellier's bankruptcy via Lefrancois, and she "...proceeded to tell him the story, which she had from Theodore, Maitre Gullaumin's servant; and although she detested Tellier, she had nothing but harsh words for Lheureux. He was a wheedler, a cringer" (152). Madame Lefrancois also brings Emma's holding Rodolphe's arm to Homais's attention.

Other supporting female characters in the book; Madame Homais, Felicite, Mademoiselle Lempereur, and Madame Tuvache; are written about in the same disparaging pattern. Consistent to Flaubert's female character development, Madame Homais is depicted as "sloppy" (120). Her children are compared to her as "...brats... always dirty, wretchedly brought up, sluggish like their mother" (98). Felicite is caught with a forty-year-old man sneaking out the back, kitchen door when he hears Madame Bovary coming (216). She also elopes and steals dead Emma's wardrobe (387). Mademoiselle Lempereur conspires with Emma to cover her affair's tracks and charges Charles for unattended piano lessons after Emma's death.

When Madame Tuvache says in reference to Emma, "Women like that should be horsewhipped" (348), I surmise Msr. Flaubert would like to punish women in such a way, perhaps with a pen rather than a horsewhip. What does the author write when characters Charles and Rodolphe face off, so rightly built up as a possible male violent overture at the end of the book? Charles, so Christ-like in his words, says, "I don't hold it against you" (395). When I read this, a wave of nausea overcomes me. Flaubert portrays men as forgiving, nonviolent, submissive, clever, debonair, and cunning, and women as lazy, stupid, frivolous, unsubmissive, gossipy, and weak.

Of all the female characters in *Madame Bovary,* two are somewhat spared from Flaubert's prejudice, specifically Berthe and Catherine Leroux. Called a "stupid old thing" (169), Leroux is rewarded at the fair for 54 years of service on the same farm. Mute, placid, humble, timid, and beaten and weathered by years of hard labor, it appears Catherine is the only type of adult female Flaubert finds venerable. Berthe is spared apparently because of her young age. However, if a sequel followed the novel, I predict that Berthe would play his next femme fatale.

Flaubert remains no more an authority on women than any other male author. A man daring enough to include so many female characters in his novel should give them range or risk revealing himself as either a woman hater or a complete fool. Personally, I dislike Flaubert's depiction of women and marvel how so many people revere this book as a classic literary landmark. Perhaps some people in this world are as fundamentally flawed as Madame Bovary, and maybe people existed like Bovary in Flaubert's day. However, a real person; whether evil or good, keen or dense, bold or timid; is never single-sided. Portraying women as fundamentally evil without giving them teeth, as Flaubert does, makes his novel weak and tiresome.

Work Cited

Flaubert, Gustave. *Madame Bovary*. The Modern Library, 1982.

Discussion Questions:
1. Identify the thesis of the essay. Does the thesis statement contain a "what" and a "so what," a significance?
2. Does the topic seem to have significant analytical and critical depth? Explain your response.
3. Does the writer adequately support her analysis with textual evidence (quotations)? Defend your response.
4. How effectively do the opening and closing paragraphs, along with the title, serve the topic and purpose of the essay?
5. Identify the strengths of the essay. What areas of improvement might you suggest?
6. Does the essay "have heart"? Does the writer's voice come through the writing? Cite specific areas of the essay that support your response.
7. Evaluate the essay holistically and provide rationale for your evaluation.

~ ~ ~

"Usage refers to linguistic etiquette,
to socially sanctioned styles of language
appropriate to given situations and audiences" (107).
—Erika Lindemann

~ ~ ~

WORD USAGE

The following word usage situations frequently arise in writing, but your computer may not detect or offer the correct usage. Fill in the spaces with the correct usage.

1. **accept**—verb "to receive";
   except—preposition "excluding"
   We _____ your invitation.
   If you _____ his first semester's grades, he has accumulated a good grade point.
   My grades appear satisfactory in every course _____ physics.

2. **affect**—verb "to influence, to cause" ("tip"—action=**verb**=**a**ffect);
   effect—noun "result"
   How did the defeat _____ the team?
   Everyone felt the _____ of the strike.

3. **all right** & **a lot**—always spelled as two words, not "alright, alot."

4. **alumnus, alumni, alumna, alumnae**—see page 141.

5. **amount**—use with singular word;
   number—use with plural word.
   She always carried a small _____ of money.
   The Bears' line displays a tremendous _____ of power.
   A _____ of fumbles occurred during the second quarter.
   He held a _____ of coins in his hand.

6. **although**—subordinating conjunction, introduces dependent clause;
   however—adverb, meaning "on the other hand" or "by contrast."
   _____ the temperature was 10 degrees below zero, I didn't feel a bit cold.
   The temperature was 10 degrees below zero; _____, I didn't feel cold.

7. **bad**—adjective, modifies noun or pronoun;
   badly—adverb, modifies verb, adjective, adverb
   The Cubs play _____.
   The stockyards smell _____.

8. **beside**—prep. "by the side of" someone or something;
   besides—adv. "in addition to" or prep. "except"
   Along came a spider and sat down _____ her.
   He owned nothing _____ his good name.
   He received a medal and five dollars _____.

9. **between**—use with two;
   among—use with more than two.
   The ball was passed _____ Phil and you.
   We earned two dollars _____ the five of us.
10. **borrow**—"to receive with the intention of returning";
    lend—"to give someone something you expect to get back"
    I _____ some money from my father.
    Lisa didn't want to _____ me any of her clothes.
11. **bring**—denotes motion toward a place;
    take—denotes motion away from a place
    _____ my book here.
    _____ my book there.
12. **can**—expresses ability;
    may—expresses permission or possibility
    _____ I accompany you to the dance?
    _____ you type 3,000 words per minute?
13. **could of, should of, would of**—of is not a verb;
    correct = **could have, should have, would have**
    The composition instructor should of given us more work.
    The composition instructor should _____ given us more work.
14. **due to** or **due to the fact that**—use since, because, or because of,
    unless **due** functions as predicate adjective.
    Nonstandard: Due to the fact that it rained so much, the game is cancelled.
    Correct: Because it rained so much, the game is cancelled.
15. **fewer**—use with a plural word;
    less—use with a singular word.
    I encounter _____ health problems than I did 10 years ago.
    I save _____ money than I did 10 years ago.
16. **good**—adjective, modifies a noun;
    well—adverb, "perform an action capably" or adjective "in good health," "satisfactory"
    The Cardinals played _____ against the Cubs.
    Violet sang _____ in the concert.
    Herman does not feel _____ after eating four pizzas.
    Otto appears to be in _____ health.
    Ellen looks _____ in that new, blue dress.
    His clothes never fit him _____ .

17. **imply**—"to suggest something";
    infer—"to interpret, to conclude" from.
    > A writer or speaker _____ to a reader or listener.
    > A reader or listener _____ from a writer or speaker.
18. **in**—"located within";
    into—"from the outside into"
    > We were all gathered _____ my grandparents' living room.
    > Joe just walked _____ my office.
19. **irregardless**—drop **IR**—should be **regardless**.
    > _____ of the score, our team won.
20. **it's**—"it is";
    its—possessive
    > Dubuque proudly boasts of _____ hills.
    > _____ not too late.
    > _____ a long way to Tipperary.
    > The dog chewed on _____ bone.
21. **lay**—"put or place" (lay, laying, laid, laid);
    lie—"rest or recline" (lie, lying, lay, lain)
    > Last night Homer _____ in his bed all night.
    > Waldo _____ his gun on the table.
    > _____ the dish on the counter.
    > I plan to _____ in the sun this afternoon.
22. **leave**—"to go away from";
    let—"to allow or permit"
    > I am _____ my past life behind.
    > I will _____ him have my answer soon.
    > We will _____ if you _____ us.
23. **like**—preposition, introduces a phrase;
    as or **as if**—subordinating conjunction—introduces a clause.
    > She looks _____ a queen.
    > She does _____ she wishes.
24. **principal**—(noun or adjective) noun: "person in a high position or important role"; adjective: means "chief" or "most important;" also, "a sum of money lent or borrowed."
    principle—(only a noun) guiding rule or fundamental truth
    > Kay provides the _____ income in our family.
    > The _____ of your high school acts like your "pal."
    > It opposed his _____ to give easy grades.

I pay the _____ on my homeowner's loan.

25. rise—"to go up" (rise, rose, risen);
raise—"to force something up" (raise, raised, raised)
    The sun is _____ in the sky.
    The farmer _____ two chickens and two daughters.

26. set—"to put or place";
sit—"to seat yourself"
    Please _____ down.
    Please _____ your glass down.

27. than—used in comparisons;
then—adverb of time
    Hilda seems stronger _____ Waldo.
    She ate breakfast and _____ brushed her teeth.
    _____ the waiter handed us the bill.
    Our house costs more _____ theirs.

28. double negative—**can't hardly, can't scarcely** (hardly and scarcely are negatives when combined with <u>not</u>), **can't help but; no, nothing, none** combined with **not**.

    Examples of Nonstandard Usage:
    I can't hardly tell the difference between this year's cars and last
        year's.
    There wasn't scarcely enough food for everyone.
    Haven't you no ticket?
    I can't help but admire his courage.
    She hasn't nothing to do.
    He didn't give me none.

PRACTICE 8B: Word Usage   Correct word usage errors in the following sentences. Some may be correct.

1. They have met less students from UNI than from NICC.
2. How will the new policies effect the students?
3. Besides my instructors, my friends have been pushing me to study.
4. Both of the women giving speeches are alumnae of NICC.
5. The cash prizes were divided between the six winners.
6. Researchers are studying the effects of the new drug.
7. I could of written a better essay if I had edited more closely.
8. I hope you will take your children when you come to Florida this summer.
9. As you grow older, you will find less chances to change jobs.

10. She excepted our congratulations with deep appreciation.
11. The amount of pizzas Zelmo can eat astounds me.
12. I see growing awareness of good writing among the students.
13. With three gifts to choose from, Waldo couldn't decide which one to accept.
14. The composition instructor complained about the amount of papers not turned in.
15. In his novels, Hemingway implies that war unjustly costs many innocent lives.
16. Mother is borrowing us $5,000.
17. I asked my friends to leave me go with them to the gym.
18. His comments inferred that he did not agree with the new policy.
19. Should writers be held responsible for what readers infer from their works?
20. If he had behaved like he should, he wouldn't be steeped in trouble now.
21. The composition instructor left us use the writing lab after class.
22. Bring a computer with you when you fly to North Buenie.
23. Zelmo had made a large amount of friends.
24. The response shows how much the readers were effected by the essay.
25. I can't hardly read your essay.

PRACTICE 8C: Word Usage   Correct the word usage.

1. You might of found it hard to finish your assignment for Tuesday.
2. Leave me give you some good writing tips.
3. Beside his interest in poetry, Waldo also enjoys drama.
4. The volcano has been acting like it might erupt.
5. The instructor asked the class less questions than he had prepared.
6. What effect will the new assignment have on the class?
7. I can't find nothing else to worry about.
8. Paula seldom edits as good as she should.
9. I'll bring my portfolio to Herman's room when I go.
10. Due to the storm, classes were cancelled last Friday.
11. Someone had ought to bring snacks to class.
12. I must have laid in bed for an hour after the alarm sounded.
13. Because of his cold, Donald did not feel good yesterday.
14. A heavy mist laid in the valley.
15. The temperature is raising.

16. The documents laying on my desk need my signature.
17. I plan to lay in bed all day Saturday.
18. Marian did good on her math exam.
19. You might have found less friends than he.

PORTFOLIO IN PROGRESS

The Demonstration Portfolio, submitted near the end of the course, allows you to get responses, improve, and revise earlier pieces as the course progresses. In addition, you will continually self-reflect on your growth as a writer, determine ways to improve your writing, and prepare entry slips for your Demonstration Portfolio. The Entry Slip-Reflection ideas suggested in the "Portfolio in Progress" section at the end of Chapter 2 may help you reflect on your writing. Keep track of your self-reflections by dating them, labeling them, and saving them in a secure place (notebook, journal, computer) so you can draw on these ideas as you prepare your portfolio entry slips

GLAD, BAD, SAD, OR MAD

The following sentences are taken from student writings. Note how the misuse of language or failure to edit affects meaning. Evaluate the sentences by rating each one as GLAD (witty), BAD (accidental error), SAD (misuse of language), or MAD (a little off center).

1. I live out in the country.
2. I road the bus to school each day.
3. The best way to avoid udder humiliation is not to lie at all.
4. Ms. Smith has a presents about her that actually makes you look forward to learning.
5. While working at the human society, we gave dogs baths, brushed them, and fed them.

CHAPTER 9

More Student Writings

This chapter contains numerous pieces of student writing which fit writing projects contained in this book. Student samples are included rather than professional writers' models because, as Erika Lindemann writes in *A Rhetoric for Writing Teachers*, "Excellent papers show students that they can use language effectively, that what you're asking them to do doesn't require some peculiar magical power granted only to professionals" (135).

SAMPLE STUDENT WRITING

Significant Place

The Mississippi's View of Life
by Stacia Riccio

In Dubuque, Iowa, I can see many beautiful scenes from the River Walk. I sit here on huge, cement steps that stretch out over the Mississippi. Their triangular shape makes it easy to see the entire river. I scan over the landscapes and catch a whiff of all the fish in the river. When I look around, I know an artist's hand created this place. With all the memories here, I couldn't forget the River Walk and the scenes near it. Its beauty and calm feeling stick with me wherever I go.

The Illinois bridge takes over the right side of the river. Its dark gray color blends in with the night sky like a criminal hiding out. Only its bright lights give it away. An otter swimming about catches my eye. The darkness makes it hard to see him in detail, but I hear the splaaaash he makes. Fish near him put on a show by flipping out of the water as the moon reflects off rings of ripples they make on the surface.

I feel my legs start to itch from the rough cement, so I shift a bit to make the itch go away. I look up to see, against mixtures of blues and blacks, glittery twinkles in the night sky. Clouds of mist make a blanket for the man in the moon. His smile of light reflects like pieces of broken glass scattered along the Mississippi. This scene makes me hear Andy Williams' song "Moon River" in my head. A sweet breeze kisses my cheek and distracts me from my thoughts for a moment.

Off the cliff to the right, fuzzy fingers of moss tightly grip resisting rocks. Waves crash against them making a swooooosh and swaaaaash. Their battle goes on through the night while whispering trees share gossipy stories. Their branches hold hands and hug each other like good friends. It reminds me of my good friends and the times we share here.

I shift my eyes to focus on the river. The current's hungry mouth could swallow Jonah in an instant. Some seagulls riding the river fall victim to the current's swift motion and are launched down the river. The excited flapping of their wings gives a hint that they enjoy the ride. Across the river, I see a train. Its horn sings a tune while its wheels keep the beat. The old, creaky bridge to my left starts to turn. As the train crosses, it passes me, and I can see it in more detail.

I become overwhelmed by scattered gems of light in a little city behind me. Buildings holding these gems act like display cases lifting up bright colors for all to see. The cars floating on the highways throw in their tune as their wheels bump against the road. Busy yet quiet nights of Dubuque flow throughout the years. The view from the River Walk shows different personalities of Dubuque never seen before.

I hear footsteps coming toward me, so I turn back toward the river. A young couple holding hands talk quietly as they walk. As they pass me, their voices are hushed, and I get a sniff of his musky cologne and her sweet perfume. A few steps behind them, an older man walks his beagle hound. I say hi in a quiet voice. Shifting the cigarette in his mouth, he says, "Hey there," in a rough voice. His cigarette smoke makes me cough a bit, but I giggle after seeing his beagle hound kick up grass with his hind legs. I watch them walk off and wonder how many different feet must have walked along the River Walk through the years.

The way the River Walk is laid out attracts visitors' interest. Old-fashioned lamps line the edge of the walkway and reflect their light off the smooth, pink and tan tiles. Flowers hanging in pots on the lamps wave at me with beautiful colors. The pathway always reminds me of the yellow brick road from *The Wizard of Oz*. Many times my friends and I have locked arms together as we skipped along and sang, "We're Off to See the Wizard" on this walkway.

It feels as if time pauses or is put on hold here. My dozing is interrupted by the sound of smooth jazz. I look for the location of the music and notice some tikki lamps surrounding a group of tables. The music is coming from a jazz band performing at the River Walk Restaurant. I hear laughter while people cut some rug on the dance floor. What a perfect spot for a little restaurant — scenic, romantic, relaxing, and lively all in one little space. Waitresses and waiters hurry around balancing trays of food that I bet smell wonderful.

The tikki lamps chase away early season fish flies. Fish flies hum their songs as they flock to areas of light. I know from experience that they also like to flock inside my mouth. Yuck! From the corner of my eye, I see tiny, dark shapes fly through the air. When I hear little squeeeeaaks, I know the dark shapes are bats. They remind me of tie fighters from *Star Wars* swooping around catching fish flies for dinner.

A circle structure made out of stone ends the journey of the River Walk. The broken steps to the left look weathered and rustic. A field of emerald green grass surrounds them and reminds me of medieval Ireland. In the distance, the Shot Tower stands tall and strong. I can't believe it survived the Civil War era. The Shot Tower's age amazes me every time I see it. The old Star Brewery sits next to the Shot Tower. So much history exists behind the River Walk and these buildings.

Down at the other end of the River Walk sits a large, pink gazebo. The lights on the ceiling make an inner, small circle. Its deep steps lead down to a little beach of sand, and in the water, a sign on a buoy states, "Please, no wading." Another buoy floats next to a lonely dock waiting for some company from a boat. In the morning, jet skis, speed boats, and many other fun water toys will fill it.

Statues of abstract art stand spread out between the Grand Harbor Hotel and River Walk. Local artists put their work on display here for people to see as they walk. A piece of art made from silver metal looks as if a rain drop is connected to a smaller one. Art similar to this lines the edges of the River Walk. I always enjoy trying to figure out what each piece looks like, if anything at all.

The glitter in the sky now intensifies against the pure black sky. The night air becomes cooler, and a chill runs down my spine. My legs also become cold from the icy feeling of the cement steps I sit on. Some tourists stop in front of me and block my view for a second but walk off, and I can see in front of me again. The tourists take a quick picture of the rustling trees across the river. The mountains of trees across the river have become a sea of black motion.

As I yawn, I get a taste of the river's mist. The cool mist refreshes my dried-out mouth. Night fully covers the sky and makes it easy to see the towers of flickering lights. Near me, a little pavilion sits off the bank of the river. Eight picnic tables sit inside of it waiting for an event to take over. At that same spot, my friends and I have gone swimming and enjoyed riding boats up and down the river.

I let the scene take me away from the everyday life. The swift sounds made by the waves hitting the rocky cliffs keep my ear entertained as the moon acts like a beautiful night light. The River Walk's beauty shows all year round, but I like it most during summer nights. Something about the moon's reflection hitting the river and the twinkling lights all around keep me coming back to the River Walk. I love the peace and quiet of this beautiful location, and I will continue to come to the Mississippi River Walk to relax and meditate as often as possible.

Discussion Questions:

1. What place is the author describing, and what camera angle does the writer take?

2. What dominant impression does the writer try to establish in the piece?

3. Point out specific examples of sense imagery and figurative language. Analyze the effectiveness of the writer's use of sense imagery and figurative language.

4. Analyze the effectiveness of the title, introduction, and conclusion. How well do they support the topic?

5. Identify the strengths of this essay. What areas of improvement would you suggest?

6. Does the writer "have heart" in the essay? What specific aspects of the piece support your response?

7. Evaluate the effectiveness of the piece holistically and provide rationale for your evaluation.

SAMPLE STUDENT WRITING
Significant Event

Send to Me My Spring
by Angela Frohling

Life does not always go as planned. Human nature allows us to take life for granted. But ordinary events can sometimes become some of life's biggest challenges. Even though they are often filled with heartache and pain, they offer valuable learning experiences. Becoming a mother seemed to me like a natural event. God blesses parents with children every day. But after years of hormone treatments and surgery, I realized my trip down this road might never start.

Discovering my pregnancy with Kate became a short-lived joy. I went to Northwest Clinic in Thief River Falls, Minnesota, for severe pain in my side. Dr. Krepp, who was just as excited over my newly found pregnancy as I, became concerned. My first pregnancy, diagnosed as tubular, needed to be removed. I traveled from delight to despair in two short hours. But I awoke to smiling faces and hugs. I was still pregnant. Kate did not show up in my ovarian tubes. Her disappearing act on the original tests remained a mystery. After fourteen long days, Kate made her first appearance on the ultrasound. Both of my doctors assured me everything looked normal. With all the hurdles cleared, I could relax and enjoy my pregnancy.

I took my pregnancy seriously; after all, I was told I may never conceive children. I couldn't wait to wear maternity clothes. I collected every baby book written and read children's stories aloud to my barely swollen stomach. I took "evening sickness" on as a welcoming sign. Nick, my husband, and I took birthing classes offered at Northwest Medical Center. Life seemed to be traveling according to nature's plan.

On the morning of Wednesday, October 2, 1991, my road to motherhood took an unexpected detour. I awoke to severe pressure and could barely walk. Clearing the sleep from my mind, I recalled the strange feelings of the night before. I called my doctors and was advised to lie down and call back if I felt contractions. Two hours later I arrived in the emergency room.

Dr. Schueneman looked ghostly white standing at my bedside holding my hand. "Angela, you are in labor," he said softly. "I'm sending you to United Hospital in Grand Forks. They have a Neonatal Intensive Care Unit (NICU) there. The ambulance is waiting for you on the dock. Kate is 25 weeks along; she can make it. Everything will be fine."

In the ambulance, I lay motionless and unable to breathe. The drive from Thief River Falls to Grand Forks, North Dakota, normally took 45 minutes. On this day, 25 minutes seemed too long. An all new staff and insensitive doctor met me at United Hospital, and my new diagnosis brought devastating news. With my labor moving too quickly, my baby would most likely die during delivery.

Kate Louise Frohling entered this world at 9:14 that evening. No cries broke the air as a team of specialists and nurses whisked her from my sight. Thirty minutes later I made my way to the emergency room to meet my daughter. Fighting with all her might, she appeared tinier than one pound, four ounces. She lay in a sea of wires and tubes. Fine, blond hair covered her small head, and she owned incredibly long fingers and toes. I felt an overwhelming love for this child. No amount of medical hardware could stand in my way. I kissed my finger and gently placed it on her cheek. I caressed her hand, and she gripped my finger as if to say, "It'll be OK, Mom." I watched with tear-filled eyes as the team loaded Kate into a new ambulance for her trip to a more advanced NICU in Fargo.

At that point, Kate had exceeded everyone's expectations. Babies born at 25 weeks gestation age teeter on the borderline of life and death. Some can survive seemingly unscathed; others survive with a nightmarish list of health complications, and some don't survive at all. Female babies claim a higher survival rate than males, one plus for our side. Premature infants lack the characteristic baby fat. They resemble small, finely tuned athletes rather than "Gerber" babies, a trait which makes a parent want to converse with them on an adult level rather than ramble the usual baby talk.

Nick and I arrived at St. Luke's in Fargo the following afternoon. After learning the protocol for entering the NICU, we stepped into a new world. Attired in green scrubs, I stood in utter amazement of my daughter's new surroundings. A brightly lit room greeted me along with two long rows of isolates, those clear boxes premies are placed in. All the wires, tubes, and machines seemed out of proportion to the small babies they were sustaining. Kate's bed stood in a far corner that seemed surprisingly cozy. I approached cautiously, afraid I would accidentally touch something untouchable. Motionless from the drug Pavlon used to keep her quiet, she appeared peaceful and content. A soft, pink ribbon taped to her blond hair filled my heart with warmth.

"Nick and Angela?" a soothing voiced questioned.

"Yes," we answered in unison.

"I'm Shelly; I will be Kate's day nurse. You have a beautiful daughter; she is a real fighter; we are amazed at her will."

"How is she?" I asked apprehensively.

"Well, she is stable right now. The doctors are anxious to talk with you. They'll be in soon. I'll show you what we are doing for Kate. She is such a sweetheart."

Four doctors were handling Kate's case. As the doctors entered the NICU, in a flurry of white lab coats and clipboards, I prayed for better news than they delivered. Kate's age was closer to 23 weeks than 25 weeks as first calculated. This became a huge factor on her delicate time scale. Kate's lungs were too underdeveloped to handle oxygen. Drugs were given to strengthen them. Waiting was all we could do.

I spent every possible moment with Kate. Always trying to stay upbeat, I never wanted her to hear me cry. I told her funny stories, read aloud to her, or just held her hand. After returning from a quick trip to Target, I filled Kate in on my adventure. "Kate, guess what your goofy mother did?" I rambled. "I was in such a hurry to come see you that I forgot to pack underwear and socks! You'll soon figure out that Mommy can be a little spacey. You might want to pack your own suitcase when we go on a trip. I'll buy you one with Barbie on it."

I turned to see Shelly wiping tears from her eyes. "Shelly, what's wrong?" I asked.

"It's just so unfair that you have to go through this. You love Kate so much, and you are already a great mom."

"If something happens to Kate, I don't want her to leave this world wondering if I loved her or not. I don't care if she's perfect or if she's sick."

We gave each other a long hug and shed our tears in silence. I became quite close to Shelly and Kate's night nurse, Pat. Parents were encouraged to spend as much time as possible with their infants. Pat and Shelly recorded every minute we spent with Kate; a pattern developed. Whenever I left the unit or kept silent for more than 15 minutes, Kate's vitals would begin to fall. Being called back to the unit, especially at night, I found my voice and touch could bring her vitals up again in five to ten minutes.

Sunday morning greeted us with worried faces in the NICU. Kate was failing. The doctors feared brain hemorrhaging, and Kate's lungs were rupturing faster than the oxygen could be absorbed. Kate did not look well; her skin had taken a darker hue, and she was not responding to my voice as quickly. Sunday became a long day. Until then, I had convinced myself I would be taking Kate home in a few months. Reality stood on my doorstep. Tests were ordered, and a full staff consultation was set up for the following morning. I spent Sunday evening pacing the courtyard of the Ronald McDonald House where Nick and I stayed. I had spent hours on my knees in the hospital chapel praying the decision before me would never come. If God wanted her, He should take her quietly. My selfishness wanted her to stay. Would she think I gave up on her? Could God forgive me?

After a sleepless night, Monday morning arrived with blue sky and an autumn sun. Fallen leaves tickled the pavement outside the hospital windows. Our meeting started at 10 a.m. Shelly and Pat, both on their day off, joined the meeting. Kate's test results revealed a brain hemorrhage of 90%; her organ systems were beginning to shut down. Kate's best interest would be served if we stopped treatment. The room fell still. After an unbearable silence, I looked up from my tattered Kleenex to find everyone's eyes upon me. I needed to give the final answer; I needed to actually say it out loud! I could not speak. Fear took over my body, and I began to sob.

Pulling in a long breath, I cried, "I will let her go."

Scrubbing for the last time, I realized I would not walk out of the NICU the same person in a few hours. My life would be forever changed. The walk to "Kate's World," as I named it, played out in slow motion. Nurses, one by one, stopped their care-giving for a brief moment to give an approving nod. I requested a priest and Last Rites. A small, white, curtained partition gave Kate her first taste of privacy. Pat and Shelly had placed a delicate, pink gown on Kate. A small, gold cross necklace draped her tiny neck. Kate looked like a true angel. Kate was placed in my arms for the first and the last time. Dr. Nielsen slowly stepped forward, his voice almost poetic. "All you have to do is nod your head, Angela. I will take out the ventilator only when you are ready."

"Will she feel any pain?" I cried.

"No, we gave her a small dose of morphine to ease her discomfort."

"How long do I have?"

"You can take as long as you want. I won't do anything until you are ready."

An hour slipped away. A gentle peace warmed me, and I knew she was ready. I slowly nodded my head.

Kate left this world a few minutes later, cradled in my arms.

On a cold day in January, close to Kate's original due date, a poem I have never been able to erase landed in my mind.

> I stand
> among you now
> like the wintering tree
> with open arms
> now empty
>
> I sway in life's
> bitter cold breeze
> praying and hoping
> God will send to me soon my spring.

God did send me a spring. After an emergency surgery to stop labor at 16 weeks, five-and-a-half months of ABSOLUTE bed rest and medication, Reese Lawrence Frohling arrived on July 1, 1994. Reese's blue eyes twinkle when he laughs, and his heart shines like gold. I look upon my son as a true gift.

Through the trials of my children, I have learned the preciousness of life. Without my growth in faith and strength, Kate's life would have been lived in vain. To honor her life and courage, I needed to move forward with more than bitterness and tears. This lesson helped me face my journey with Reese and many other unexpected seasons in this life. In those few short days of October 1991, Kate taught me never to let a day pass without showing the important people in my life they are loved.

Discussion Questions:

1. What event is the writer relating? What point of view is used and how effectively does it work?

2. What point or significance does the writer try to establish in the piece?

3. Evaluate the author's use of dialogue. How does it enhance or detract from the story?

4. Analyze the effectiveness of the writer's use of descriptive details, such as sense imagery and figurative language.
5. Analyze the effectiveness of the title, introduction, and conclusion. How well do they support the topic?
6. Does the writer "have heart" in the essay? What specific aspects of the piece support your response?
7. Identify the strengths of this essay. What areas of improvement would you suggest?
8. Evaluate the effectiveness of the piece holistically and provide rationale for your evaluation.

SAMPLE STUDENT WRITING

You're the Expert

Bringing Pictures to Life
by Missy Richard

I love to scrapbook and create new pages in my book every week, so I guess people could call me an expert in this area. Scrapbooking is not just gluing pictures on a page; it involves colors, precious moments, and expressions. The hobby of scrapbooking helps me relax. When I scrapbook, I am able to express my feelings about the events of each picture by using techniques other than words. As I create each page of my scrapbook, I smile as memories of the past are brought back to life.

The first step of scrapbooking requires picking out pictures. This takes a lot of my time. As I scramble through overflowing shoeboxes full of pictures, the sides of the boxes begin to tear as the pictures fight their way out. "If only I had these in photo albums," I say to myself, "this would be much easier." As I sort through each shoebox, I keep in mind that all of the photos on one page should connect with each other. When selecting pictures, I choose various photos of one event. The images might relate to a birthday party, a day at the zoo, or a football game. I pick many pictures from one occasion and begin creating my page.

I perform this next step easily. I now begin to arrange the pictures to be put on the page. Some people may think the order of the pictures seems unimportant, but putting the pictures in order gives the page meaning. I arrange my pictures according to their importance to me and not always in the order they happened. Positioning the pictures by importance better expresses my feelings toward the event of the page and gives it more meaning.

After arranging my pictures, I use my special scissors to cut the edges uniquely. I love the snip, snip of the scissors; it sounds familiar to me. Some of my scissors cut jagged edges; some cut rounded edges. I determine which edge I want on each picture in relation to the mood the picture gives off. If the picture includes my wild cousin dancing, I use the jagged edge to show a party-effect. If the picture shows my sister sleeping, I use the rounded edge to show the calmness of the picture. Cutting the right edge on the picture highlights the effect and mood of that picture.

Now comes the sticky part. After cutting edges on my pictures, I glue the pictures down in my chosen order. While I am gluing each photo, a napkin sits next to me, ready to wipe off the glue, which seeps from under each picture as it gasps for air. I wait for the glue to dry so I know that the pictures are unquestionably secure. Watching glue dry is like watching the second-hand move around the clock, so during this time, I pick out colors of crayons and construction paper for my next step.

Choice of color, one of the most important components of creating my page, takes time and thought. The color must coordinate with the mood of the picture. The inviting color of lavender shows the warmth and mystery of a picture. Shades of blue bring out the tranquility and harmony of a picture. The bright hues of orange and red show courage and endurance while the tones of pink and yellow illustrate love and happiness. Putting color around a picture emphasizes the mood of that image for everyone to see.

After surrounding each picture with its coordinating color, the final steps of creating my page are getting close. Some pictures, even with special-cut edges and harmonizing colors, are not fully expressed. Next to these pictures, I add special words or expressions. My *Scrapbooking Quote Book* sometimes comes in handy for this purpose. If I don't use a catchy quotation from this book, I write a sentence or two describing what is happening in the picture. Adding words to my page gives it a personal feeling.

The final step to creating my page involves writing the date of when the event occurred. While creating each page in my scrapbook, I sometimes get lost in the moment. Handling each picture makes me feel as if the event is taking place at that very minute. I feel as if I am reliving the occasion. After designing my page and writing the date in the bottom corner, I come back to reality. That event, although now only a memory, will come back to life many times as I revisit this page of my scrapbook. After designing each page according to this series of events, I finally complete my scrapbook. Most of the scrapbooks I make, I keep for myself. I love looking through old scrapbooks and reliving the events of each page. As I look back through the book, some pages bring tears, and some bring laughter. I smile because this scrapbook, a treasure, will last forever.

My favorite page includes photos of my grandpa and me. This page holds a special place in my heart because my grandpa is not with me anymore. I designed this page with almost every color possible to capture my grandpa's personality. Grandpa made me feel warm, loved, happy, and at peace when he was alive. I loved spending as much time as possible with my grandpa, and looking at this page brings back those memories I experienced with him.

On occasion, I make scrapbooks for my friends or for other members of my family. Giving scrapbooks as gifts provides me as much joy as when I keep them for myself. I love watching others, who are smiling through their tears, as they look through the book and remember special, past events of their lives. I know the scrapbook brings them happiness, and that makes me happy. A scrapbook, the gift that keeps on giving no matter who receives it, brings pictures to life.

Discussion Questions:

1. What concept, activity, or hobby does the writer explain? Does the writer seem like an expert on the topic, and does the writer's personal voice come through? How can you tell? Identify the writer's purpose.

2. Is the writing geared to a novice's level of understanding? Explain your answer.

3. Evaluate the title, introduction, and conclusion. How effective are they? Explain your responses.

4. Identify any writing strategies (figurative language, sense imagery, dialogue humor, satire, etc.) that the writer uses, and evaluate their effectiveness.

5. Does the writer "have heart" in the essay? What specific aspects of the piece support your response?

6. Point out the strengths of this essay. What improvements for the piece would you suggest?

7. Evaluate the effectiveness of the piece holistically and provide rationale for your evaluation.

SAMPLE STUDENT WRITING
Convince Your Readers
Letter for Change

Not Nagging, Just Advising
by Luke Wiederholt

Dear Mom,

Many times I've heard friends and relatives beg you to stop smoking. But their strategies have failed, so I want to try a new way—this letter. It kills me to see you light each new cigarette because I know each drag harms you greatly. I want to make you consider kicking the bad habit, but I want to do it without nagging and making you angry. I know you have smoked since age eighteen, so quitting this habit will not be easy, yet far from impossible.

I hope you understand how much you mean to our family. If you keep smoking, our wonderful relationships may not last as long as we hope because smoking, on average, reduces life expectancy by ten years. I can't imagine your not living long enough to see your grandchildren because smoking caused one of its many deadly diseases. Thinking of this makes me sad and depressed. I tried to think of an advantage to smoking, but I couldn't come up with one. Instead, I thought of how smoking causes cancer, heart disease, asthma, and emphysema.

Beyond the health issues, smoking yellows your teeth, and it smells. Furthermore, smoking has burned a huge hole in your purse over the years. By saving the seven dollars that you spend on each pack of cigarettes, you could buy things you NEED. I calculated that you have spent over $10,000 on cigarettes throughout your lifetime. You could have easily bought a dream car or invested the money and earned lots of interest instead of spending it on cigarettes. Mom, I hope you know that the rest of the family and I care more about you than to let these negative aspects of smoking affect you.

You may think that quitting smoking now may not help because you have been smoking too long. Wrong! If you choose to stop smoking, many positive results will occur. The smell of your car, your home, your hair, and your breath will immediately improve after you quit. By quitting, you will immediately reduce the risks of heart attack, stroke, emphysema, and lung diseases. I want you to realize the positive effects of quitting smoking.

Also, please consider that smoking not only harms you but also harms the people around you. Second-hand smoke harms other people just as the smoke you inhale from your cigarettes harms you. Also, the smoke from cigarettes stains the paint in your house. When you take a picture off the wall, you will see that black outlines of cigarette smoke remain around the outline of the frame.

You may find the first step in the quitting process the hardest. You need to WANT to quit. Wanting to quit will show that you care not only about your own health but also about our family. And I know that you want nothing more than to please your family. You might consider one of the following two ways of quitting. Try to reduce the amount of nicotine that you put into your system each day. By doing this, your body won't "need" as much nicotine on a daily basis. If this method seems too hard, I recommend your attending a hypnosis session to help you quit smoking.

You might also try a few simpler procedures to help make the quitting process easier. First, make a chart of reasons why you want to quit. Keep this list handy so any time you crave a smoke, you can look at it and know why you shouldn't smoke. Next, note where you smoke the most. Try to avoid these places at all costs while you are involved in the quitting process. By not being in these places, you might be able to quit more easily. If you are carrying cigarettes, get rid of them. If the cigarette isn't there, you can't smoke it.

Mom, I wrote this letter not because I want to complain to you but rather because I care about you, and I know how much the rest of the family cares about you, too. I hope that you will take my advice and concern into consideration and seriously think about quitting smoking. Please make plans to break this addiction soon. I promise you will immediately notice the positive effects of not smoking. Good luck. I love you always.

Your son,
Luke

Discussion Questions:

1. Identify the problems and the need for changes the writer proposes. What ways does the writer suggest to bring about the changes? What does the writer present as advantages of the changes?

2. Are concrete examples of the situation and possible changes presented? If so, identify these.

3. Analyze the tone of the piece. Does it seem appropriate for the purpose of the essay? Why or why not?
4. Does the essay provide an opening, a clear thesis, and a strong conclusion that work effectively for this topic? Support your answer.
5. Does the writer "have heart" in this essay? What specific aspects of the piece support your response?
6. Cite the major strengths of the essay. What ideas do you suggest for improvement?
7. Evaluate the essay holistically and provide rationale for your evaluation.

SAMPLE STUDENT WRITING

Convince Your Readers
Letter to the Editor

Money Doesn't Grow on Trees
by Nikolai Doffing

To: Editor, *Telegraph Herald,* Dubuque, Iowa

I recently came across several articles from different periodicals that reported the new state budget for Iowa and the spending gap between the revenue and expenses. I noticed that the money needed for the government's spending represents an amount significantly larger than the state government's income. The fact that the state government would even think of spending more money than its income concerns me. I find it hard to understand how a government could let this happen. I hope to convince the state legislature to lead the rest of the state government to balance the budget better so Iowa will not go into further debt and the burden will not fall onto future generations.

To put the budget and debt situation into perspective, I will provide an example of what happens when a family acquires debt through a credit card. When families fail to completely pay off their credit card payments, the payment accrues interest, and they become indebted to their lenders. The debt increases if they continue not to pay the full credit card payments. When they finally pay off their credit card payments, the families end up paying more money for their purchases than they are valued at. The credit card payments also keep them from using their money in more productive ways. If the family does not watch or budget their money, their negligence will result in significant amounts of debt.

Like this example, the state government needs to minimize the debt and spending in the budget.

To eliminate the debt, I propose cutting funds from programs that do not help Iowa to either save money or reduce spending. If the state government implements a program that the federal government has already established, the state government program should be canceled. Also, the state government should reduce funding for programs in relation to economic development and labor programs. Local governments know more about their respective communities and will know how to spur their communities' economic growth and support their labor programs better than the state government. The state government should also eliminate funding for research studies that do not provide a profit to the state or produce a significant benefit to the state's well-being.

Iowa also needs to capitalize on efficient motor vehicles and natural gas. The state should eliminate all government vehicles that do not operate efficiently. New electric and hybrid vehicles have proven to consume fuel in much smaller portions than traditional cars, and they will save the government significant amounts of money. Because it will cost a lot of money to replace the vehicles, Iowa should purchase the new vehicles in small amounts over a larger period of time so it would not lose money. Natural gas is starting to become a large source of fuel in Iowa, and continuing to use it will save money from importing fuel from other countries. Not only will the state government save money that would have been used for fuel, but Iowa will also become one of the leading states in green technology.

Since Iowa consists mostly of flat farmland, the government needs to take advantage of the layout by installing more windmills and solar panels. Windmills provide free energy from the wind, and they do not cost a lot of money to install. With more windmills, Iowa's government can transfer its energy to electricity and save money by not spending more money on more expensive electrical sources. Solar panels also provide an excellent source of natural energy that can be transferred into electricity. Solar panels cost little to maintain, and they only need the sun to operate.

To create a higher state income, fines on misdemeanors and traffic citations should be raised. With thousands of Iowans committing traffic violations every day, a slight increase in the fines will generate more money for the state. Fine increases should not include just traffic violations. A fine increase should be implemented for all parking violations and other minor offenses. The higher fines will potentially reduce the violations and traffic accidents as well.

Also, red-light cameras should be installed at every major intersection in Iowa. A red-light camera takes a picture of a vehicle if it drives through a red light when it crosses an intersection. The cameras will eliminate the need for a patrol officer to cite the violation. When a patrol officer is not needed to charge the offender with the traffic violation, the officer can be used to concentrate on other issues in the community. The cameras will also catch more violators and generate more income for the state.

To pay off the debt, the state legislature needs to develop a payment plan and stick with it. Legislators should devise a schedule to consistently pay off debt the state has acquired. If the government sticks with the plan, Iowa will hopefully become debt-free within a few years. When legislators write the state budget each year, they should put ten percent of the budget aside and use it for paying the debt that the state owes. A similar plan is used by many families across the country to eliminate their debts, and it has been proven successful.

With the debt paid off, the state legislature can use the extra money to help the citizens of Iowa. The money can be used to strengthen the education system. With stronger education, the state can hire more teachers to increase the intelligence and effectiveness of Iowa's students. Iowa students will become more educated than students from other states, and they will raise our stance and role in our country. The money can also be used to grant more funding to environmental, scientific, and technological research at the state-funded universities such as Iowa State University and The University of Iowa.

The extra money could also be used to enhance the flood and tornado protection. In the wake of the recent floods in eastern Iowa, it has become evident that more money is needed to fund the flood prevention and protection services. With the extra money, river cities such as Cedar Rapids can construct more effective flood prevention walls and levees. Because of the likelihood of tornados every year, money is needed for more effective early warning systems. State emergency organizations could also benefit from the extra money when they participate in flood and tornado relief efforts.

The money should also be used to benefit Iowa's law enforcement.

With high crime rates, law enforcement officials stress the need for more officers on patrol. The extra money can be used to hire more officers. With more officers on patrol, crime rates will potentially drop, and officer injuries will also decline. The money can be used to upgrade the state police's old cars to newer, faster, and more efficient cars.

I hope that the State House of Representatives and Senate will consider my proposals. Our state is sinking in debt, and it should not be run this way. If the state legislature implements these changes, Iowa will prosper and become one of the leaders in this country in economic growth, public safety, and environmental technology. With these changes, Iowa can show the other states how to operate an economy and promote wise spending. Becoming monetarily indebted to someone or an organization should not be accepted as the way of living. If Iowa can eliminate the debt our state owes, we citizens can enjoy a freedom that has not been experienced for a long time.

Sincerely,

Nikolai Doffing

Discussion Questions:
1. Identify the problem and the need for change the writer proposes. What ways does the writer suggest will bring about this change? What advantages of the change does the writer present?
2. Are concrete examples of the situation and possible changes presented? If so, identify these.
3. Analyze the tone of the piece. Does it seem appropriate for the purpose of the essay? Why or why not?
4. Does the essay provide an effective title, an opening that attracts attention, a clear thesis, and a sound conclusion? Support your answer.
5. Identify the strengths of the essay. What ideas do you suggest for improvement?
6. Does the piece of writing "have heart"? Cite specific areas of the essay that support your response.
7. Evaluate the essay holistically and provide rationale for your evaluation.

SAMPLE STUDENT WRITING

Comparison-Contrast

My Heroic Nuisance
By Kelsey Kieler

Dave Barry once said, "To an adolescent, there is nothing in the world more embarrassing than a parent." Once, at thirteen years of age, I viewed my parents as nuisances, and I became convinced their precise goal focused on ruining my teenage social life. They applied strict rules and felt they needed to know everything about my existence. However, currently six years older and a bit wiser, I analyze my parents' actions differently; they transformed into my heroes. I realize they rarely established a rule without a sensible purpose lurking in the shadows. As an adult, I respect and appreciate their guidelines on employment, education, chores, curfew, parties, discipline, and family love.

The day of my thirteenth birthday, Natalie and Mandy, my older sisters, advised me to save any scrap of money I could. "Just remember, when you turn sixteen in our household, you grow up. Mom and Dad want you to pay for your own car, clothes, and gas." I encoded their reminder; employment would show its ugly face in a short three years. "I thought I wasn't technically considered an adult until I'm eighteen. That's what the law says," I would counter. Nonetheless, at age sixteen, I became employed at the Southwest Health Center Nursing Home as a food service worker. I dreaded working for five hours after school, but I enjoyed the extra cash. By adulthood, I learned to accurately budget my income. I set aside eighty dollars a month for fuel and two-hundred-fifty dollars for my car payment. I kept half of the remaining money for shopping and stored the other half in my savings account at the Dupaco Community Credit Union. Today, I confess if my parents hadn't stopped paying for my "wants," my financial planning would not exist.

Similar to most female adolescents, my primary interests in middle and high school were directed toward cute boys, gorgeous hair, and brand-name clothes. Receiving a D- on a vital algebra quiz easily rolled off my shoulders. Of course, when Mom and Dad received my report card at parent-teacher conferences, that nearly failing grade mattered more than I expected. After the first semester of my freshman year at Cuba City High School, my parents expected no grade lower than a B+. As a current college student at Northeast Iowa Community College,

I thank my parents for their persistent high expectations regarding education. I graduated from Cuba City High School with a 3.92 grade-point-average and five thousand dollars in scholarships. As former president Bill Clinton once acknowledged, "Every parent knows a good education is a gift that keeps on giving for a lifetime." Today, I couldn't agree more.

Each afternoon, after an unbearably tedious eight hours of class periods, I trudged home and imagined what my "To Do" list would entail. Typically, it involved emptying the crammed dishwasher, organizing my chaotic bedroom, or dusting the wooden furniture. Occasionally, I received the pleasure of scrubbing the nearly shining kitchen floor or washing the rainfall debris from the exterior of our first-floor house windows. As a selfish teenager, I would grumble, "This is totally ridiculous. Why do they make *me* do this? It's not like they have anything more important to do. Seriously, they should know I have places to go and people to see." Even though I detested household chores, I matured to realize my parents were trying to teach me a valuable lesson; I can help others without expecting something in return. Because of this, I developed a generous and noble attitude.

The memorable words, "Make sure you're home by curfew," were permanently planted in my mind throughout my four years of high school. I cynically rolled my eyes and obstinately argued, "My friends are allowed to come home whenever they want, so why should I have to be home at a specific time?" I never received an answer to this question, but rather I caught "the glare," which warned I'd better return by ten o'clock sharp. I attentively glanced at the neon-blue digital numbers on the screen of my Motorola cell phone and obediently moseyed through the front door at quarter to ten each night. Surprisingly, as an adult, I salute my parents for setting early night curfews. I understand their concern for my safe arrival home and realize their attempt to create boundaries. Without these boundaries, I could have easily attended drinking parties, suffered careless car accidents, or smoked illegal drugs like many of my former friends. My parents rescued me from potentially destructive experiences.

After pleading to host a slumber party following the homecoming dance my sophomore year, my mother's words came as no surprise. "You know the rules, Kelsey. You are allowed to have three friends stay overnight or six friends to leave by eleven." My promises to stay quiet, fall asleep early, or keep the house clean rarely fazed my mother; after all, she knew better because she survived my older sisters. Until I matured, I failed to understand her logic. Dustin, my thirteen-year-old brother, constantly invites friends over. Deafening rock music blares through the air vents, and they carelessly leave video games strewn across the basement floor. Any hope for relaxation disappears. Now, I empathize with my mother's desire for a peaceful environment and a tidy house. I understand the necessity of setting limitations on social gatherings when raising teenagers.

When I turned fifteen, my parents revealed their fearless approach on proper discipline. I tended to gossip with Lynn, my best friend, until two in the morning, so they seized my cell phone. When I refused to accept the answer "no," I wouldn't hear the answer "yes" for an agonizing two weeks. After quarreling with Dustin or allowing my grades to slip, I could expect to reside within the blank walls of my bedroom for a dragging seven days. Naturally, I thought this grounding business seemed irrational; I never imagined I'd understand their logic. By taking away my most prized possessions when I disobeyed the rules, they taught me the importance of respect for authority. At present, I catch myself determining decisions based on the consequences that may follow. I admire my parents' strength to stand their ground through my several tiresome temper tantrums.

As an adolescent, I dreaded hearing the words, "We're having a family night." My family wasn't exactly awarded the highest position of my social chain, but my parents insisted we spend one night a week together. They enjoyed making me a social outcast and found acute humor in my protest, "This is totally social suicide." However, as my closest friends dwindled after graduation, my family remained. I admired their loyalty and love for me, especially when I treated them poorly. I learned the importance of creating strong and loving relationships with each member of my family.

I, similar to most teenagers, failed to recognize my parents in a positive manner. I chose to remain blinded by their regulations. I refused to consider how I could benefit from their punishments or how education could impact my life so immensely. However, as each year passed, I began to realize the valuable lessons my parents taught me not only about life but also about raising mischievous children. When I decide to build a family of my own, I plan to raise my children with the same integrity and patience my parents demonstrated. When my children develop into teenagers and view me as a nuisance in their lives, I hope they realize someday I just might become their hero.

Discussion Questions:

1. Identify the issues/ideas that the writer is trying to compare/contrast. Can you identify the writer's thesis?
2. Can you identify the writer's purpose (the so what) of the essay?
3. Are concrete examples presented to show specific points of comparisons and contrasts? If so, identify these.
4. Explain the organization the author uses and comment on its effectiveness.
5. Analyze the tone of the piece. Does it seem appropriate for the purpose of the essay? Why or why not?
6. Does the essay provide a title and opening that attract attention and a strong conclusion? Support your answer.
7. Identify the strengths of the essay. What ideas would you suggest for improvement?
8. Does the piece of writing "have heart"? Cite specific areas of the essay that support your response.
9. Evaluate the essay holistically and provide rationale for your evaluation.

SAMPLE STUDENT WRITING

Definition of Abstract Term

Freedom: Never to be Taken for Granted
By Carissa Oberbroeckling

What is freedom? Everyone I asked to define freedom offered a different response. The two-year-old I encountered last weekend would define freedom as ripping off his continuously present diaper and running through the house with pure excitement. A sixteen-year-old, who just received his or her license, would consider freedom to be driving to the mall without the supervision of a parent. A nineteen-year-old, who recently moved away from home and entered a large university, would define freedom as doing a keg stand at a frat party and then streaking through mid-campus in order to be accepted into a fraternity. A green card means freedom to a migrant worker who has crossed the border seeking a life of riches. A ninety-year-old man may consider freedom as still holding a valid license and living alone in the house he has owned for the last fifty years. Freedom to a soldier returning from Afghanistan is being able to eat dinner with his or her family without worrying about being hit by flying shells or bombs. Different stages of the life process offer different perspectives on how freedom is defined and valued.

Freedom may be defined as the power to do, say, or think as one pleases. Is freedom free? In the United States of America, freedom came at a high price. Wars were fought. Many brave men and women sacrificed their lives. Treaties were signed, laws were written, and bills were passed. The most important piece of written documentation is known as the Declaration of Independence. Every year Americans celebrate Independence Day on the Fourth of July to remember our founding forefathers and show our pride for the patriots that have shaped this great country. The flag serves as our national symbol for freedom, which represents the states as being united. The National Anthem serves as another reminder as the words are sung before every baseball game and other sporting events, "O'er the land of the free, and the home of the brave."

The opposite of freedom would be described as slavery. Slaves were forced to work for a person or household against their will. Those born into a slave family would probably never be given the opportunity to taste freedom. Most slaves are treated like a piece of property that is walked, tilled, and hunted on. Not all slaves were treated horribly; some were kept in good health and were given a minimal workload in order to keep them healthy. Thankfully, slavery became illegal in United States in the late eighteen hundreds.

Another example of how freedom came about includes the Civil Rights Movement. The movement began when a black woman named Rosa Lee Parks was arrested for refusing to sit in the rear of a city transportation bus in Montgomery, Alabama, in 1955. Desegregation followed the Civil Rights Movement, which gave blacks more freedom than they had experienced before slavery. In the last few years of the movement, southern blacks were granted the right to vote. Not only were blacks able to vote, but also anyone over the age of eighteen was allowed to vote.

Political freedoms can vary in importance as opposed to individual freedoms. The younger generations tend to take their political freedoms for granted more than the older generations. Five of the political freedoms that I highly value include freedom of education, freedom of movement, freedom of religion, freedom of speech, and freedom of thought. When I chose to attend NICC, I used my freedom of education. In writing this paper, I am using the freedom of thought and speech in voicing my personal opinions.

We live in an era where freedom is restricted but not as harshly as the past. For example, when I turned sixteen, I couldn't go to the Department of Transportation, get a mug shot taken, and legally drive. Oh, no! First, I needed to pass my driver's education course by taking a series of tests, attending many hours of lectures, and spending a minimum of twenty hours behind the wheel with an instructor. Once I finished the course, I unwillingly took a final exam and passed. Then, I took my certificate of successful completion of the course to the Department of Transportation. Once there, I took yet another test of hearing and vision. Finally, I was able to get a hideous picture taken, but in return, I held a piece of plastic which allows me to drive legally. After everything I went through to receive my license, I now hold responsibilities to abide by the rules of the road, leaving me with some freedom but not complete freedom.

In order to live in a free, civilized society, laws must be followed. This, in essence, takes some of our freedoms away, but without these laws restricting our freedom, total chaos could occur. For example, freedom to bear arms doesn't give citizens the freedom to carry a weapon openly without consequences. The more the freedoms are abused, the stricter the laws become. Situations that abuse the freedom to bear arms include drive-by shootings, school shootings, assault with deadly weapons, and an increased number in violent homicides, just to name a few. Over a hundred years ago, ranch owners typically hung their shotguns above their doors. Today, citizens are required to apply for a permit, and an extensive background check is completed in order to legally own a firearm.

Freedom can mean something different to every individual depending on his/her age, gender, religion, or ethnicity. For me, freedom means having the ability to choose what career path I want to take and what college I will pursue my education at in order to achieve that goal. Freedom also means choosing where I want to work and live and what type of vehicle I drive. As I mature, I am starting to realize the responsibilities that come with freedom. The soldiers that have died on the battle fields have paid the highest price so all of us in the United States of America can enjoy our freedoms, and that should never be taken for granted.

Discussion Questions:

1. What abstract term has the writer chosen to define? Identify the writer's thesis. Is the thesis effective?
2. List the methods the writer uses to define the term. How effectively does the writer use these methods?
3. Identify the point, the <u>so what</u>–the significance of the essay.
4. Do you as a reader understand the term better after reading this piece? Why or why not?
5. Analyze the effectiveness of the title, the introduction, and the conclusion.
6. Explain the strengths of the essay. What aspects might improve the essay?
7. Does the writer "have heart" in the essay? What specific aspects of the piece support your response?
8. Evaluate the essay holistically and explain your rationale for that evaluation.

SAMPLE STUDENT WRITING

Research Essay—MLA Format

Rachel Hellewell

Instructor Jim Brimeyer

ENG 106: Composition II

15 April 2017

Defining and Treating ADD: My Daugther's
Tigger Behavior

Thesis: Attention Deficit Disorder, a real medical condition, can be successfully treated.

I. Attention Deficit Disorder has become a dreadful societal plague.

    A. At times, regular kid's behavior is mistaken for ADD.

    B. Those with ADD demonstrate an overabundance of attention, not a deficit.

II. The causes of ADD vary with each case.

    A. Many believe ADD is caused by bad parenting and lack of discipline.

    B. ADD is inherited and contains genetic influences.

III. Family doctors, pediatricians, and psychiatrists can diagnose ADD.

    A. Parents and teachers must assist in diagnosis of ADD.

    B. A Conner's computer test most often helps determine ADD.

IV. ADD can be treated in a number of ways.

    A. Nutritionists suggest a dramatic change of diet.

    B. Herbal supplements have helped some ADD patients.

    C. Behavior modification benefits some patients.

    D. Medication seems to be the most popular and productive treatment.

Hellewell 1

Defining and Treating ADD: My Daughter's Tigger Behavior

Nervously I sat outside my daughter Lacey's second grade classroom awaiting her parent-teacher conference. Since her kindergarten, I dreaded hearing what the teachers would say about my bright and beautiful daughter. Always full of energy, incoherent chatter, and silly antics, she often seems just like Tigger from "Winnie the Pooh," making all those around her seem like Eyores. Although she frustrated and exhausted her parents, she had always delighted our family, but school had become another matter. Starting with her kindergarten teacher, my husband and I would hear about the downside to Lacey's Tigger behavior. "Can't sit still; won't stay seated; often writes letters backwards; pesters other kids; never pays attention," and the list goes on.

"Lacey is a very bright and creative child," the second grade teacher, Mrs. Johnson, reassured me, just before she hit me with uglies. "She has such a hard time paying attention and staying on task. I can tell that she is very smart, but her writings and other schoolwork are so messy and confusing. It is hard to tell how much she understands and is learning." Finally during this teacher conference, I faced the facts and asked one question I dreaded, "Do you think Lacey might have Attention Deficit Disorder?"

Cautiously, Lacey's teacher replied, "Many of her classroom attention and behavior problems may be consistent with those of someone with Attention Deficit Disorder." There it was, the ugly truth I had refused to face for two-and-a-half years. Now that I had finally said it out loud, the full impact of it hit me. What now? Whom do I talk to? How will they know if she has an attention disorder? If she does, what next?

Like bumper cars in a noisy amusement park, question after question crowded my thoughts. One thought took formation just to be knocked aside by the next more desperate and dire thought. That night at the parent-teacher conference, my journey to educate myself about ADD began. Through research and tenacity, I would find a way to help heal my daughter. I faced my biggest problem when I realized that finding straightforward answers becomes difficult when it comes to ADD. Even the experts do not agree on the specifics. The medical research and case study of my own daughter proves, thankfully, that Attention Deficit Disorder, a real medical condition, can successfully be treated in a number of ways.

Attention Deficit Disorder (ADD) is often written as AD(H)D, the H standing for hyperactivity. For simplicity, I will refer to the condition as ADD, encompassing the disorder with and without hyperactivity. ADD, a neurological syndrome, affects the functions of the brain and nervous system. It is characterized by several behavior traits. The top three—distractibility, impulsiveness, and restlessness—are displayed from childhood on in people with ADD. Some of these traits may be found in all people from time to time but are extremely intensified and consistent in those with ADD, causing them major problems in their everyday lives. People mistakenly think that normal childish behavior will be seen as ADD behavior. As children, we all remember behaving naughtily and giving adults a hard time. Some people worry that we are diagnosing our children with disorders when they simply behave as we remember children should. When asked if Tom Sawyer would have been labeled ADD for his adventurous and rambunctious antics, Dr. Edward Hallowell, an authority on ADD and author of *Answers to Distraction*, replied, "We only diagnose children who are suffering in their lives at not being able to control their own behavior or focus their own mind, and with correct diagnosis we will relieve their pain" (17). I, like many other parents of ADD children, want to help my daughter because I see her struggle, not because I want to throw a wet blanket on her personal party. Despite what many people think, children do not consider having this disorder fun. It frightens and confuses them and limits their potential.

I find it ironic that attention deficit has become the main focus of ADD, for those afflicted display an overabundance of attention, not a deficit. They simply pay attention to too many things and not to the ones they need to. When making the decision whether or not to tell my daughter that she had been diagnosed with ADD, I came across a children's book that sums up Lacey's attention problem best: "Dad explained that I have eagle eyes; I notice everything. But eagles know when to stop looking around and zoom in on their prey. Me, I just keep noticing more things and miss the catch" (Gehret 14). Although my husband and I agreed that Lacey did not need to know about the ADD diagnosis, she was told about her eagle eyes. She feels proud of this gift and knows she needs to work on focusing and zooming in.

Many people consider ADD a new and novel ailment. Media and society labeled it as the disease of the nineties and strongly opposed the use of "new and experimental drugs" in the treatment. Truth be told, the disorder has been recognized and studied in North America since 1902. Although the name has changed several times over the years, the symptoms of ADD have been recognized and documented consistently by physicians and psychiatrists. In addition, the medication being used to treat ADD was pioneered, tested, and put into use over six decades ago (Mate 7). Those most opposed to the existence of ADD and the medication used to treat it lack knowledge on the subject. Life for those with ADD is challenging enough without this constant, ignorant criticism and social pressure.

Although many adults suffer from ADD, our children are currently most affected and in need of healing. Children with ADD often get into trouble at home and in school and find making friends difficult. Left untreated, ADD can severely affect a child's self-esteem and chance for social and academic success. Undiagnosed and untested ADD can

Hellewell 4
devastate parents and other family members as well. Parents of children found to suffer from ADD are three times more likely to divorce than parents of unaffected children because of the stress, self-blame, depression, and pressure parents suffer because of untreated ADD symptoms (Wodrich 20).

A lack of inhibition can be used to explain almost all ADD behaviors. This lack of inhibition ultimately leads to many other ADD problems. Dr. Hallowell explains:

> They often lack the intermediate reflective step between impulse and action. This can be charming and innovative, or it can be annoying and disruptive, depending upon the impulse and the action. People with ADD neither inhibit nor shape their responses as automatically as those who do not have ADD. This leads, directly or indirectly, to almost all of the other symptoms associated with ADD. (5)

As with anything else, ADD also comes with good traits. People with ADD display dynamic energy, creativity, intuitiveness, loyalty, kindness, and extreme intelligence. Many famous and respected people in American history have shown signs and symptoms of ADD, although it was not recognized as a disorder then. Thomas Edison, inventor of the light bulb and countless other inventions, is believed to have been affected by ADD. Writing left by Edison and his mother describe classic ADD symptoms. Although his ADD symptoms got him thrown out of school at a young age, Edison learned to use them to his advantage. He often worked on as many as forty inventions at a time. When one lost his interest, he moved to another. Thomas Hartmann's book *Attention Deficit Disorder* stresses that many other men; including Ben Franklin, Ernest Hemingway, and Sir Richard Francis Burton; were also suspected of being affected by ADD (133-43).

Those afflicted with ADD cannot always demonstrate their

vast intelligence. The problems the negative ADD traits cause can overshadow the positive traits. My daughter faced this very thing several times at home and in school. Lacey often made up imaginative stories that she wanted to tell and write down, but because of the ADD, she could not relay or record them. Before she could get half the story out, she would get distracted and forget. Even though we tried to comfort and encourage her, she felt "stupid," forgetful, and hopeless. The negative qualities can harm and defeat the strengths of the good qualities, leaving them wasted and unrealized. With treatment for ADD, the negative parts will recede, and the positive qualities can take center stage.

Scientists and parents alike are racing to discover the causes of ADD. Scientists must know more about ADD origins to treat and cure it. Parents desperately want to discover the causes not only to help their children but also to release them from the ultimate blame that society has placed on them for their children's disorder. Many see ADD as a recent societal problem caused by bad parenting and a lack of discipline. This line of reasoning could not stray further from the truth. ADD, as a diagnosed medical disorder, needs treatment, not punishment.

The latest scientific evidence tells us that ADD is inherited and contains genetic influence. Nongenetic factors such as premature birth or maternal alcohol and tobacco use have also been linked to the causes of ADD, but child-rearing techniques have never been seriously suspected in scientific and medical opinion. The National Attention Deficit Disorder Association (NADDA) research shows that disciplining those with ADD will simply worsen, not improve, behavior. The NADDA states simply that "one can't make a paraplegic walk by applying discipline. Similarly, one can't make a child with a biologically-based lack of self-control act better by simply applying discipline alone" ("Myths" 2).

Once the condition is suspected, ADD can be diagnosed reliably by a family doctor, pediatrician, or child psychologist.

Hellewell 6

Since these individuals are often not well acquainted with the individual being diagnosed, they consult parents and teachers for a history of behavioral tendencies. Parents and teachers complete a questionnaire called The Conner's Scale, which rates the child's behavior. Parents and teachers provide invaluable information to the practitioner because of the time each has spent observing the child in normal settings. In addition, the child goes through a series of computer tests and games that also aid the diagnosis. These tests, called the Conner's Continuous Performance Tests, compare the responses of two thousand other children with the child in question's responses. After analyzing the questionnaires, computers tests, and in-office observations, professionals can make reliable diagnoses.

How is ADD treated? Many a child's problems and pains have been kissed away and fixed with a simple Band-aid and an encouraging "all better" from Mom and Dad. As children grow, it seems that their parents can magically cure any childhood ailment. This makes the issue of Attention Deficit Disorder a sensitive one. For the first time, parents must face the fact that they cannot make their child "all better" through love and encouragement alone. Instead, they must choose from options such as nutrition modifications, homeopathic herbal supplements, behavior modification, and medication to treat ADD.

Many nutritionists believe the symptoms consistent with ADD to be caused by allergic reactions and sensitivities to certain foods. Nutritionists recommend a drastic change in diet as a cure for ADD. Removing foods containing artificial flavoring, preservatives, dyes, and other additives, as well as "provoking foods" (91) such as milk and eggs from the ADD child's diet is recommended by Marcia Zimmerman, author of *The ADD Nutrition Solution*. This approach means implementing drastic changes in the way the entire family shops, cooks, and eats. Unfortunately while many hyperactive symptoms have been shown to improve with diet, attention and distractibility have not been improved.

Because my daughter's problems with ADD excluded hyperactivity, the only aspect of ADD diet improves, I decided to forgo a major life-changing diet approach. I turned my sights instead to other natural alternatives in the form of herbal supplements. The holistic experts at Ultimate.org, a website dedicated to alternative, natural medication, suggested that because ADD results from "neurotransmitter imbalance" in the brain, correcting that imbalance using amino acid supplements becomes the logical and natural treatment approach ("Neurotransmitter" 8). In fact, several companies and organizations offer forms of herbal "Ritalin" which they claim yield amazing results. Unfortunately, none of these claims have been proven through documented studies. Herbal supplements sound tempting, but because they are unproven, I continued my search for well-established and effective interventions.

Behavioral treatments became the next treatment option to come under my research scope. Altering behavior in those with ADD involves training and practice. Behavior management begins with identifying the behavior in need of being eliminated and deciding what behavior would better replace it. It ends with identifying the consequences of the problem behavior and assigning a logical consequence that will discourage the ADD child from repeating the behavior. Parents must learn many new skills and techniques to help manage and improve their child's behavior. The techniques they learn will help them handle the toughest aspects of parenting an ADD child, but these techniques must fit the nature of the child. Simply put, what works for one child will not work for all children.

At this point in treating an ADD child, it is best to seek advice and instruction from ADD written material and ADD experts. Although many great parenting books have become available, they do not apply or help with many of the problems the parents of ADD children face. Although emotionally taxing and time-consuming, behavioral treatments have been shown, over time, to immensely benefit those with ADD. Despite the benefits, major Health and Human Service studies have shown that children treated with medication alone showed more progress and improvement over time than those children treated with just behavioral management. This discovery led me to research the medication used to treat Attention Deficit Disorder.

Considering the time, money, and results, medication has become the most popular treatment available for controlling ADD. Many parents hesitate, with good reason, at the thought of placing children on medication. Martin Irwin, M.D., Director of the Children and Adolescent Psychiatry program at New York State University, explains that "there is a wide gulf between the public's misperceptions and misinformation about the medication and the vast research showing that Ritalin and other medication, when used properly, are safe and effective" (Wodrich 157). Contrary to popular belief, taking these medications does not "change" the child's personality nor harm him or her with dangerous side-effects. According to Dr. Steven Haas of the Dubuque Family Practice, "The most common side-effects are a temporary loss of appetite and trouble sleeping. If side-effects do occur, they most often last only for the first few weeks of treatment."

The immediate results and benefits of medication cannot be denied. Medication has effectively improved ADD behavior in 70 to 90 per cent of children over the age of five. The children who take the medications prescribed for ADD such as Ritalin and Adderall "not only are less impulsive, restless, and distractible but are also better able to hold important information in mind, to be more productive academically, and to have more internalized speech and better self-control," according to Russell Barkley, Director of Psychology and Professor of Psychiatry and Neurology at the University of Massachusetts

Medical Center. Barkley further states, "As a result, children tend to be better liked by other children and to experience less punishment for their actions, which improves their self-image" (6).

So, I had discovered that I had many misconceptions about treating ADD with medication. Before beginning my research, I was strongly opposed to using psychiatric medication to treat children. I had always thought it a little sick that parents give children mind-altering drugs. When I thought of a kid on Ritalin, I pictured a normally fun-loving and rambunctious child slumped down in a school chair "doped" out of his or her mind, half-asleep, and drooling. Before my own daughter Lacey showed signs of ADD, I considered myself one of those people who thought that lazy parents would not take responsibility for their bad parenting and labeled their kids "ADD" so they could "sedate" and "drug" them. My thinking has changed greatly since then. I now know that medication can become extremely helpful in treating this disorder.

Medication, however, should not be considered the "cure-all" for ADD; it only treats the symptoms. Dr. Daniel T. Moore insists that "parents should not be content in just dealing with the symptoms of ADHD. They should be more positive and attempt to help the child outgrow or at least compensate for their ADHD symptoms" (11). Moore, along with the National Institute of Mental Health, suggests the combined treatment of medication and behavioral modification.

Having decided on the medication and behavior route, my husband and I put Lacey on Adderall once a day medication for ADD. We chose Adderall on our doctor's advice because with her taking it once a day, we need not tell anyone, and her school need not administer it to her. We wanted to see the results of the treatment without any prejudiced notions from those for or against medication. We also wanted to see if Lacey's teacher noticed improvement without first expecting it. Along with medication, my husband and I also modified our parenting techniques to better accommodate Lacey's disorder.

Aside from the Adderall's minor appetite side-effect, which lasted about a week, Lacey's negative behaviors changed overnight. Lacey had always experienced problems wetting her pants. She would do this several times a day, but never at night. We had taken her to several doctors and a specialist who could find no cause or cure. After her second day on medication, she stopped and has not experienced an "accident" since. We were impressed with the immediate results but hoped to get a less biased opinion from those who did not know about her diagnosis and treatment. My husband and I felt that only time would tell if we had done the right thing.

Once again I found myself sitting in a tiny, uncomfortable, kid-size chair outside my daughter's classroom awaiting another conference. After all the research I went through to locate the optimum treatment for Lacey, I held high hopes. Those hopes were shattered earlier in the day when Lacey had given me her report card. It appeared that nothing had changed. Although the report card contained none of the handwritten, negative comments I was used to seeing on Lacey's cards, her academic marks had not improved much. I sat dejectedly expecting to hear the same speech from the teacher I had become familiar with over the years, which included a rundown of my daughter's faults.

I walked into the classroom after my agonizing wait and to my surprise received a warm smile and an excited "you must be so proud of Lacey" from her teacher, Mrs. Johnson. I was speechless. She must have noticed the confused look on my face and straightened the whole thing out for me. Lacey had improved so much in class in the last few months that she had moved to an advanced math class and up two reading groups. Her report card had not reflected this because of the simple report card system the school uses. According to her teacher, she had

Hellewell 11

improved one hundred percent in several areas since the last conference. Mrs. Johnson showed me a journal that Lacey had been writing since September. I could have sworn that two different children had written the journal. The improvement in handwriting and storytelling amazed me; finally, my Tigger could put all her silly and outlandish stories into print. Mrs. Johnson also told me about Lacey's behavior in class toward her classmates. She had made several friends in the last two months and was enjoying school more.

I drove home that night in a happy daze. I could not wait to tell my husband about our genius daughter. My long journey down the information and research highway had finally come full circle. It began at this year's first teacher's conference when I finally admitted to myself that Lacey suffered from ADD. Though this journey had become a long and rocky one, I would not have changed it for the world. The improvements that Lacey has made socially and academically have been well worth the time and trouble. Although Lacey will always be Tigger at heart, treatments help to redirect her destructive and uncontrollable "woopdie dooper looptie looper ally ooper bounce." Once Lacey's out-of-control bounce was redirected, all those who knew her could see past that distracting bounce we know as ADD to experience and appreciate all of her good and amazing qualities. I encourage anyone who thinks he/she or a loved one may suffer from ADD to seek diagnosis. This disorder, when successfully treated, can become an amazing gift. Treatment may help unlock unlimited potential. The benefits could be astounding.

Works Cited

Barkley, Russell A. "Attention-Deficit Hyperactivity Disorder." *Scientific American*, Sept. 1998, pp. 1-8.

Gehret, Jeanne. *Eagle Eyes*. Verbal Image, 1991.

Haas, Steven G. Personal interview. 8 Mar. 2017.

Hallowell, Edward M., and John Ratey. *Answers to Distraction*. Bantam, 1996.

Hartmann, Thomas. *Attention Deficit Disorder*. Underwood, 1997.

Johnson, Becca. Personal interview. 7 Mar. 2017.

Mate, Gabor. *Scattered*. Dutton, 1999.

Moore, Daniel T. *A Comprehensive Approach to ADHD*. Drake, 2000.

Myths About ADD/ADHD. National Attention Deficit Disorder Association, 9 Feb. 2002, www.add.org.

"Neurotransmitter Deficiencies." *Ultimate Neurotransmitters-the Neuro Link*, 4 Apr. 2002, www.search.yahoo.com/yhs/search.

Wodrich, David L. *Attention Deficit Hyperactivity Disorder*. Brookes, 1994.

Zimmerman, Marcia. *The ADD Nutrition Solution*. Hen, 1999.

Questions for analysis of Rachel Hellewell's research essay:
Discussion Questions regarding content:
1. Identify the topic and purpose of the essay. Is the topic persuasive? Are you convinced by the author's claim?
2. Are concrete examples of the situation and adequate support presented? If so, identify these.
3. Analyze the tone of the piece. Does it seem appropriate for the purpose of the essay? Why or why not?
4. Do the title, opening paragraph, thesis, and conclusion function effectively? Support your answer.
5. Identify the strengths of the essay. What ideas do you suggest for improvement?
6. Does the piece of writing "have heart"? Cite specific areas of the essay that support your response.
7. Evaluate the essay holistically and provide rationale for your evaluation.

Discussion Questions regarding MLA format:
1. What pieces of information need to be included with the author identification?
2. Identify the places where the title of the essay should appear.
3. Where does the pagination begin, and what is included besides the page numbers?
4. Explain the outline format for the formal outline.
5. Explain the author's use of different parenthetical documentation on pages 3 and 4 regarding the Gehret and Hallowell references.
6. Explain the difference in the Wodrich and Hallowell references on page 4.
7. Analyze the Works Cited page; then answer the following:
   a. Analyze the variety of sources by listing the books, magazines, interviews, and web citations.
   b. Identify all aspects of information in the Barkley citation.
   c. Identify all aspects of the "Myths" citation.

GLAD, BAD, SAD, OR MAD?

The following sentences are taken from student writings. Note how the misuse of language or failure to edit affects meaning. Evaluate the sentences by rating each one as GLAD (witty), BAD (accidental error), SAD (misuse of language), or MAD (a little off center).

1. As my arms reach my waste, I slightly bend my right elbow.
2. On March 31, 1984, an angle was born— me.
3. No one would choose to look at baron land over a thickly wooded park.
4. I have learned to live each day to the fullest and not take things for granite.
5. During the sidestroke, a swimmer's arms and legs should stay in sink with each other.
6. Bartenders need to serve all the customers in a timely and responsible manor.

CHAPTER 10

Research Writing

~ ~ ~

"The first year research paper should be seen less as an introduction to the conventions of academic writing and more as an opportunity to introduce students to the genuine spirit of inquiry, to certain habits of mind that often seem to inform investigations in many disciplines" (16).
—Bruce Ballenger

~ ~ ~

Believe it or not, research will undoubtedly become a part of your life at some point beyond this course. Surely you will do research writing in various courses as you pursue your college education. In the business world, you may be called upon to research and report on a product or a service you provide. Or maybe closer to home, a doctor will prescribe a "new drug" just on the market for treatment of some medical problem one of your family members is enduring. Research can help you find information so that you can make more sound and confident decisions in your life.

Books "stack up" to good research

Research, the investigation and gathering of facts, will lead you to form an opinion about your topic, which you will state in your thesis and prove to your readers. Through research, you will learn to select, analyze, and evaluate sources and facts. From these facts, you will create a new angle of vision on your topic. Research writing may serve three purposes—expository, analytical, or persuasive. This paper will involve the third, the persuasive focus. You will research primary and secondary sources to arrive at a position, then defend or prove it.

STRUT YOUR STUFF!

Writing Project 10-1: Research Writing   Choose a **problem-solution** topic of personal interest and curiosity in which you use a selected variety of research plus logical, **persuasive** writing skills to convince readers of the validity of your topic and position. In addition to the text, your research writing must include a sentence outline, and a "Works Cited" page in MLA format or a title page, abstract, and a "References" page in APA format. You should utilize a balanced variety of sources, two being personal interviews with experts on your topic. Also, note that you are limited to two internet sources in this research project. Most importantly, let your personal voice shine through your writing. Therefore, above all, remember: **"you've gotta have heart in your writing."**

~ ~ ~

"Students should become writers who research,
rather than researchers who write" (94).
—Bruce Ballenger

~ ~ ~

SETTING A TIMETABLE

Some students think MLA stands for "Mighty Large Assignment" and APA stands for "A Prodigious Assignment." In many ways, they are right. So it may help to break this LARGE writing project into a series of more manageable stages. Your instructor may set a time frame for you to complete various stages of your research project. If not, you would do well to set up your own due dates to help you manage the depth and breadth of the research project. The following breakdown may help you organize and complete your work without added stress.

Stage   Date

1   Find research questions of personal interest and curiosity that research can help answer, and be able to explain why you want to pursue the topic.

2   After the library presentation on finding sources, locate sources and cite them in proper MLA or APA format.

3   Locate six sources and cite them in proper MLA or APA format. Take notes.

4   Locate at least six more sources (12 total) and cite them properly. Take notes.

5   Develop a Prospectus Paragraph which includes such items as: What research question or problem do you plan to address? Why is this an interesting question or problem, and why is it significant to you? How far along are you in your thinking and research? What do you expect to discover? Are you ready to formulate a preliminary thesis? If so, state it. Take notes; locate and evaluate additional sources.

6   Write a preliminary rough draft without references to determine how much you can put your research into your own words and maintain your personal voice in your research writing.

7   Revise your draft and add sources of support, a Works Cited/References Page, outline/abstract, and title page for APA.

8   Revise your research writing and prepare it for peer response.

9   Present your research writing for peer response, then revise.

10   Present your revised research writing for instructor response, then revise.

11   Revise and polish your research writing for your portfolio.

SELECTING A TOPIC

In choosing your topic, select an issue of personal interest that you care about, some problem or something puzzling or some question that research can help you answer. You might select a topic from a field of study you are pursuing or a career you are interested in. Try to choose a topic you passionately care about which has triggered your curiosity. This will lead to more accurate, honest, interesting research and writing.

For example, a mother chose to research Attention Deficit Disorder (ADD) because her second grade daughter has been diagnosed with this neurobiological condition, so the mother wanted research to help her determine whether she should agree with the family doctor to put her daughter on a medicinal drug.

A young man who enjoys deer hunting couldn't hunt at his favorite territory because the deer population there had been stricken with chronic wasting disease, so he wanted to research that disease to find out its dangers and determine his course of action.

A young college student had been placed on probation by the courts but felt the probation system was not functioning productively. He used research to examine the effectiveness of the probation system in the United States and see if any alternatives might be available.

As these three examples show, you need to choose a research topic of personal interest, which you feel passionate about, and let the research help you answer your inquiry into that topic. Your concern and passion for your topic will be reflected in your research and in your writing.

PRACTICE 10A: Research Topic Brainstorming: Make a list to answer each of the items that follow. Possibly a topic will spring from this brainstorming strategy.

1. List all topics you want to learn more about.
2. List things in your life that you deeply care about or love.
3. List goals for your life.
4. List problems, difficulties, or challenges you face.
5. List what you did today or this week.
6. List everything you thought about today.
7. List things in your life that you hate.
8. List the most urgent questions about life you can think of.

When you arrive at the topic that interests you, formulate it into a question which research can help you answer. **Be prepared to submit your topic, topic question, and your explanation of how the topic applies to your life.**

LOCATING SOURCES

Primary vs. Secondary Sources

Primary sources, a person's original words, are written by people actually involved in the subject you are researching. These might include books, articles, speeches, diaries, letters. For example, **"The 1961**

Presidential Inaugural Speech" by John F. Kennedy exemplifies a primary source.

Secondary sources are writings about the primary sources and about the authors who produce them. *Young Man in the White House: John Fitzgerald Kennedy* by I. E. Levine exemplifies a secondary source.

Obviously, primary sources qualify as the best sources in most instances—when they fit your topic and your position, of course. Avoid using "lightweight" research sources like general encyclopedias (*Americana, Britannica, Collier's, Encarta, Wikipedia*). Generally, look for current and authoritative (expert in the field) sources and realize that your pool of sources may change as you restrict your topic.

Seek a variety and balance of sources, which may be found in the options which follow. To save time, learn to browse titles and tables of contents and skim chapters and articles for information related to your topic.

1. **Books:** consult the library card catalogue, usually computerized, or consult the internet.

2. **Periodicals—newspapers, magazines, journals:** consult the original editions in the library, or consult EBSCOhost or SIRS online.

3. **Almanacs:** consult, for example, Statistical Abstract of the United States or "A Matter of Fact Database."

4. **TV Programs, Videos**

5. **CD ROMS**

6. **Internet—(LIMIT 2):** verify sources by checking for .edu or .org or .gov. Avoid commercial online sources ending in .com.

7. **Expert Interviews—(2 REQUIRED):** Preferably you will conduct these interviews face to face. If that is impossible, seek phone interview next, and e-mail interview as a last resort. As you plan your interview, call your expert to set up an appointment. Prepare questions in writing in advance. You may even wish to send these questions ahead of time to give the expert time to formulate responses. During the interview, ask the expert if he or she minds your taking notes or recording the interview. Also, ask permission to quote the expert in your paper. Send a thank-you note, along with a copy of your research paper, as a courtesy after you complete your research paper project.

Refer to Chapter 11 for citing sources in MLA format. Refer to Chapter 12 for citing sources in APA format.

CITATION STYLES

The two most utilized citation formats for college research writing are MLA (Modern Language Association) and APA (American Psychological Association). MLA is commonly used in English, foreign language, literature, and humanities courses. APA format uses a name and date system of documentation. The social sciences—psychology, sociology, anthropology, political science, economics—most often require students to use the APA format.

Other citation styles are sometimes used in other disciplines. Some life science—biology, botany, zoology, anatomy, physiology—instructors prefer the CSE (Council of Science Editors) format. Some humanities—history, philosophy, religion, fine arts—instructors insist on using the traditional, footnote CMS (Chicago Manual of Style) system of documentation. Still other specific citation styles exist, such as ACS (Manual for Authors and Editors) and AIP (American Institute of Physics). Always ask instructors in various disciplines who assign research which citation style they prefer so that you head off potential citation problems and don't waste valuable time.

Examples:

I. MLA (Modern Language Association)

Text: The greatest of all dramatists, William Shakespeare (1564-1616), has truly stood the test of time. In a seventeenth century tribute, Shakespeare's contemporary poet, Ben Jonson, writes, "He was not of an age, but for all time" (Wilson 405). And the great Bard's works still apply and appeal to twenty-first century business leaders. Businessmen and authors, Norman Augustine and Kenneth Adelman, write, "The Bard has hit the boardroom…Shakespeare's plays remain as relevant today as they were in the sixteenth century. The lessons they teach are remarkably useful in today's tough corporate universe" (xii).

Works Cited

Augustine, Norman, and Kenneth Adelman. *Shakespeare in Charge: The Bard's Guide to Leading and Succeeding on the Business Stage.* Hyperion, 1999.

Wilson, Ian. *Shakespeare: The Evidence.* St. Martin's, 1993.

II. APA (American Psychological Association)

Text: The greatest of all dramatists, William Shakespeare (1564-1616), has truly stood the test of time. In a seventeenth century tribute, Shakespeare's contemporary poet, Ben Jonson, wrote, "He was not of an age, but for all time" (Wilson, 1993, p. 405). And the great Bard's works still apply and appeal to twenty-first century business leaders, as well. Businessmen and authors, Norman Augustine and Kenneth Adelman (1999), wrote, "The Bard has hit the boardroom...Shakespeare's plays remain as relevant today as they were in the sixteenth century. The lessons they teach are remarkably useful in today's tough corporate universe" (p. xii).

References

Augustine, N., & Adelman, K. (1999). *Shakespeare in charge: The bard's guide to leading and succeeding on the business stage.* New York: Hyperion.

Wilson, I. (1993). *Shakespeare: The evidence.* New York: St. Martin's Griffin.

III. CSE (Council of Science Editors)

Text: The greatest of all dramatists, William Shakespeare (1564-1616), has truly stood the test of time. In a seventeenth century tribute, Shakespeare's contemporary poet, Ben Jonson, wrote, "He was not of an age, but for all time" (1). And the great Bard's works still apply and appeal to twenty-first century business leaders. Businessmen and authors, Norman Augustine and Kenneth Adelman, wrote, "The Bard has hit the boardroom...Shakespeare's plays remain as relevant today as they were in the sixteenth century. The lessons they teach are remarkably useful in today's tough corporate universe" (2).

References Cited

1. Wilson, Ian. 1993. Shakespeare: The evidence. New York: St. Martin's Griffin, p 405.
2. Augustine, Norman, Kenneth Adelman. 1999. Shakespeare in Charge: The Bard's Guide to Leading and Succeeding on the Business Stage. New York: Hyperion, p xii.

IV. CMS (Chicago Manual Style)

Text: The greatest of all dramatists, William Shakespeare (1564-1616), has truly stood the test of time. In a seventeenth century tribute, Shakespeare's contemporary poet, Ben Jonson, wrote, "He was not of an age, but for all time."1 And the great Bard's works still apply and appeal to twenty-first century business leaders. Businessmen and authors, Norman Augustine and Kenneth Adelman, wrote, "The Bard has hit the boardroom...Shakespeare's plays remain as relevant today as they were in the sixteenth century. The lessons they teach are remarkably useful in today's tough corporate universe."2

Footnotes:

1. Wilson, Ian. *Shakespeare: The Evidence* (New York: St. Martin's Griffin, 1993), 405.

2. Augustine, Norman, and Kenneth Adelman. *Shakespeare in Charge: The Bard's Guide to Leading and Succeeding on the Business Stage* (New York: Hyperion, 1999), xii.

WORKING BIBLIOGRAPHY

Your research project will require both library and non-library research from a balanced variety of primary and secondary sources. You will need to keep a Working Bibliography of sources you find. Note this is called a "working" bibliography because it will undoubtedly change often. You will add new sources and discard those you will not use. Put each source on a separate 3x5 index card. Be sure to note where you found the source so that you can relocate it as needed. On your index card, put the following information:

1. Author's name (last name first)

2. Title of the book or "article" (MLA—book titles *italicized* & articles with quotation marks; APA— book titles *italicized* & articles without quotation marks).

3. Publication information (city, publisher, year for book; volume, date, for article).

4. Page numbers for articles or chapters; section numbers for newspapers; volume numbers for journals.

5. Notes about the location and contents of the source.

~ ~ ~

"A list of references is a set of thank-you notes. It is our way of acknowledging that, without the people whom we reference, we would not have done the work we did. We are members of a community of scholars. References permit our readers to trace our research back to its sources" (43).

—Lee Schulman

~ ~ ~

EXAMPLES OF MLA SOURCE CARDS

Topic Card	Book—one author

Jim Brimeyer   Topic Question: Did Edward DeVere, not Will Shakespeare, write the world famous plays and sonnets?

Wilson, Ian. *Shakespeare: The Evidence*. St. Martin's, 1993.

Book—two authors	Magazine

Ogburn, Jr. *Shakespeare, the Man Behind the Name.* William Morrow, 1962.

Reed, J.D. "Some ado about who or who was not, Shakespeare." *National Geographic*, Apr. 1964, pp. 155-176.

Newspaper Article	Personal Interview

Van Matre, Lyn. "Bard Questions." *Chicago Tribune*, 17 Jan. 1992, pp. 1-3.

Schenck, Peter. Personal interview. 23 Apr. 2012.

Internet

Heckinger, Paul. "Did Shakespeare Really Write His Own Plays? A Few Theories." *BBC America*, 21 Apr. 2010, www.bbcamerica.com/ anglophenia.

TAKING NOTES

    As you take notes from the sources you have gathered, remember that your research essay will not be a "patch-work quilt" of ideas and quotations from your sources pasted together to form a paper. Rather, your research essay will consist of your ideas and writing in your personal voice with occasional, brief references from experts to support your position. You are providing readers with a fresh view and opinion of your topic, not just a summary of your research findings.

Therefore, as you research, make notes of your own ideas about your topic—your reactions, your questions, your agreements, your disagreements—rather than a set of borrowed ideas or a long list of quotations. Use a paraphrase when you wish to put an author's ideas into your own words, which you then restate or interpret. In paraphrasing, you try to capture the heart of the message of the passage and put it into your own words. Write your paraphrase in your own personal voice and style. You may also wish to summarize a passage from a source by condensing the information of the original into your own words. Whether paraphrasing or summarizing, you must document the source to give proper acknowledgement.

You may also wish to use direct source quotations, copying verbatim, a source's exact words. You might do this when you locate a memorable statement, a pearl of wisdom, or striking wording, which will help support your position. Keep quotations short. Remember that you are writing this paper in your voice and style using research for support; you are not pasting research sections together with an occasional hint of your voice and writing style. Also, on your note cards or in your notes, list the source, the date, and page of your reference for easy insertion and documentation into your research essay text.

SAMPLE NOTECARD

Ogburn, Shakespeare, the Man...p. 3

Shakes lived 1564-1616, but never left any personal autobio. notes, letters, writings, etc. "It was not until 1709 that a biography of Shakespeare was offered."(good support for DeVere)

Writing Project 10-1A: First Draft Without Sources

After you feel you have gathered enough information, write your first draft in your own words without sources. This draft helps you synthesize your research into your own ideas and words and helps you see how much you know about your topic. Furthermore, writing a draft without sources helps you retain your personal writing voice, which you've worked hard to develop, rather than succumb to a starchy, phony, fake voice of pseudo-intelligentia, which buries your writing voice. Remember, this is a draft, not the final copy, so it need not be written perfectly this first time. So as with the writing process, don't get bogged down trying to create a perfect title, introduction, or conclusion, and don't worry yet about LOC's (lower order concerns) like spelling and punctuation and usage. You will edit those aspects later. Furthermore, don't worry about the required length at this stage. Just write what you know about your topic in your personal writing voice. You will add your sources for support later by referring to one of the next two chapters.

~ ~ ~

*"The main purpose of doing research is not
to summarize the work of others but to
assimilate and to build on it and to arrive
at your own understanding of the subject"* (4).
--Joseph Gibaldi

~ ~ ~

"The distinction between being a 'writer' and being a 'researcher' implies two different ways of being in the world—a writer creates, while a researcher collects—each occupying separate domains. This separation of the act of writing and researching, and the role of the writer and researcher, is the result of a failed term paper pedagogy that extends beyond the Freshman English course. But I will argue that the first-year writing course ought to be the place where students get practice being writers who ask questions that research can help answer. I propose that we expose the artificial distinctions between writer and researcher, writing and researching that conventional pedagogy reinforces. The research essay, not the research paper, is much more likely to erase these distinctions" (16-17).

—*Bruce Ballenger*

CHAPTER 11

Writing the Draft—With Sources – MLA

~ ~ ~

"A research paper is an adventure, an intellectual adventure
rather like solving a mystery: it is a form of exploration
that leads to discoveries that are new—
at least to you if not others" (5).
—Joseph Gibaldi

~ ~ ~

Once you have written your first draft and feel you control important aspects of your topic, you are ready to move to the next stage, adding evidence and quotations. Analyze your notes to determine which facts and quotations you will incorporate into your writing to support your ideas and position. Some writers tend to over-quote; they put in too many references and detract from their own ideas and writing style. Don't let your sources overshadow your writing. Keep your quotations short. Quote short phrases, occasionally a full sentence, guardedly two sentences, rarely more. If you must include a longer passage (five or more lines of your text), use a block indented format, which may only occur once, twice at most, in your paper.

MLA—Works Cited

Every source you use in your paper needs to be listed on your Works Cited Page. Do not list works that you collected for your working bibliography but do not use in your paper. Label the page Works Cited.

Center the words Works Cited (no quotation marks, underlining, bold print or italics), and number the page(s) in sequence after the last page of your text. Double space all entries. Begin each entry at the left margin, and tab indent any other line which applies to that entry. Alphabetize entries according to authors' last names unless no author is known. Then alphabetize by the first word of the title (excluding *A, An, The*). Book or periodical titles need to be printed in *italics*.

Entry Format

The eighth edition of the MLA Handbook uses a new model containing nine separate elements. Any given citation may not contain some of the elements or repeat others, but the MLA Handbook uses the following terminology and punctuation:

1. Author.
2. Title of source.
3. Title of container,
4. Other contributors,
5. Version,
6. Number,
7. Publisher,
8. Publication date.

NOTE: To save space, the following examples are single-spaced. **Proper MLA format requires double spacing in your paper.**

BOOKS
1. Book, one author
King, Stephen. *On Writing—A Memoir of the Craft.* Scribner's, 2000.

NOTE: When listing publishers, provide only necessary information. For example, give "Harper" only for Harper and Row, Publishers, Inc. Omit business abbreviations (Co., Corp., Inc., Ltd.). Use "UP" for University Press.

2. Book, two authors
Herrington, Anne J., and Marcia Curtis. *Persons in Process: Four Stories of Writing and Personal Development in College.* NCTE, 2000.

3. Book, three or more authors

Walvoord, Barbara E., et al. I*n the Long Run: A Study of Faculty in Three Writing Across the Curriculum Programs.* NCTE, 2000.

4. Book, editor

Reynolds, Mark, editor. *Two-Year College English: Essays for a New Century.* NCTE, 1994.

5. Book, revised edition

Lynn, Steven. *Texts and Contexts: Writing About Literature with Critical Theory.* 3rd ed., Longman, 2001.

6. Book, multivolume

Granville-Barker, Harley. *Prefaces to Shakespeare.* Vol. 3, Princeton UP, 1946. 4 vols.

7. Book, translated

Hesse, Hermann. *Steppenwolf.* Translated by Basil Creighton, Bantam, 1963.

8. Book, introduction, preface, foreword, afterword

Murray, Donald M. Foreword. *Composition Instructor's Survival Guide,* by Brock Dethier, Boynton, 1999.

9. Book, work in anthology or chapter in a book

Faulkner, William. "The Bear." *Literature: Reading Fiction, Poetry, Drama, and the Essay.* Edited by Robert DiYanni, Random, 1986, pp. 218-27.

Note: When pages are listed, "p." precedes single page numbers and "pp." precedes a range of page numbers.

10. Book, published interview in a book

Campbell, Joseph. Interview. "Myth as Metaphor." *An Open Life,* by Michael Toms, edited by John M. Maher and Dennie Briggs, Harper, 1989, pp. 21-54.

11. The Bible

Good News Bible: Today's English Version. American Bible Society, 1976.

12. Two or more books by the same author.

Hemingway, Ernest. *A Farewell to Arms.* Scribner, 1929.

---. *For Whom the Bell Tolls. Scribner,* 1940.

PERIODICALS

13. Journal article, all issues for one year paginated as a volume

Engbers, Susanna Kelly. "Here We Go 'Round and 'Round: A

Process of Peer Evaluation." *Teaching English in the Two-Year College*, vol. 36, no. 4, May 2009, pp. 397-401.

Note: For journal and magazine articles, "vol." precedes the volume number and "no." precedes the issue number.

Note: Abbreviate the months (Jan., Dec.) except May, June, July.

Note: If no author is given, alphabetize according to the first main word (other than A, An, The) of its title.

14. Journal article, each issue newly paginated

Sowder, Wilbur H., Jr. "The Thing's the Play, Doing Hamlet." *English Journal*, vol. 82, no. 4, Apr. 1993, pp. 65-67.

15. Magazine article, weekly or monthly

Lazarus, Edward. "Four Myths About the Supreme Court." *Time*, 8 June 2009, pp. 30-31.

16. Newspaper article

Swenson, Jim. "Emotional ceremony honors veterans." *Telegraph Herald* [Dubuque, IA], 12 Nov. 2017, 19A.

NOTE: If the city of publication is not included in the name of a locally published newspaper, add the city in square brackets, not underlined, after the newspaper name.

17. Interview—published

Kline, Kevin. "Bottom as a Romantic Figure: An Interview with Kevin Kline." Interviewed by Mike LoMonico. *Shakespeare*, vol. 32, no. 2, 1999, pp. 5-7.

OTHER SOURCES

18. Interview – face to face, phone, e-mail

Brimeyer, James L. Personal interview. 15 July 2017.

Brimeyer, James L. Phone interview. 15 July 2017.

Brimeyer, James L. E-mail interview. 15 July 2017.

19. VIDEOTAPE or DVD

Wuthering Heights. Directed by David Skynner, performance by Robert Cavanah, Orla Brady, Anchor Bay Entertainment, 1998.

20. CD-ROM

Grammar for the Real World. Knowledge Adventure, 1998.

21. TV or Radio Program

Doctorow, E.L. "Television interview with Bill Moyers." *A World of Ideas with Bill Moyers*, PBS, 1989.

22. Online book

Bronte, Emily. *Wuthering Heights*. 1847, The Project Gutenberg eBook, 2007, www.gutenberg.org/files/768/768-h/768-h. htm.

23. Online magazine with URL

Kleiner, Carolyn, and Mary Lord. "The Cheating Game." *U.S. News & World Report*, 22 Nov. 1999, www.docsfewbanks. com/pdf/world-news-article-4.

24. Online magazine with DOI (Digital Object Identifier)

Yazdani, Masoud, and Donald Bligh. "Computer-supported cooperative learning in a virtual university." *Journal of Computer Assisted Learning*, vol. 15, no. 1, 18 June 2002, pp. 2-13, ERIC, doi:10,1046/j.365-2729.1999.151071.x.

Note: DOI provides a direct link to identify and locate published, internet locations. Citing a DOI is preferable to citing a URL.

25. Work from a library subscription service

Wakefield, Lawrence. "Cooling Trend in America." *Futurist*, May-June 2002, vol. 15, Academic Search Premier, EBSCO.

Note: If the service gives only the starting page number of the article's original print publication (e.g. i"), give the number followed by hyphen, a space, and a period: "p. 192 -."

❖ **Other MLA citations not included in this book may be found in** *MLA Handbook*. 8ᵗʰ ed. New York: The Modern Language Association of America, 2009.

PRACTICE 11A: MLA Citations Use the information about American author William Faulkner and his works provided in the following items to create an MLA Works Cited Page with correct order, indentation, and necessary punctuation.

1. A biographical magazine article about William Faulkner's life appears in the June 2000 issue of *Biography Magazine*. The five-page article began on page 97, ran to page 99, and continued on pages 112 and 113. The article was written by Melissa Burdick Harmon and was entitled "William Faulkner: The Sound and the Fury of a Self-Destructive Life."

2. Irving Howe, Distinguished Professor of English at the City University of New York, wrote a book entitled *William Faulkner,*

a Critical Study. This third edition of the book was published in 1975 by The University of Chicago Press.

3. A written interview called "WILLIAM FAULKNER: AN INTERVIEW" appears on pages 67 to 82 in the book *William Faulkner: Three Decades of Criticism*. The book was co-edited by Frederick J. Hoffman and Olga W. Vickery. The book was published in New York in 1960 by Harcourt Brace. The person who interviewed Faulkner was Jean Stein.

4. A face-to-face interview was completed with Professor Gene E. Uss, noted Faulkner expert, on March 21, 2017.

5. At web site <http://www.olemiss.edu/depts/english/ms-writers/dir/faulkner_william/>, John B. Padgett, professor of English at the University of Mississippi, wrote an article dated December 12, 2002, called "William Faulkner" for the on-line magazine *The Mississippi Writer's Page*. The article was retrieved from the on-line site on May 4, 2017.

NOTE: *Online sources may require combining documentation information.*

PRACTICE 11B: Creating Sources—MLA   Using MLA format, create a source to fit each of the following entries. Use humor, if possible, but keep it in good taste.

1. A book by a single author
2. A book by two authors
3. An article in a weekly magazine
4. An article in a daily newspaper
5. An internet article in a journal
6. A video
7. A face-to-face interview

PLAGIARISM

Plagiarism, purposely offering another's writing or ideas as your own, constitutes ethical dishonesty. The Northeast Iowa Community College Student Catalog and Handbook defines plagiarism as follows: Students are plagiarizing if they:

use direct quotes without quotation marks and textual citation of the material; paraphrase without crediting the source; present another's ideas as their own without citing the source; submit material developed by someone else as their own (this includes purchasing or borrowing a paper or copying a disk); or submit a paper or assignment for which so much help has been received that the writing is significantly different from their own.

In addition, research papers are readily available for purchase on the internet. Submitting a lifted paper of this nature also constitutes plagiarism and ethical dishonesty. These papers are usually easily detectable because they frequently lack depth and because they stray from a writer's personal voice, which causes instructors' alarms to sound and red flags to rise.

You need to give credit by documenting your sources for direct quotations; paraphrases or summaries; tables, charts, diagrams, or graphs; and specific examples, figures, or facts. As a guideline, remember: **When in doubt, document!**

PRACTICE 11C: Avoiding Plagiarism in MLA Format   Read the passage and its citation. Next, analyze each sample and indicate whether it is plagiarized or cited satisfactorily; then, explain your analysis.

ORIGINAL PASSAGE:

When it's successful, the research essay encourages students to own their own words and the insights they glean from following those words. And just as it revives the notion of authorship effaced by the objective report of the conventional term paper, it strengthens the rhetorical relationship between writer and reader. As my students become writers who research, rather than researchers who have to write, I hope they expand the role they claimed earlier in the course as writers of personal essays.

From: Ballenger, Bruce. *Beyond Notecards: Rethinking the Freshman Research Paper*. Heinemann, 1999. (The passage is taken from page 94.)

1. Research writing expert Bruce Ballenger believes that students write successful research papers in their own words (94).

2. Students should become writers who research, rather than researchers who have to write.

3. Research writing expert Bruce Ballenger hopes that research writers "expand the role they claimed earlier in the course as writers of personal essays" (94).

4. The book *Beyond Notecards* suggests that "students become

writers who research, rather than researchers who have to write" (Ballenger 94).

5. When research writers compose in their own words, they revive the notion of authorship effaced by the objective report of the conventional term paper.

USING CITATIONS

Use **leads** (beginning, middle, end) or **blend** your sources into your writing in a smooth, seamless way. Leads may offer an explanation or commentary on the quotation's purpose and may establish the authoritative expertise of the person being quoted. MLA style requires that leads be written in **present tense** and that all quotations are placed within quotation marks or blocked (double indentation of five or more lines of the your text). Use parenthetical references to document the author's last name and the exact page numbers. No punctuation or abbreviation for page or pages is needed inside the parentheses. If you blend the author's name into your context, place only the page number in parentheses. The works cited entry will provide other publication information (publisher, date, volume, total pages, etc.). Remember, you document sources to credit your references and to provide a list for readers to investigate if they so choose.

~ ~ ~

"In a way, quotations are orphans: words that have been taken from their original contexts and that need to be integrated into their new textual surroundings... The point we want to emphasize is that quoting what 'they say' must always be connected with what you say" (40).
Gerald Graff and Kathy Birkenstein

~ ~ ~

LEADS & CITATIONS

Beginning Lead, One Book with Two Authors

This research paper must focus on persuasion as its rhetorical purpose. Persuasion will enable the writer to defend his or her argument convincingly. James D. Lester and James D. Lester, Jr., noted research writing experts, argue, "Persuasion enables you to reject the general attitudes about a problem and to affirm new theories, advance a solution, recommend a course of action, and invite the reader into an intellectual dialogue" (11).

Work Cited

Lester, James D., and James D. Lester, Jr. *The Essential Guide to Writing Research Papers*. Longman, 1999.

Middle Lead, Personal Interview

Drafting the research essay text can pose problems for some college writers. "Students should write their first drafts without sources," suggests Jim Brimeyer, composition instructor at Northeast Iowa Community College. "This helps writers digest and synthesize their research while writing in their personal voice." Furthermore, writers using research should avoid a "patch-work quilt" of strung together quotations or sources and should avoid depending on one source for the bulk of their references.

Work Cited

Brimeyer, James L. Personal interview. 16 Jan. 2017.

End Lead, Internet Source

The MLA (Modern Language Association) documentation format is well known and widely used by scholars and students. "MLA guidelines are also currently used by over 125 scholarly and literary journals, newsletter, and magazines with circulations over one thousand; by hundreds of smaller periodicals; and by many university and commercial presses," states the MLA Web Site.

Work Cited

MLA Style. Modern Language Association of America. 1 Sept. 2000, www.mla.org.

Block Quotation, Article

Writers using research must write in their own personal voice. Writers must remember that this academic assignment calls for them to write using research for support, NOT to research and use writing for support. The article "Giving Voice to Your Nonfiction" states:

> Your leads, your verbs, your descriptions, or your quotes can convey subliminal messages that evoke responses, conscious or subconscious, to your writing. But a single stylistic technique alone does not always give you voice. Your overall success at finding the

voice for your writing depends ultimately on the way you blend all the ingredients of your writing. It depends on your ability to massage language to suit your needs. (Brooks 26)

Writers can write livelier, more readable research prose by retaining their personal writing voice rather than adapting a phony, starchy style influenced by research quotations.

Work Cited

Brooks, Terri. "Giving Voice to Your Nonfiction." *Writer's Digest,* Sept. 1990, pp. 26-32.

Secondhand Source, an Author's Published Account of Another's Remarks

Regarding the correct usage of who/whom, James Thurber says, "The number of people who use 'whom' and 'who' wrongly is appalling. To address a person one knows by a 'Whom are you?' is a mark either of incredible lapse of memory or inexcusable arrogance" (qtd. in Zinsser 170). Obviously Mr. Thurber was not burdened with many other things to worry about in life.

Work Cited

Zinsser, William. *On Writing Well.* 2nd ed., Harper, 1980.

Embedded Quotation, Book with One Author

The introduction to *Beyond Notecards* suggests that we teachers and students view the research paper not so much as an exercise in using proper conventions and mechanics of quoting and citing sources, but rather as a "spirit of inquiry, to certain habits of the mind that often seem to inform investigations in many disciplines" (Ballenger 16).

Work Cited

Ballenger, Bruce. *Beyond Notecards: Rethinking the Freshman Research Paper*. Heinemann, 1999.

NOTE: When embedding quotations, try to keep the quoted portion to one or two lines of your text.

AVOID THE FOLLOWING:

✓ **Floating (Hanging) Quotation – a reference without a lead.**

This research paper must focus on persuasion as its rhetorical purpose. Persuasion will enable the writer to defend his or her argument convincingly. "Persuasion enables you to reject the general attitudes about a problem and to affirm new theories, advance a solution, recommend a course of action, and invite the reader into an intellectual dialogue" (Lester and Lester 11). The writer will use logical, supporting, research evidence to persuade the reader to act or at least consider the writer's position.

Work Cited

Lester, James D., and James D. Lester, Jr. *The Essential Guide to Writing Research Papers*. Longman, 1999.

✓ **Beginning paragraphs with a quotation.**
"Persuasion enables you to reject the general attitudes about a problem and to affirm new theories, advance a solution, recommend a course of action, and invite the reader into an intellectual dialogue" (Lester and Lester 11), argue the authors of *The Essential Guide to Writing Research Papers*. You, the writer, will use logical, supporting, research evidence to persuade the reader to act or at least consider your position.

Work Cited

Lester, James D., and James D. Lester, Jr. *The Essential Guide to Writing Research Papers*. Longman, 1999.

PRACTICE 11D: Leads   Develop (1) a different lead (beginning, middle, end), plus one embedded quotation, written in MLA format (present tense), (2) a parenthetical citation, and (3) a Works Cited entry for the passages that follow.

(A) "In the thousands of years before him, or the 400 years since, no writer has profoundly captured the heart and admiration of the human race as has William Shakespeare. His plays have forever enlarged our comprehension of those inner forces that drive and haunt, agonize and madden people. Yet we know little of his private world and the source of his astounding genius. We do not have a single letter or memoir or diary note in his hand."—This excerpt is taken from the opening page 35 of an eight-page article in the October 1986 issue of *Readers' Digest*. The article is entitled "The Shakespeare Nobody Knows," and it is written by Leo Rosten.

(B) Shakespeare "is indeed himself in many ways in character what one can only describe as Christ-like; that is gentle, kindly, honest, brave and true, with deep understanding and quick sympathy for all living things."—This item is found on page 207 of a book entitled

Shakespeare's Imagery and What It Tells Us, published in 1958 in Cambridge, England, by the Cambridge University Press. The book is written by Caroline Spurgeon, a renowned Shakespearean scholar.

(C) "We also have the anecdotes of Shakespeare's godson William D'Avenant about him, but scholars tend not to take D'Avenant's tales as seriously as perhaps they should because Will D. got loaded one night and told people that he was Shakespeare's bastard son."—This information is gleaned from the following web site: <http://www. jetlink.net/~massij/shakes/author/html>—on August 24, 2017. This article entitled "The Authorship Issue" is written by J. Massi and was placed on-line on Monday, April 21, 1997.

(D) "Every time I reread a play by Shakespeare, I see something more that I missed in my earlier readings. Shakespeare's plays are not exhaustible." – This was stated on July 15, 2017, in an interview with Jim Brimeyer, Shakespeare instructor at Northeast Iowa Community College.

MLA FORMAT - PAPER LAYOUT

Use good quality 8.5" x 11" white paper and a high quality, clear printer. Print on one side only, and use 12 pt. font, preferably Times New Roman typeface. Set one-inch margins for each page: bottom, right, left. **Double-space the text throughout, including outline, quotations, and works cited page.** Set paragraph indentations to one-half inch. Some instructors require a title page and/or outline while others do not.

Heading and Title

If no title page or outline is required, begin at the right margin, one-half inch from the top of page one. Type your last name, space, and 1. Double-space. On the left margin, type your full name, your instructor's name, the course and number, and the date on four separate lines. Then center the title, but do not italicize it, use quotation marks around it, type it in all capital letters, or bold it. Double-space between the title and first line of text.

Your name

Your instructor

Course name and number

Day Month Year

(*Double-space→*)

Title

Title Page

   If a title page is required, center the title one-third of the way from the top. Do not underline the title, italicize it, put quotations marks around the title, or put it in all capital letters. Then skip a space and center *by*; then skip a space and print your name, address, city, state, and zip code. Move most of the way to the bottom where you will print the course number and course name. On the next line, print your college's name. Then skip a space and print *Instructor*: followed by the instructor's name. Skip a space and center the day, month, year, using no commas.

<u>Title Page Model</u>

Title

by

Your name

Address

City, State Zip

Course number and course title

College/University Name

Instructor: title, first, last name

Day Month Year

Pagination

Type your last name followed by the page number (Arabic 1, 2, 3, 4...) in the upper right hand corner of each page of your text, one half inch from the top and against the one-inch right margin. Pagination should begin with page one of your text. A one-page outline needs no page number. However, for an outline of more than one page, use lower case Roman numerals following your name (ex. Jones ii).

Outline

If your instructor requires a formal outline (topic or sentence), attach it to the front of the paper. In the upper left corner, type (double-spaced) your name on line 1, instructor's name on line 2, the course title and number on line 3, and the date (day month year) on line 4. Then center the title of your paper at the top of the first page of your outline. Next, type and underline the word <u>Thesis</u> followed by a colon. Then type your thesis, double-spaced below the title. Use Roman numerals for level one, capital letters for level two, Arabic numbers for level three, and lower case letters for level four. At any level, you must provide at least two items. A topic or phrase outline must show parallel grammatical structure, and a sentence outline must be written in complete sentences. Since the outline provides a simple roadmap for readers, list only main points of your paper, and keep the length of the outline to a page, a page and one-half at most. Remember: **double-space the outline**.

<u>Outline Form</u>

Title

<u>Thesis</u>:

I.

    A.

        1.

            a.

            b.

        2.

    B.

II.

Using Sources

Remember: research writing means using your writing supported by the research. It does not mean pasting together a number of long quotations with your writing tying the quotations together. You are a writer who uses research, not a researcher who uses writing to develop the research essay. Therefore, use short quotations only as necessary to support an important idea, to clarify technical terms, or to strengthen your position by using the words of an expert or authority. Smoothly blend quotations into your text using present tense leads (Williams emphasizes, "...) and embedded quotations to identify your sources. Use vivid tag verbs (Jones argues, claims, concludes, endorses, observes, refutes, suggests...) to add more life and focus to the quotations and sources. Try to favor direct quotations rather than paraphrasing or summarizing your sources. Avoid hanging (floating) quotations, which are not tied to your text. Limit the length of the quotations, and as a guideline, limit long quotations to one, two at most, block quotations (five or more lines of your text).

Works Cited Page

Type your last name and page number at the upper right-hand corner. Center the words Works Cited. List all sources used in your paper alphabetically by last name of the author. If no author is available, alphabetize by the first main word of the title, excluding A, An, The.

Appendix

If your text refers your readers to an appendix which follows the Works Cited page, center the word Appendix; add identifying capital letters for more than one appendix. Double-space and type the title of the appendix (without italics or all capitals or underlining or bold). Double space; indent to the one-half inch mark, and type your text.

"Should my research appendix be added or removed?"

SAMPLE RESEARCH PAPER (Modified)—MLA FORMAT

Deanne Wulfekuhle

Instructor Jim Brimeyer

ENG 106: Composition II

9 April 2017

Testing: Stop the Madness!

<u>Thesis</u>: Standardized tests harm children more than they help children; therefore, children should not be given standardized tests.

I. Standardized tests are used to measure intelligence.

   A. Testing starts the moment of birth.

   B. The results are used to compare students across the U.S.

II. As a young child, I didn't believe anyone looked at the scores.

   A. The tests aren't graded.

   B. The scores are only compared to other students.

III. Timed tests cannot measure intelligence.

   A. Timing tests add extra pressure to the students.

   B. The timing requirement remains unfair and inaccurate.

IV. Testing techniques inaccurately measure intelligence.

   A. Many testers have never taken a multiple-choice test before.

   B. Multiple-choice tests cannot possibly measure how well a student can read or write.

V. Tests waste everyone's time.

   A. Too much emphasis is placed on test scores.

   B. One test can take three days of class time.

Wulfekuhle 1

Testing: Stop the Madness!

Some parents say, "APGAR; what is APGAR?" Many parents may not even realize that their child is tested not once, but twice within the first five minutes of life. Testing starts the moment of birth and continues throughout life. APGAR tests measure newborns for appearance (color), pulse (heartbeat), grimace (reflex), activity (muscle tone), and respiration (breathing). The test is given at one minute and at five minutes after birth. Unfortunately, the APGAR test only starts the testing madness!

Remember the week long standardized tests we all took in grade school? Now, my own children are taking these same tests. I often ask myself, "Do teachers look at the results of these tests? Does anyone look at the results?" In a few years, I will be teaching my own classroom. I will be distributing these same standardized tests to my own students. For these reasons, I decided to research this subject. Should we give our young children one standardized test across the nation to prove intelligence? No, we shouldn't. Standardized tests harm children more than they help them; therefore, children should not be given standardized tests.

Standardized tests supposedly measure what students have learned about a particular school subject. Measuring students across the nation according to one test cannot possibly measure students equally or fairly. For example, how can students in rural Oregon be compared with students from urban Florida, and more importantly, why would anyone want to compare them? When students take these tests, they feel the pressures of scoring high.

Unfortunately, most students fail to put forth their best effort. They only are interested in getting the tests finished. Kids don't need the extra pressures of scoring high on a multiple-choice test just to make the school or themselves look good. Schools should focus more on teaching children rather than on testing and comparing children.

Furthermore, a major problem with standardized testing occurs because the standardized tests do not match or align with the curriculum that students are learning. Testing should be used as a part of student learning, but if the items on the test don't match the material being taught, the test cannot be considered a valid measure of learning. Nancy S. Cole, President of Educational Testing Service, states:

> Large numbers of educators set specifications, write questions, and review most tests in wide use. However, without a clear understanding of how to align tests with teaching, such processes are hollow. One of the failings of the reform era is our limited progress in understanding this alignment. (1)

Schools should not be funded according to how their students perform on certain tests. Gerarda Kepler, a psychology teacher at Northeast Iowa Community College, says, "Schools should not be paid according to the results from their test scores. In fact, schools that score lower on tests need more funding than schools that score high on tests. Many times, the schools that score lower are located in poverty areas of the county." George W. Bush's plan, "No Child Left Behind," may have caused low scoring schools to dramatically drop their scores even lower. These schools actually need more funding to better educate their children and to introduce new technology to their students.

Alfie Kohn, an author who believes standardized tests simply waste time, jokes in *Kappan* Magazine, "Don't let anyone tell you that standardized tests are not accurate measures. The truth of the matter is that they offer a remarkably precise method for gauging the size of the houses near the school where the test was administered!" (349) Kohn believes that affluent families and schools are better able to afford products to help them raise their test scores even higher. Kohn also states in his

Wulfekule 3

book, *The Case Against Standardized Testing,* "When poorer schools manage to scrape together enough money to buy materials to help them improve their test scores, it's often at the expense of books and other educational resources they really need" (37).

Another problem with standardized testing, multiple-choice format, should also be investigated. How can filling in dots measure intelligence? Kids need to learn how to take a multiple-choice test before they can actually score well on one. Many elementary age children have never experienced a multiple-choice test before. Standardized tests supposedly measure intelligence in many different subjects. Reading, writing, vocabulary, math, and other subjects are included on the tests. If tests check to see how well children can read and write, then the tests should contain reading and writing. How can reading and writing be tested when reading and writing are excluded from the tests? Most tests consist of filling in dots! This kind of testing cannot possibly measure how well children can read, write, or comprehend.

According to Louise Ames, author of *Child Care and Development,* "One of the most important ways the mind reveals itself is through the things the child says" (73). But yet, when standardized tests are given in school, no speaking is allowed! Many times standardized tests contain fill-in-the-dots, essays, or matching testing instructions, which are all inaccurate measures of intelligence.

Sandy Klaus, elementary school principal at the Starmont Community School District, says, "The tests are unfair because half of the test is set up to pass, and half of the test is set up to fail. "Why would anyone want to set up a test that only half of the questions could be answered correctly? This becomes hard for some parents to understand. Klaus wishes that the public would understand that if their school scores low, it doesn't necessarily mean that the system's standards are lower than other schools'.

Wulfekuhle 4

The school may be teaching things that are not being tested. Students may actually be learning far above expectations.

According to Anita Woolfolk, author of *Educational Psychology*, "Standardized test scores not only are inaccurate measures of intelligence, but they are (many times) misinterpreted because the numbers are thought to be a precise measurement of a student's ability. No test provides a perfect picture of a person's abilities; a test is only a small sample of behavior" (530).

Can the results of standardized tests be used as useful tools for determining anything? "Intelligence should be defined as whatever intelligence tests measure," author Benjamin Lahey states in *Psychology*. "We cannot be very   confident that intelligence tests are very good at measuring intelligence, but intelligence tests are fairly good at picking out those individuals who perform well on tasks that seem to require intelligence" (267). Then I ask myself why the tests are named intelligence tests?

Kids feel enough pressure these days; they should not face the pressures of scoring well on standardized tests besides. Schools should spend more time teaching students than testing them. It would not bother me one bit if my children would never take another standardized test as long as they live! Testing starts on the APGAR test, and it continues throughout life. When will we ever STOP THE MADNESS?

Wulfekuhle 5

Works Cited

Ames, Louise. *Childcare and Development.* Lippinott, 1970.

Cole, Nancy S. "Determining What is to be Taught: The Role of Assessment." Eisenhower National Clearinghouse, 1999, www.worldcat.org/title/assessment-that-informs-practice.

Keppler, Gerarda. Personal interview. 15 Mar. 2017.

Klaus, Sandy. E-mail interview. 1 Feb. 2017.

Kohn, Alfie. "Fighting the Tests: A Practical Guide to Rescuing Our Schools." *Kappan,* vol. 82, no. 5. Jan. 2001, pp. 348-357.

- - -. *The Case Against Standardized Testing.* Heinemann, 2005.

Lahey, Benjamin. *Psychology.* McGraw, 1998.

Woolfolk, Anita. *Educational Psychology.* Allyn, 1980.

CHAPTER 12

Writing the Draft—With Sources – APA

~ ~ ~

"As an introduction to research, first year students should be encouraged to embrace their topics with wonder, passion, and a strong desire to find out, rather than to prove" (128).
—Bruce Ballenger

~ ~ ~

Once you have written your first draft and feel you control important aspects of your topic, you are ready to move to the next stage, adding evidence and quotations. Analyze your notes to determine which facts and quotations you will incorporate into your writing to support your ideas and position. Some writers tend to over-quote; they put in too many references and detract from their own ideas and writing style. Don't let your sources overshadow your writing. Keep your quotations short. Quote short phrases, occasionally a full sentence, guardedly two sentences, rarely more. If you must include a longer passage (40 or more words), use a block indented format, which may only occur once, twice at most, in your paper.

APA—References

Every source you use in your paper needs to be listed on your

Reference Page. Center the term "References"; do not underline, use quotation marks, or italicize it. Number the page(s) in sequence after the last page of your text. Double space all entries. Begin each entry at the left margin, and tab indent any following line which applies to that entry. Alphabetize entries according to authors' last names unless no author is known. Then alphabetize by the first word of the title (excluding *A, An, The*). Book or periodical titles need to be printed in italics. In APA format, write the titles like ordinary sentences: capitalize only the first word of a title, the first word following a colon within a title, and proper names.

Entry Formats:
Books:

Author(s). (Year). *Book title*. City, State: Publisher.
NOTE: do not add the state to commonly known large cities like Chicago, New York, Los Angeles, Dallas. Omit unneeded terms, such as *Publishers, Co.,* or *Inc.,* but retain the words *Books* and *Press.*
Periodicals:

Author(s). (Year, date). Article title. *Publication title*, volume number (for journal), issue number in parentheses (if applicable): page numbers.

NOTE: Capitalize all significant words of periodical titles.

NOTE: To save space, the following examples are single-spaced. **Proper APA pagination requires double spacing in your paper.**
BOOKS

1. **Book, one author**
   King, S. (2000). *On writing—A memoir of the craft*. New York: Scribner.
NOTE: If no author is given, alphabetize according to the first main word (other than *A, An, The*) of its title, then the date (in parentheses).

2. **Book, two or three authors**
   Herrington, A. J., & Curtis, M. (2000). *Persons in process: Four stories of writing and personal development in college*. Urbana, IL: NCTE.

3. **Book, four or more authors**
   Walvoord, B. E., Hunt, L. L., Dowling, H. F., Jr., & McMahon, J. D. (2000). *In the long run: A study of faculty in three writing across the curriculum programs*. Urbana, IL: NCTE.

4. **Book, editor**
   Reynolds, M. (Ed.). (1994). *Two-year college English: Essays for a new century*. Urbana, IL: NCTE.

5. **Book, revised edition**
   Lynn, S. (2001). *Texts and contexts: Writing about literature with critical theory* (3rd ed.). New York: Longman.

6. **Book, multivolume**
   Granville-Barker, H. (1946). *Prefaces to Shakespeare* (Vols.1-4). Princeton, NJ: Princeton University Press.

7. **Book, translated**
   Hesse, H. (1963). *Steppenwolf* (B. Creighton, Trans.). New York: Bantam Books. (Original work published 1929).

PERIODICALS

8. **Journal article, all issues for one year paginated as a volume**
   Wilson, S. (2000). When computers come to English class. *Teaching English in the two-year college*, 27(4), 387-399.

NOTE: If no author is given, alphabetize according to the first main word (other than *A, An, The*) of its title, then the date (in parentheses).

9. **Journal article, each issue newly paginated**
   Tye, B. B., & O'Brien, L. (2002). Why are experienced teachers leaving the profession? *Phi Delta Kappan*, 84(1), 24-32.

10. **Magazine article, weekly or monthly**
    Wolffe, R., & Hirsch, M. (2003, February 3). Target: Iraq: will war make us more secure? *Newsweek*, 22-28.

11. **Newspaper article**
    Campbell, C. (2007, December 9). O'Connor book remembers 'spirit of Wahlert'. *Telegraph Herald [Dubuque, IA]*, p. 1C.

12. **Interview - published**
    LoMonico, M. (1999). Bottom as a romantic figure: An interview with Kevin Kline. *Shakespeare*, 3(2), 5-7.

OTHER SOURCES

13. **Interview – face to face, phone, e-mail**
    Do not include in your reference list personal interviews, e-mail, telephone conversations, lectures, and like communications that cannot be consulted by your readers. Instead, provide an in-text citation by using the name of the person, the words *personal communication*, and the full date.

Example: According to NICC Shakespeare instructor J. L. Brimeyer, Shakespeare lived during the Elizabethan Age of British Literature (personal communication, January 28, 2017).

14. VIDEOTAPE or DVD

Mallon, T. (Producer), & Hale, C. & Wyche-Smith, S. (Writers). (1988). *Using student writing groups* [videotape]. (Available from Wordshops Productions, 3832 North Seventh Street, Tacoma, WA 98406)

15. CD-ROM

Vashem, Y. (1997). *Return to life: The story of the Holocaust survivors* [CD-ROM]. Jerusalem: Icons LTD.

16. TV or Radio Program

Moyers, B. (1989). Bill Moyers interviews Sisslea Bok. *A world of ideas with Bill Moyers.* New York: Public Broadcasting Service.

17. Online book

Freud, S. (1911). *The interpretation of dreams* (3ʳᵈ ed.). (A.A. Brill, Trans.). Retrieved February 5, 2017 from PsychWeb web site: http://www.psychwww.com./books/interp/toc.htm

18. Online magazine

With DOI (Digital Object Identifier)

English, S., & Yazdani, M. (2002, June 18). Computer-supported cooperative learning in a virtual university. *Journal of Computer Assisted Learning,* 15(1), 2-13. doi:10.1046/ j.1365-2729.1999.151071.x

(NOTE: DOI provides a direct link to identify and locate published, internet locations.)

Without DOI (Digital Object Identifier)

Kleiner, C., & Lord, M. (1999, November 22). The Cheating game. *U.S. News & World Report.* Retrieved February 5, 2017 from http://nl4.newsbank.com

19. Work from a library subscription service

Weber, P. (1993, July/August). Saving the coral reefs. *Futurist,* pp. 28-33. Retrieved June 8, 2017 from SIRS Knowledge Source database (SIRS Researcher).

NOTE: Other APA citations not included in this book may be found in *Publication manual of the American psychological association.* (2010). (6ᵗʰ ed). Washington, DC: APA.

PRACTICE 12A: APA Citations   Use the information on brain research and its connection to learning provided in the following items to create an APA Reference page with correct order, indentation, punctuation, etc.

1. In 2002, Mel Levine, M.D. wrote a 13-chapter book entitled *A Mind at a Time*. The book was published in New York by Simon & Schuster.

2. The book *Making Connections: Teaching and the Human Brain* was published by the Association for Supervision and Curriculum Development (ASCD) in Alexandria, Virginia. The copyright date on the book is 1991. The book was co-authored by Renate Nummela Caine and Geoffrey Caine.

3. Daniel Coleman, Ph.D., wrote an article entitled "The New Thinking on Smarts." This article began on page 4 and ended on page 7 of *USA Weekend*, a weekly magazine. The article came out on Sept. 8, 1995.

4. The third edition of Tony Buzan's book entitled *Use Both Sides of Your Brain* was published in New York in 1991 by Penguin Books.

5. In an on-line magazine, *Brain & Mind Electronic Magazine* on Neuroscience (February-May 2001, issue # 12), Renato M.E. Sabbatini, professor of neuroscience at the State University of Campinas, Brazil, wrote an article "The Evolution of Intelligence." The article was retrieved on February 4, 2017, at the following web site: http://www.epub.org.br/cm/n11/mente/eisntein/rats.html.

6. The 30-minute video "Thinking Allowed" was released in 1988 by Thinking Allowed Productions, 5966 Zinn Drive, Oakland, California 94611. It was written by Virginia Satir and produced and directed by Arthur Block.

PRACTICE 12B: Creating Sources—APA   Using APA format, create a reference to fit each of the following entries. Use humor, if possible, but keep it in good taste.

1. A book by a single author
2. An article in a daily newspaper
3. A book by two authors
4. An internet article in a journal
5. An article in a weekly magazine
6. A video

PLAGIARISM

Plagiarism, purposely offering another's writing or ideas as your own, constitutes ethical dishonesty. The Northeast Iowa Community College Student Catalog and Handbook defines plagiarism as follows: Students are plagiarizing if they:

> use direct quotes without quotation marks and textual citation of the material; paraphrase without crediting the source; present another's ideas as their own without citing the source; submit material developed by someone else as their own (this includes purchasing or borrowing a paper or copying a disk); or submitting a paper or assignment for which so much help has been received that the writing is significantly different from their own.

In addition, research papers are readily available for purchase on the internet. Submitting a lifted paper of this nature also constitutes plagiarism and ethical dishonesty. These papers are usually easily detectable because they frequently lack depth and because they stray so far from a writer's personal voice, which causes instructors' alarms to sound and red flags to rise.

You need to give credit by documenting your sources for direct quotations; paraphrases or summaries; tables, charts, diagrams, or graphs; and specific examples, figures, or facts. As a guideline, remember: **When in doubt, document!**

PRACTICE 12C: Avoiding Plagiarism in APA Format   Read the passage and its citation. Then analyze each sample and indicate whether it is plagiarized or cited satisfactorily; then, explain your analysis.

ORIGINAL PASSAGE:

When it's successful, the research essay encourages students to own their own words and the insights they glean from following those words. And just as it revives the notion of authorship effaced by the objective report of the conventional term paper, it strengthens the rhetorical relationship between writer and reader. As my students become writers who research, rather than researchers who have to write, I hope they expand the role they claimed earlier in the course as writers of personal essays.

From: Ballenger, Bruce. (1999). *Beyond notecards: Rethinking the freshman research paper*. Portsmouth, NH: Heinemann.
(This passage is taken from page 94.)

1. Research writing expert Ballenger (1999) urged students to write successful research papers in their own words (p. 94).
2. Students should become writers who research, rather than researchers who have to write.
3. Ballenger (1999) hoped that research writers "expand the role they claimed earlier in the course as writers of personal essays" (p. 94).
4. The book *Beyond Notecards* suggested that "students become writers who research, rather than researchers who have to write" (Ballenger, 1999, p. 94).
5. When research writers compose in their own words, they revive the notion of authorship effaced by the objective report of the conventional term paper.

USING SOURCES AND QUOTATIONS

Use **leads** (beginning, middle, end) or **blend** your sources into your writing in a smooth, seamless way. Leads may offer an explanation or commentary on the quotation's purpose and may establish the authoritative expertise of the person being quoted. APA style requires that leads be written in **past** or **present perfect tense** and that all quotations are placed within quotation marks or blocked (40 or more words). Use parenthetical references to document the author's last name, year, and the exact page numbers. Use *p.* or *pp.* for page or pages inside the parentheses. If you blend the author's name into your context, place only *p.* and the page number in parentheses. Most online sources do not provide page numbers. Therefore, use the abbreviation *para.* plus the paragraph number (para. 7). The references page entry will provide other publication information (publisher, date, volume, total pages, etc.). Remember, you document sources to credit your references and to provide a list for readers to investigate if they so choose.

~ ~ ~

"In a way, quotations are orphans: words that have been taken from their original contexts and that need to be integrated into their new textual surroundings... The point we want to emphasize is that quoting what 'they say' must always be connected with what you say" (40).
Gerald Graff and Kathy Birkenstein

~ ~ ~

LEADS & CITATIONS

Beginning Lead, One Book with Two Authors
This research paper must focus on persuasion as its rhetorical purpose. Persuasion will enable the writer to defend his or her argument convincingly. Lester and Lester (1999), noted research writing experts, argued, "Persuasion enables you to reject the general attitudes about a problem and to affirm new theories, advance a solution, recommend a course of action, and invite the reader into an intellectual dialogue" (p. 11).

Reference
Lester, J. D., & Lester, J. D., Jr. (1999). *The essential guide to writing research papers*. New York: Longman.

Block Quotation, Article
Writers using research must write in their own personal voice. Writers must remember that this academic assignment calls for them to write using research for support, NOT to research and use writing for support. Brooks's (1990) article "Giving Voice to Your Nonfiction" stated:

> Your leads, your verbs, your descriptions, or your quotes can convey subliminal messages that evoke responses, conscious or subconscious, to your writing. But a single stylistic technique alone does not always give you voice. Your overall success at finding the voice for your writing depends ultimately on the way you blend all the ingredients of your writing. It depends on your ability to massage language to suit your needs. (p. 26)

Writers can write livelier, more readable research papers by retaining their personal voice rather than adapting a phony, starchy style influenced by research quotations.

Reference
Brooks, T. (1990, September). Giving voice to your nonfiction. *Writer's Digest*, 26-32.

Secondhand Source, an Author's Published Account of Another's Remarks
According to Shaughnessy's study (as cited in Lindemann, 1982), students' writing errors do not result from "carelessness or irrationality but rather from thinking" (p. 229). Shaughnessy's study was based on essays written by first year students entering City College of New York.

Reference
Lindemann, E. (1982). *A rhetoric for writing teachers*. New York: Oxford University Press.

Embedded Quotation, Book with One Author
The introduction to *Beyond Notecards* suggested that we teachers and students view the research paper not so much as an exercise in using proper conventions and mechanics of quoting and citing sources but rather as a "spirit of inquiry, to certain habits of the mind that often seem to inform investigations in many disciplines" (Ballenger, 1999, p. 16).

Reference
Ballenger, B. (1999). *Beyond notecards: Rethinking the freshman research paper*. Portsmouth, NH: Heinemann.

NOTE: When embedding quotations, try to keep the quoted portion to one or two lines at maximum.

AVOID THE FOLLOWING:
✓ **Floating (Hanging) Quotation—a reference without a lead.**
This research paper must focus on persuasion as its rhetorical purpose. Persuasion will enable the writer to defend his or her argument convincingly. "Persuasion enables you to reject the general attitudes about a problem and to affirm new theories, advance a solution, recommend a course of action, and invite the reader into an intellectual dialogue" (Lester & Lester, 1999, p. 11). The writer will use logical, supporting, research evidence to persuade the reader to act or at least consider the writer's position.

Reference
Lester, J. D., & Lester, J. D., Jr. (1999). *The essential guide to writing research papers*. New York: Longman.

✓ **Beginning paragraphs with a quotation.**
"Persuasion enables you to reject the general attitudes about a problem and to affirm new theories, advance a solution, recommend a course of action, and invite the reader into an intellectual dialogue" (Lester & Lester, 1999), argued the authors of *The Essential Guide to Writing Research Papers.* You, the writer, will use logical, supporting, research evidence to persuade the reader to act or at least consider your position.

Reference

Lester, J. D., & Lester J. D., Jr. (1999). *The essential guide to writing research papers.* New York: Longman.

PRACTICE 12D: Leads   Develop (1) a different lead (beginning, middle, end) written in APA format (past or present perfect tense), plus one embedded quotation, (2) a parenthetical citation, and (3) an APA Reference page entry for each of the passages that follow.

(A) "In the thousands of years before him, or the 400 years since, no writer has profoundly captured the heart and admiration of the human race as has William Shakespeare. His plays have forever enlarged our comprehension of those inner forces that drive and haunt, agonize and madden people. Yet we know little of his private world and the source of his astounding genius. We do not have a single letter or memoir or diary note in his hand."—This excerpt is taken from the opening page 35 of an eight-page article in the October 1986 issue of *Readers' Digest.* The article is entitled "The Shakespeare Nobody Knows," and it is written by Leo Rosten.

(B) Shakespeare "is indeed himself in many ways in character what one can only describe as Christ-like; that is gentle, kindly, honest, brave and true, with deep understanding and quick sympathy for all living things."—This item is found on page 207 of a book entitled *Shakespeare's Imagery and What It Tells Us,* published in 1958 in Cambridge, England, by the Cambridge University Press. The book is written by Caroline Spurgeon, a renowned Shakespearean scholar.

(C) "We also have the anecdotes of Shakespeare's godson William D'Avenant about him, but scholars tend not to take D'Avenant's tales as seriously as perhaps they should because Will D. got loaded one night and told people that he was Shakespeare's bastard son."—This information was gleaned from the following web site: <http://www. jetlink.net/~massij/shakes/author/html>—on August 24, 2017. The article entitled "The Authorship Issue" was written by J. Massi and was placed on-line on Monday, April 21, 1997.

APA FORMAT—PAPER LAYOUT

Use good quality 8.5" x 11" white paper and a high quality, clear printer. Print on one side only, and use 12 pt. font, preferably Times New Roman typeface. Set margins at one inch for top, bottom, and sides of each page. Double-space the text throughout, including title page, abstract, and references page. Tab paragraph indentations to one-half inch.

Title Page and Running Head

The title page requires three double-spaced items: (a) running head, (b) title, (c) writer's name and institutional affiliation. The term Running head: and a shortened title in all capital letters (50 characters maximum) should appear against the upper left margin of all pages, including the title page. It also appears at the upper left-hand corner of the title page. The title is centered and appears in the upper portion of the page. The writer's name and institutional affiliation are centered. Include the instructor's name, course and section, and date **only if the instructor requests that information.**

Running head: AUTHENTIC ASSESSMENT   1

Authentic Assessment:

Productive Change for Learning

Jim Brimeyer

Northeast Iowa Community College

Professor Ed U. Kation
Educational Evaluation 7H: 999
February 10, 2017

Pagination

In the upper right-hand corner, type the page number against the right margin on the same line as the shortened title in all capital letters, which is placed against the left margin. Number all pages including the title page.

Abstract

If your instructor requires an abstract, include it as page two of your paper. Center the word Abstract. Without indenting, write one paragraph (between 75-120 words) which summarizes your paper.

Text

Begin the text on a new page with the shortened title in all capital letters, which is placed against the left margin, followed by number 3 in the upper, right-hand corner. Double-space and center the full title. Double-space and begin typing your text.

References

Remember: research writing means using your writing supported by the research. It does not mean pasting together a large number of long quotations with your writing to tie the quotations together. You are a writer who uses research, not a researcher who uses writing to develop the research essay. Therefore, use short quotations only as necessary to support an important idea, to clarify technical terms, or to strengthen your position by using the words of an expert or authority. To identify your sources, smoothly blend quotations into your text by using **past** or **present perfect** tense leads (*Abrams emphasized*, or *Abrams has emphasized*,) and embedded quotations. Use references' last names only. Use vivid tag verbs (Jones *argued, claimed, concluded, endorsed, observed, refuted, suggested…*) to add more life and focus to the quotations and sources. Try to favor direct quotations rather than paraphrasing or summarizing your sources. Avoid hanging (floating) quotations, which are not tied to your text. Limit the length of the quotations, and as a guideline, limit long quotations to one, two at most, block (40 or more words) quotations. In APA style, long quotations are blocked at one-half inch from the left margin.

References Page

Type your shortened title in all capital letters on the top line against the left margin and page number against the right margin. Center the word References. List all references used in your paper alphabetically by last name of the author. If no author is available, alphabetize by the first main word of the title, excluding *A*, *An*, *The*.

Appendix

If your text refers your readers to an appendix which follows the references page, center the word Appendix; add identifying capital letters for more than one appendix. Double-space and type the title of the appendix (without italics, without all capitals, without underlining, without bold). Double-space; indent to the one-half inch mark, and type your text.

"Should my research appendix be added or removed?"

SAMPLE RESEARCH PAPER (Modified)—APA FORMAT

Running head: THE SLIPPERY CLIMB   1

The Slippery Climb: Financial Security for Retirement

Carol Wissing

Northeast Iowa Community College

Instructor Jim Brimeyer

English 106: Composition II

May 1, 2017

THE SLIPPERY CLIMB   2

Abstract

More and more Social Security experts are predicting that the Social Security system established in the 1930's will be depleted by the 2030's. The baby boomer children will come to retirement age at that time and require more money in returns than the system will take in as revenue. The United States government needs to institute major changes in the Social Security system to protect it for the future. Furthermore, individual citizens must plan ahead and prepare financially for their retirements because Social Security, even if it exists later in this century, will not offer enough dividends for retirees to live on.

THE SLIPPERY CLIMB   3

The Slippery Climb: Financial Security for Retirement

Feelings of frustration, futility, and inadequacy plague millions of Americans as they attempt to manage their finances. People of retirement age often feel as if their money has betrayed them and vanished with the night. Trying to prepare for retirement makes many people feel like field mice that desperately and repeatedly engage in futile efforts to climb up a slippery, stone wall. Amid ominous reports of the eventual demise of Social Security, consumers must view saving for retirement as a vital part of their present financial management.

As scores of Americans age, they must develop plans to sustain themselves through retirement. America's demographics have changed as the number of persons aged 65 and older has tripled since 1940. The proportion of the population reaching retirement age will continue to swell as 76 million baby boomers begin to reach age 65 in 2011. By 2030, Americans beyond age 65 will comprise 20% of the population, up from 13% today (McCune, 1998, p. 10). This already increased elderly population, combined with 76 million, predicts an ominous future for Social Security.

Pins (1998) wrote, "The system the U.S. government has chosen to take care of its elderly is in trouble. The search for a solution may pit old against young as everyone poses the same question: What about me?" (p. 8A). Therefore, consumers must exercise financial caution and plan carefully for retirement. Social Security simply cannot be counted on for retirement. Laurel Beedon (2003), senior policy advisor for the Public Policy Institute at the American Association of Retired Persons (AARP), wrote, "Not even the most ardent advocates of Social Security are saying that Social Security can or should be a worker's only source of retirement income" (para. 3). Americans must initiate retirement savings plans as early as possible in their lives to protect their long-term future financial welfare.

THE SLIPPERY CLIMB   4

At present pace, financial experts have said that "by 2029, the combination of interest and taxes will fall short of expenditures and the trust fund securities, the principal, will have to be tapped. The trustees project that in 2032, if no changes are made, the trust funds will be exhausted" (Beedon, 2003, para. 8). Americans can no longer rely on Social Security to provide for their golden years as Franklin D. Roosevelt envisioned when he established the system in the late 30's. Americans should be saving for retirement, but Michelle Spencer, of the Consumer Credit Counseling Service of Iowa, stated, "Unfortunately, the 50 and over age group haven't been saving" (personal communication, March 20, 2017).

What can the United States Government do to remedy the Social Security problem? It could raise revenues, but according to Schieber and Shoven (1999):

It would take an immediate payroll tax increase of between 4.5 and 5 percentage points to make Social Security permanently solvent. Now we are talking about as much as two years' worth of earnings over a lifetime— two years of your children's professional lives. The stakes are high here, and policy proponents are playing with your family's money. So you'll want to pay close attention to this debate. (p. 412)

Another possible governmental action would be reducing benefits, but that would cause a further burden to citizens who have paid their taxes throughout their lives and presently live on Social Security. The U.S. Government could also consider increasing the full retirement age to 68 or higher, thereby protecting Social Security from bankruptcy. The Government could also consider reducing revenue and benefits and letting citizens keep more earned income to invest in private retirement plans.

Our government must act immediately to protect its citizens

THE SLIPPERY CLIMB   5

by salvaging Social Security. As Allen (1995) observed, "The most serious threat to Social Security is the federal government's fiscal irresponsibility. Regaining control of our fiscal responsibility is the most important step that we can take to protect the soundness of the Social Security trust funds" (p. 125). If our government won't protect its citizens and its Social Security system, then citizens must individually start now to protect themselves by consistent, lifetime savings plans aimed toward retirement. Americans must cast off their old attitudes about the "security" in the Social Security system and realize it's "every man, woman, and mouse for him or herself" on a financially slippery climb toward retirement.

THE SLIPPERY CLIMB   6
References

Allen, S. J. (1995). *Violation of trust*. Fairfax, VA: The Seniors
    Coalition.

Beedon, L. (2003, January 3). *Social security now and in the
    future*. Retrieved March 14, 2017 from http://www.umc-
    gbcs.org

McCune, J. C. (1998, April). The future of retirement.
    Management Review, 10-16.

Pins, K. (1998, December 7). A generational debate. *Des
    Moines Register*, p. 8A.

Schieber, S. J. & Shoven, J. B. (1999). *The real deal*. New Haven,
    CN: Yale Press.

Discussion Questions regarding APA format:

a. Cite all pieces of information needed on the title page.

b. Where should the Running head: appear?

c. How many characters should the Running head (shortened title) be limited to?

d. On what page does the first page numbering appear?

e. Identify where the complete title of the research essay should appear.

f. Count the number of words in Ms. Wissing's Abstract. Does it qualify? State the word count parameters for an APA Abstract.

g. Explain the difference in parenthetical documentation in the McCune and Pins citations on page 3 of Ms. Wissing's paper.

h. Explain the differences in the Beedon reference and the Schieber/Shoven reference on page 4 of the Wissing text.

i. In APA citation format, what is the word requirement for using a block quotation?

j. Explain how Ms. Wissing cited her personal interview source on page 4 of her text.

k. Analyze Ms. Wissing's Reference page; then respond to the following:

   (1) Analyze the variety of sources by listing the number of books, magazines, web cites, newspapers, etc.

   (2) Identify all aspects of information included in the McCune reference.

   (3) Cite all aspects of information included in the Pins reference.

CHAPTER 13

Good MECHANICS
Keep Writing Motors Running Smoothly

~ ~ ~

"Concentrate on the mundane housekeeping jobs,
like fixing misspellings and picking up inconsistencies.
There'll be plenty; only God gets it right the first time
and only a slob says, 'Oh, well, let it go,
that's what copyeditors are for'" (212).
—Stephen King

~ ~ ~

COMMA PLACEMENT

In addition to dates and addresses, place commas in sentences in three situations—**introductory** elements, **interrupting** elements, or **intertwining** elements.

INTRODUCTORY   Word, Phrase, Clause

Word, **SENTENCE.**

Yes, sentence.

No, sentence.

Oh, sentence.

Well, sentence.

Phrase, **SENTENCE.** (phrase = group of words without subject or predicate)

1. Prepositional Phrase—"Clue words."

The following list includes some commonly used prepositions:

after	behind	of	toward
among	below	off	under
around	between	on	up
as well as	during	over	with
at	from	through	within
before	in	to	without

Examples of Prepositional Phrases:

over the river   through the woods

to Grandmother's house

2. Participle Phrase

> *Present Participle (-ing)—*

Driving down the highway at a moderate speed, Waldo was able to avoid the crossing deer.

> *Past Participle (-ed, -en, -d, -t)—*

Written for composition class, the essay drew rave reviews.

> *Present Perfect (Having + past participle)—*

Having selected a topic, Fritz began writing his essay.

Clause, **SENTENCE.** (clause = group of words containing a subject and predicate) Complex Sentence

Adverb Clause "Clue Words":

The following words commonly begin an adverb clause:

after	before	since	whenever
although	even though	unless	where
as	if	until	wherever
because	once	when	while

NOTE: No comma is required when these clause "clue words" appear after the sentence clause.

Examples of Adverb Clauses:

> When the moon comes over the mountain, the wolves begin to sing.

The wolves begin to sing when the moon comes over the mountain.

COMMA PRACTICE 13A: Place commas in the following sentences. In front of each sentence, write W (Word), P (Phrase), or C (Clause) to indicate the reason for your comma placement.

1. Oh I almost forgot today's class.
2. In my opinion commas can confuse even the best writers.
3. Expecting the worst we planned for the exam.
4. Tripped in the hallway by Ralph Jim was carried to the doctor's office.
5. Before the half the Packers jogged into the locker room.
6. When the game ended the Hawks had won again.
7. Because writing is challenging I must put forth good effort.
8. Harry are you chilly on top?
9. Typing for only ten minutes Hilda finished the forty-five page essay.
10. If students study hard they usually do well in college.
11. Having studied for only ten minutes Waldo approached the quiz apprehensively.
12. While the Cubs lose the Cardinals continue to win.

COMMA PRACTICE 13B:

1. Compose a sentence with an introductory word.

2. Compose a sentence with an introductory phrase.

3. Compose a sentence with an introductory clause.

~ ~ ~

Regarding the comma, "When in doubt,
leave it out."
—Mark Twain

~ ~ ~

INTERRUPTING **Word, Phrase, Clause**
  SEN, *interrupting word*, **TENCE**
    John, too, writes well.
    I feel, Tom, that you write well. (Direct Address)
  SEN, *interrupting phrase*, **TENCE.**
    Eldred, on the other hand, struggles with his essays.

Homer, in my opinion, writes like Hemingway.
This, my dear friend, presents quite a challenge. (Direct Address)

**Appositive—renames or describes:

Ralph, my older brother, earns the bucks in our family.
My toughest class, Advanced Nuclear Trigonometry, presents quite a challenge.

SEN, *interrupting clause*, **TENCE**.

(Complex Sentence)

(Clue Words: **who, whom, which, where, whose**)

Non-restrictive—adds interesting or useful information but is not necessary for meaning. Set it off with commas so readers see it as helpful but not essential information.

Walter, who teaches at NICC, loves to write poetry.
Walter, whom I admire, teaches at NICC.
Walter's latest poem, which I love, uses a great deal of imagery.

Restrictive—adds essential information; do not set it off with commas so that readers see it as a necessary part of the sentence. Because *that* can specify rather than simply add information, its clause usually requires no commas.

The poem that I need to search for is written by Robert Frost.

COMMA PRACTICE 13C: Place commas in the following sentences. In front of each sentence, write W (Word), P (Phrase), or C (Clause) to indicate the reason for your comma placement.

1. Kay too teaches elementary students.
2. Shakespeare my favorite dramatist wrote 37 wonderful plays.
3. Yes Herman you suffer from a bad case of halitosis.
4. Bob Hope a terrific comedian instilled laughter into the hearts of most Americans.
5. Early computers large and immobile have been replaced by smaller models.
6. Kay my lovely wife teaches third grade.
7. Mr. Ed who talked like a human ate like a horse.
8. Buenie where I was raised can be missed in the blink of an eye.
9. My dad whom I greatly respected placed a fair and valid curfew on his sons.
10. My cousin the technological genius repairs broken computers.
11. Karen Morris who was offered four scholarships will attend NICC this fall.

12. The computer working quickly and accurately processed useful information.

COMMA PRACTICE 13D:

1. Compose a sentence with an interrupting word.

2. Compose a sentence with an interrupting phrase.

3. Compose a sentence with an interrupting clause.

INTERTWINING—joins Words, Phrases, Clauses, Sentences.

Series (list) of words, phrases, clauses. (Use one less comma.)
I enjoy baseball, basketball, football, and golf. (words)
I love playing the piano, attending concerts, writing essays, and eating pizza. (phrases)
I enjoy a picnic when the weather feels warm, when the sky looks clear, and when the food is provided. (clauses)

Mini-Series:
The secretary impresses us as a competent, personable professional.

Compound Sentence: SENTENCE, conjunction SENTENCE.
Joining Words: **for, and, nor, but, or, yet, so (FANBOYS)**
Gene has washed his old car, and he hopes to attract a buyer.
Our former boss demanded a high standard of work, but our new boss favors quantity over quality.
We can stay home and eat lamb, or we can go out for pizza.

Compound Sentence: SENTENCE; word, SENTENCE.

Glue Words:	...; additionally,...	...; also,...
...; consequently,...	...; furthermore,...	...; however,...
...; indeed,...	...; still,...	...; then,...
...; therefore,...	...; thus,...	

Gene has washed his old car; therefore, he hopes to attract a buyer.
Our former boss demanded a high standard of work; however, our new boss favors quantity over quality.
We should not have put off writing our essay; instead, we should have started the process as soon as it was assigned.

Compound Sentence: SENTENCE; SENTENCE.

Gene has washed his old car; he hopes to attract a buyer.

Our former boss demanded a high standard of work; our new boss favors quantity over quality.

We should not have put off writing our essay; we should have started the process as soon as it was assigned.

PRACTICE 13E: Use commas and/or semicolons to punctuate the following sentences. In front of each sentence, write S (Series), MS (Mini-Series), or Cd (Compound Sentence) to indicate the reason for your comma placement.

1. I visualize a quiet relaxing pleasant and peaceful office.
2. She liked the instructor when he was kind when he was patient and when he left the class.
3. Our computer expert acted fairly smart but sometimes he suffered from an e-mail virus.
4. The eighty-year-old couple married they spent their honeymoon on the mountain slopes of Vail.
5. I need to earn some extra money therefore I teach some extra classes.
6. The instructor stumbled into the classroom bumped into the desk kicked a chair and laughed in relief.
7. Most of us loved the class but Zeke considered it boring.
8. We worked on the essay for hours but never handed it to the professor.
9. I put in long hours at my job yet I could do even more.
10. Joe does not fear snakes nor do turtles frighten him.
11. You must honor the college policies or suffer the consequences.

PRACTICE 13F:

1. **Compose a sentence containing a SERIES of words, phrases, or clauses.**

2. **Compose a COMPOUND SENTENCE with a conjunction (FANBOYS).**

3. **Compose a COMPOUND SENTENCE without a conjunction (use semicolon).**

DATES & ADDRESSES   Use a comma to separate items in dates and addresses.

DATES: Use a comma between the day of the month and the year and also after the year when it does not end the sentence. Do not use a comma between the month and the day. Do not use a comma when only the month and the year are used.

ADDRESSES: Consider the street number and street name as one item and the state and zip code as one item. Each additional item is followed by a comma. No comma is used between the state and the zip code.

> I was born on July 19, 1947, at Mercy Hospital in Dubuque, Iowa 52002.
>
> I was born at Mercy Hospital in Dubuque, Iowa, on July 19, 1947.

PRACTICE 13G: Dates and Addresses   Compose a sentence that tells the date of your birth, the city and state of your birth, and the hospital of your birth.

Composing Compound-Complex Sentences

Compound-complex Sentence

Two or more independent clauses
+ one or more dependent clauses

Some possible compound-complex sentence patterns:

- **Compound-complex Sentence (compound with a coordinating conjunction, complex with an introductory clause)**

    Introductory Clause, sentence, conjunction sentence.

    Example: If students revise essays promptly, they reduce their stress, and they usually produce better portfolios.

- **Compound-complex Sentence (compound without a coordinating conjunction, complex with an introductory clause)**

    Introductory Clause, sentence; word, sentence.

    Example: If students revise essays promptly, they reduce their stress; furthermore, they usually produce better portfolios.

- **Compound-complex Sentence (compound with a coordinating conjunction, complex with an interrupting clause)**

    Sen, interrupting clause, tence, conjunction sentence.

Example: Students, who revise essays promptly, reduce stress, and they usually produce better portfolios.

* **Compound-complex Sentence** (compound **without** a coordinating conjunction, complex with an interrupting clause)

    Sen, interrupting clause, tence; word, sentence.

    Example: Students, who revise essays promptly, reduce stress; furthermore, they usually produce better portfolios.

Note: an introductory clause may also precede the second independent clause in a compound-complex sentence, and an interrupting clause may be placed in the second independent clause of a compound-complex sentence.

PRACTICE 13H: Composing Compound-Complex Sentences

1. Compose a compound-complex sentence (compound with a coordinating conjunction, complex with an introductory clause).

2. Compose a compound-complex sentence (compound without a coordinating conjunction, complex with an introductory clause).

3. Compose a compound-complex sentence (compound with a coordinating conjunction, complex with an interrupting clause).

4. Compose a compound-complex sentence (compound without a coordinating conjunction, complex with an interrupting clause).

PRACTICE 13I: Comma Usage   Analyze the passage, and place commas as needed. Above each comma, place the corresponding number from the list below to designate its usage in the passage.

1—introductory word	4—interrupting word	7—intertwining series
2—introductory phrase	5—interrupting phrase	8—compound sent.
3—introductory clause	6—interrupting clause	9—date or address

Professor I.M. Snoring had spent countless hours researching his area of expertise advanced microscopic photosynthesis. He was planning a lecture for his 8 a.m. class the following Monday. After many hours in the library Professor Snoring had accumulated a large stack of notes. He then organized them in outline form and he placed them in a three-ring binder. The professor was pleased with his work and anxiously awaited the opportunity to share his expertise with his class.

When the night before the lecture arrived Professor Snoring stayed up late into the evening reviewing his notes. After about five hours of study he grew tired and decided to get some rest. At 6:30 a.m. he heard his alarm go off and he immediately jumped out of bed. He brushed his teeth put on his best sweater and ate his Corn Flakes. In an eager frame of mind he hopped on his Honda motorcycle and headed for his office.

Although the traffic slowed him a bit Professor Snoring arrived at the campus in good time found a spot close to his office and tied his motorcycle to a tree. He briskly walked to his office and unlocked the door. On the floor he found a letter from his brother Waldo who lived at 1032 High Lane Filmore Iowa which was dated May 1 2009. Waldo who was born three years before the professor farmed 380 acres just off Highway 151. In the letter Waldo said he was planning a vacation trip to Millville Iowa and hoped the professor would join him. Professor Snoring decided to respond to the request at a later time.

Then Professor Snoring left for his eagerly anticipated 8 a.m. lecture. The students groggily entered the lecture hall after their long weekend. The professor began his lecture as late-comers continued to straggle in one by one but that did not derail the professor's speech. After one hour and fourteen minutes of non-stop lecture the professor finally looked up from his notes to find numerous listeners fast asleep. The professor became undone halted his lecture picked out a student in the back of the room and said "Say John would you please wake up that student who is sleeping in the seat next to you?"

In reply the startled John stammered "You wake him up yourself Professor Snoring. You put him to sleep."

PRACTICE 13J: Overall Practice: Compose sentences to fit each of the patterns listed below. Edit punctuation carefully.

1. Introductory word

2. Introductory phrase

3. Introductory clause

4. Interrupting word

5. Interrupting phrase

6. Interrupting clause

7. Series of words, phrases, or clauses

8. Compound with conjunction (FANBOYS)

9. Compound without conjunction (semicolon)

10. Date and Address

11. Compound-complex with either an introductory clause or an interrupting clause

APOSTROPHE

~ ~ ~

"Using the apostrophe correctly is a mere negative proof: it tells the world that you are not a thicko" (105).
~ Lynne Tress

~ ~ ~

NO! NO! NO!

The apostrophe indicates possessive case of a noun, **not plural of a noun.**

Milton has written three essay's for composition class.

Waldo has cooked lunch for us three times' this week.

NO! NO! NO!

The apostrophe indicates possessive case of a noun, **NOT contractions for "is" or "has."**

Mildred's writing her third essay of the semester.

Hilda's written a poem for her portfolio.

Alfred's a good dancer.

1. **Add an apostrophe and an s to form the possessive of a singular noun, of a plural noun not ending in s, and of an indefinite pronoun.**

the man's car	the witness's responses	(singular nouns)
the boss's office	Mary's desk	
the men's glee club	the women's coat room	(plural nouns)
the children's choir	people's rights	
anybody's game	everyone's future	(indefinite pronouns)
someone's work	nobody's fault	

NOTE: add an apostrophe alone to "hard to pronounce" singular words.

Miss Phillips' election   Moses' laws   Euripides' plays

2. **Add only an apostrophe to form the possessive of a plural noun ending in s.**

the bosses' cars   ladies' coat room   attorneys' offices

PRACTICE 13K: Apostrophe   Make the following examples possessive.

a. today _____ assignments
b. boss _____ tirade
c. job _____ pressures
d. workers ___ duties
e. attorney _____ fees
f. attorneys ____ parking lot
g. men _____ basketball league
h. anybody _____ guess

3. **Possessive pronouns (my, his, hers, its, ours, yours, theirs) never require an apostrophe to show possession.**

The victory is ours. (not our's)
The dog chased its tail. (not it's)

Remember: it's = it is.

4. **The last word takes 's to show possession in compound nouns, names of business firms, and two nouns showing joint ownership.**

father-in-law's profession	mother-in-law's cooking	(compound nouns)
brother-in-law's job	Attorney General's statement	

Sears Roebuck's insurance plan
Honkamp Krueger's employees (business firms)

Tom and Geri's cat   Mom and Dad's car   (joint possession)

NOTE: Place 's after each item if you want to show individual possession.

Tom's and Geri's cats   Mom's and Dad's cars
(individual possession)

5. **Add 's to form the plurals of certain signs, numbers, letters, and words.**

four t's and two s's   all 6's and 7's
14 and's in the letter   too many which's in writing

6. **Use an apostrophe in a contraction to show that letters or figures are left out.**

has not = hasn't   is not = isn't
they are = they're   class of 1988 = class of '88
it is = it's

PRACTICE 13L: Apostrophe   Add apostrophes as needed.

1. Stephen King and John Grisham novels
2. Tom, Dick, and Harry project
3. four -s and four -i in Mississippi
4. Rodgers and Hammerstein *The King and I*
5. Tom, Dick, and Harry bikes (each own a bike)
6. Its time for the secretarial staff to take its coffee break.
7. Dont snore.

PRACTICE 13M: Apostrophe   Add or delete apostrophes in the following sentences.

1. The womens' basketball team won it's sixth consecutive game.
2. The girls choir will sing for the mens glee club.
3. Weve won the clients confidence.
4. Before Fridays rain, Charleys goat ate eight acres of grass and felt an ache in its stomach.
5. My mother-in-laws cooking has become famous in three states'.
6. When your editing you're drafts, check carefully to dot your is and cross your ts.

PRACTICE 13N: Apostrophe   Provide the correct possessive forms in the following paragraph:

The students essays show good use of the writing process. Student writers revision strategies have been used effectively. Everyones focus on improving his or her writing style is encouraging. Each students editing is also improving. Strunk and Whites book, *Elements of Style*, seems to be helping all the writers knowledge of style. People from miles around Peosta will flock to read the students wonderful writings.

SEMICOLONS

1.   Use a semicolon between two sentences to form a compound sentence without a coordinating conjunction or with a transitional word such as *consequently, furthermore, however, instead, otherwise, then, therefore.*

> Writers must practice their craft; they will then see improvement in time.
> Writers must practice their craft; otherwise, they will not see improvement.

2.   Use a semicolon between items in a series (list) containing internal punctuation.

> In the literature class, the students read *Things Fall Apart*, an African novel; *Madame Bovary*, a French novel; *Wuthering Heights*, a British novel; and *Antigone*, a Greek drama.

COLONS

1. Use a colon after a preceding complete sentence to introduce a list, a quotation, or an appositive.

> My typical day includes the following: an early breakfast, two

morning classes, two afternoon classes, reading interesting essays, walking for exercise, a hearty supper, and a good night's sleep.

Analyze this passage from *Henry IV, Part I* by Shakespeare: "What is honor? A word. What is in that word 'honor'? What is that 'honor'? Air...Honor is a mere scutcheon" (133-135; 139-140).

Students should now recognize the syntactical meaning of the compound sentence: two independent clauses joined by comma and conjunction or by a semicolon.

2. **Use a colon after the salutation of a formal letter, between hours and minutes, to show ratios, between title and subtitle, between chapter and verse of Biblical references, and between city and publisher in reference entries.**
Dear Professor Wright:
9:20 a.m.
The ratio of students to teacher is 11:1.
Teaching and Performing: Ideas for Energizing Your Classes
1 Corinthians 13:1-13
Dubuque, IA: McGraw-Hill.

DASHES

(Type two hyphens with no space before or after them.)
1. **Use dashes for emphasis and to set off appositives that contain commas.**
Everything I touched today—my car, my computer, my TV, my stove—broke down in seconds.

PARENTHESES

1. **Use parentheses to enclose brief explanations or interruptions.**
After serving her husband his normal breakfast (bacon, eggs, hash browns, toast, fruit, coffee, juice), Mildred went back to bed.

2. **Use parentheses around letters or numbers labeling items in a series.**
The portfolio should contain the following items: (1) an introduction, (2) an example of a full process, (3) revised essays, (4) entry slip reflections, (5) a diagnostic essay, (6) personal inclusions, and (7) a metacognitive conclusion.

ITALICS

1. **Italicize the titles of magazines, newspapers, pamphlets, books, plays, films, radio and television programs, book-length poems, ballets, operas, long musical compositions, record albums, CD's, legal cases, and names of ships or aircraft.**

   Newsweek (magazine)   *Telegraph Herald* (newspaper)
   Math (play)   *Walden* (book)
   Field of Dreams (film) *Cheers* (TV Program)

   Do not italicize, underline, or use quotation marks around titles of religious works.

   Bible   Koran   Ten Commandments   Torah

2. **Italicize foreign words used in an English sentence.**

   The students became accustomed to Professor Wright's *modus operandi.*

END PUNCTUATION

1. **Use periods to end statements and commands.**
   This composition class requires lots of writing and thinking.
   Turn in all essays on Thursday.

   Also, use periods in abbreviations. Do not add a second period if the sentence ends with a period indicating an abbreviation.

   Mr.   Mrs.   Ms.   Dr.   B.A.
   M.A.   Ph.D.   R.N.   B.C.   A.D.

   Ms. Jones recently completed her course work for her Ph.D.

2. **Use a question mark following a direct question.**
   How many students have completed the writing assignment?

3. **Use one exclamation mark to indicate emotion or emphasis.**
   When Zelmo received his essay and saw his grade, he shouted,
   "A miracle!"

QUOTATION MARKS

1. **Use quotation marks for titles of songs, poems, short stories, lectures, courses, chapters of books, and articles in newspapers, magazines, or encyclopedias.**
   "On Top of Ol' Smokey" (song)

"Young Goodman Brown" (short story)
"Cultures Through Literature" (course)
"The Road Not Taken" (poem)

2. For quotation marks in dialogue, see pp. 54-56.

CAPITALIZATION

1. **Capitalize the first word of a sentence and the first word of a direct quotation.**
   When the instructor requested the assignment, Herman muttered, "My dog ate it."

2. **Capitalize proper nouns and adjectives:**
   Specific Individuals
   Michael Jordan   William Shakespeare   Dad   Grandma

(NOTE: do <u>not</u> capitalize a family relationship that follows an article or possessive pronoun: my dad, her grandma, an uncle, my grandpa.)

Specific Places and Geographical Areas
Pacific Ocean   Europe
Institutions, Organizations, Government Departments
the Supreme Court   Northeast Iowa Community College
St. Louis Cardinals
Historical Events, Documents, Periods
the Renaissance   the French and Indian War
the Bill of Rights
Days of the Week, Months, Holidays
Monday   May   Father's Day
Religions and Sacred Terms
Allah   Christian   Zeus   the Bible
Races, Nationalities, and Languages
Caucasians   Arabs   Irish
Trade names
Banana Republic   Toyota   HyVee
Titles preceding, but not after, a proper name
President Mark Smith   Mark Smith, our president
Professor Waldo Wright   Waldo Wright, my professor
Titles of books, articles, plays, films, songs, stories, poems, essays, paintings
Tom Sawyer   "The Star-Spangled Banner"

SPELLING

1. **Write *i* before *e* except after <u>c</u> or when sounding like *a* as in neighbor and weigh.**

   receive   ceiling   brief

   relief   believe   eight

2. **If a word (sit) ends in a consonant (*t*) preceded by a vowel (*i*), double the final consonant before adding a suffix which begins with a vowel (sitting).**

   admit = admitted   slam = slammed   occur = occurring

3. **If a word ends in a silent *e*, drop the *e* before adding a suffix that begins with a vowel.**

   come+ing = coming

   write+ing = writing

   debate+able = debatable

   When *y* is the last letter of a word preceded by a consonant, change *y* to *i* before adding a suffix—except those suffixes beginning with *i*.

   hurry = hurried   lady = ladies   happy = happiness

   beauty = beautiful

NOTE: when forming the plural of a word that ends in *y* preceded by a vowel, add *s*.

   play = plays   donkey = donkeys

Consult a reputable dictionary for variations and exceptions.

GLOSSARY of Editing FUNdamentals

1. **Adjective**—a word that modifies (describes or limits) a noun or pronoun.

   "It's a <u>beautiful</u> day in the neighborhood."

2. **Adverb**—a word that modifies (describes or limits) a verb, adjective, or another adverb.

   The cow strolled <u>utterly gracefully</u> across the pasture.

3. **Appositive**—a word, phrase, or clause that renames the noun preceding it.

   My sister, <u>the brain in the family</u>, owns five buildings.

4. **Article**—the words *a, an, the*.

5. **Case**—the form, or use of a word, that shows its relationship to

other words in a sentence. The three cases are nominative (subject, predicate nominative, direct address), objective (direct object, indirect object, object of preposition), and possessive (ownership, possession).

> *I prefer to type the letter. (nominative)*
> *Kay gave me the keys to the car. (objective)*
> *I gave my checkbook to Kay. (possessive)*

6. **Clause**—a group of words containing a subject and a predicate and forming a part of a compound or complex sentence. There are two kinds of clauses—independent (main) and dependent (subordinate).

   Dependent (Subordinate) Clause—a clause introduced by a subordinate element. It depends on the rest of the sentence for meaning. A subordinate clause does not express a complete thought and cannot stand alone. It must be attached to the main clause as a part of a sentence. The three kinds of dependent clauses are adverb, adjective, and noun.

   > *He will attend the Hawkeye game if the Hawks promise to win. (adverb)*
   > *I am grateful to the student who edited my work. (adjective)*
   > *I remember what the boss said. (noun)*

   Independent (Main) Clause—a clause that is not introduced by a subordinate element. A main clause does not modify. It usually can stand alone as a simple sentence.

   > *Time passes quickly when one is writing.*
   > *I knew a fellow who was born in Buenie.*

   Nonrestrictive Clause—could be omitted without changing the meaning of the sentence and should be surrounded by commas.

   > *Zelmo, who thinks he's high and mighty, fell flat on his face.*

   Restrictive Clause—could not be omitted from the sentence. Without this clause, a sentence would change in meaning or be misunderstood.

   > *The book that Waldo wrote is selling well.*

7. **Complex Sentence**—contains one independent clause and one or more dependent clauses.

   > *After the Cardinals whipped the Cubs, we celebrated.*
   > *We agreed with what Homer suggested.*

8. **Compound Sentence**—contains two or more independent clauses but no dependent clauses. Clauses may be joined either by a comma + coordinating conjunction (for, and, but, or, nor, yet, so) or by a semicolon.

> *Waldo believes everyone, but Hilda needs proof.*
> *Waldo believes everyone; Hilda needs proof.*

9. **Compound-Complex Sentence**—contains two or more independent clauses and one or more dependent clauses.

> *Sally met the Chicago students, who landed at the airport, and she escorted them to NICC.*

10. **Gerund Phrase**—a phrase starting with a gerund, the -ing form of a verb. The entire gerund phrase is used like a noun.

> *Earning a passing grade seemed tougher than I thought.*
> *The strawberry picker was fired for sitting down on the job.*

11. **Helping Verbs**—a verb phrase consists of the main verb and one or more helping (auxiliary) verbs. Helping verbs are used with main verbs to express changes in tense, voice, or mood. Note the helping verbs (italicized) in the following examples:

> *has* practiced   *will be* practicing
> *should have* practiced   *should have been* practicing

Common helping verbs:

be (am, is, are, was, were, been)	have, has, had	ought
can, could	may, might	shall, will
do, does, did, done	must	should, would

12. **Infinitive Phrase**—a phrase introduced by an infinitive (to + verb). It may be used as a noun, an adjective, or an adverb. Try not to split the *to* from the rest of the verb.

> *To refuse the gift seemed foolish. (noun—subject)*
> *Work to do was not hard to find. (adjective, adverb)*

13. **Number**—refers to singular (one) or plural (two or more).

> *Each person should have their coats on. (Number agreement error)*
> *All people should have their coats on. (Correct)*

14. Participle Phrase—a phrase starting with a participle. The entire phrase is used like an adjective.

> *We watched the instructors <u>figuring our grades</u>.*
> *<u>Booed beyond belief</u>, the referee forfeited the game.*
> *<u>Having finished my tax form</u>, I sent in the balance.*

15. Participle—a verb form used as an adjective or adverb. It may modify a noun or pronoun. It can take an object.

> *<u>Gasping</u>, I sucked in air.*

16. Phrase—a group of related words not expressing a complete thought and without a subject and verb.

> *over the river*   *running down the hall*
> *through the woods*   *having opened my book*
> *to Grandmother's house*

17. Predicate—the particular word or words that express the action in a sentence. The simple predicate is the verb.

> *Harold <u>read</u> the essay to his peer response group.*
> *Pierre <u>reads, writes, and speaks</u> French fluently.*

18. Prepositional Phrase—a phrase starting with a preposition and used to modify other words.

> *Gloria stepped <u>to the edge of the dock</u>.*

19. Run-on Sentence—two or more independent clauses run together without proper punctuation.

> *The secretary used the new computer, she bought it in Chicago.*   (splice)
> *The secretary used the new computer she bought it in Chicago.*   (fused)

20. Sentence—a group of words expressing a complete thought and containing a subject and predicate.

21. Simple Sentence—contains one independent clause and no dependent clauses.

> *Margo types 421 words per minute.*

22. Sentence Fragment—a group of words that does not express a complete thought and is used incorrectly as a sentence. Often a

fragment is a dependent clause or a phrase.
The pretty girl in the blue dress.
Walking into my office yesterday morning.

23. **Subject**—that part of the sentence that does the action (exception: passive voice). The subject can be found by asking, "Who or what did the action?"
George Washington chopped down a cherry tree.
John and Nancy work in the Writing Center.

24. **Subordinating Conjunction**—a word that introduces a dependent adverb clause. Examples: after, although, as, as if, as though, because, before, if, since, unless, until, when, whenever, where, wherever, while.

25. **Verbal Phrase**—a phrase introduced by a verbal, a word derived from a verb, but used as a noun, adjective, or adverb. The three kinds of verbals are participle, gerund, and infinitive.

26. **Voice**—Active voice is preferred over passive voice.
Active Voice—the subject performs the action of a sentence.
The instructor presented a lecture on voice.
Passive Voice—the subject is the receiver of the action. The word by generally indicates passive voice.
A lecture on active voice was presented by the instructor.

Works Cited

Adler, Richard, and Jerry Ross. "Heart." *Damn Yankees*, CPP/Belwin, 1987.

Andersen, Richard, and Helene Hinnis. *The Write Stuff: A Style Manual for Effective Business Writing*. National Press, 1990.

Ballenger, Bruce. *Beyond Notecards: Rethinking the Freshman Research Paper*. Boynton, 1999.

Barnet, Sylvan. *A Short Guide to Writing About Literature*. 4th ed., Little Brown, 1979.

Barry, Marilyn R., and Thiru Yaso. "Digging in! Dynamics of Assessing General University Competencies by Portfolio." *The Portfolio Standard*, edited by Bonnie S. Sunstein and Jonathan H. Lovell. Heinemann, 2000, pp. 83-93.

Bradbury, Ray. *Zen in the Art of Writing*. Bantam, 1992.

Buscaglia, Leo F. *Personhood: The Art of Being Fully Human*. Fawcett, 1978.

Cheuse, Alan, and Nickolas Debanco. *Talking Horse*. Columbia UP, 1996.

Danziger, Elizabeth. *Get to the Point*. Three Rivers, 2001.

Ebersole, Mark C. *A Humor Anthology on Higher Education*. Fordham UP, 1992.

Elbow, Peter. *Writing With Power*. Oxford UP, 1981.

---. *Writing Without Teachers*. Oxford UP, 1973.

Fitzgerald, F. Scott. *The Great Gatsby*. Scribner, 1925.

Frost, Robert. "Out,Out—" *Literature, Structure, Sound, and Sense*, edited by Laurence Perrine, 5th ed., Harcourt Brace, 1988, pp. 624-25.

Gibaldi, Joseph. *MLA Handbook for Writers of Research Papers*. 6th ed., MLA, 2003.

Graff, Gerald, and Cathy Birkenstein. *They Say, I say: The Moves That Matter in Academic Writing*. W.W. Norton, 2006.

Graves, Donald H., and Bonnie S. Sunstein. *Portfolio Portraits*. Heinemann, 1992.

Hammerstein, Oscar. "Getting to Know You." Williamson Music, 1951.

Hamp-Lyons, Liz, and William Condon. *Assessing the Portfolio*. Hampton, 2000.

Hemingway, Ernest. *A Farewell to Arms*. Scribner, 1957.

Holmes, Marjorie. "Writing From the Heart." *Chicken Soup for the Writer's Soul*, edited by Jack Canfield and Mark Victor Hanson, Health Communications, 2000.

King, Stephen. *On Writing—a Memoir of the Craft*. Scribner, 2000.

Kirby, Dan and Tom Liner. *Inside Out: Developmental Strategies for Teaching Writing*. Boynton, 1981.

Langer, Judith. "Research on the Enterprise of Writing Instruction." *Ways of Knowing: Research and Practice in the Teaching of Writing*, edited by James S. Davis and James D. Marshall, Iowa Council of Teachers of English, 1988, p. 54.

Lindemann, Erika. *A Rhetoric for Writing Teachers*. Oxford UP, 1982.

Lyons, Bill. "The PQP Method of Responding to Writing." *English Journal*, vol. 70, no. 3, Mar. 1981, pp. 42-43.

Marius, Richard. *A Writer's Companion*. McGraw-Hill, 1999.

Meyers, Chet, and Thomas B. Jones. *Promoting Active Learning: Strategies for the College Classroom*. Jossey-Bass, 1993.

Miles, Robert, et al. *Prose Style, A Guide*. 2nd ed., Prentice Hall, 1991.

MLA Handbook for Writers of Research Papers. 8th ed., The Modern Language Association of America, 2016.

Murray, Donald. *Shoptalk: Learning to Write with Writers*. Boynton, 1990. (p. 57-Sinclair Lewis, p. 114-Updike).

Murray, Donald. *The Craft of Revision*. Holt, Rinehart, Winston, 1991.

Perrine, Laurence. "Fifteen Ways to Write Five Hundred Words." *Exploring Language*, edited by Gary Goshgarian, 5th ed., Scott Foresman, 1989.

Provost, Gary. *100 Ways to Improve Your Writing*. Mentor, 1985.

Schmit, John S., and Deborah A. Appleman. "Portfolios and the Politics of Assessing Writing in Urban Schools." *The Portfolio Standard*, edited by Bonnie S. Sunstein and Jonathan H. Lovell, Heinemann, 2000, pp. 83-93, pp. 181-194.

Schulman, Lee. *Teaching as Community Property*. Jossey-Bass, 2004.

Scott, Dewitt H. *Secrets of Successful Writing*. Reference Software, 1989.

Shakespeare, William. *Henry IV, Part One*. Edited by David Bevington, Bantam, 1988.

Shakespeare, William. *Macbeth*. Edited by David Bevington, Bantam, 1988.

Shakespeare, William. *Richard III*. Edited by David Bevington, Bantam, 1988.

Sidney, Sir Philip. "Astrophel and Stella." *The College Survey of English Literature*, edited by Alexander M. Witherspoon. Harcourt, 1951, p. 210.

Straub, Richard. A *Sourcebook for Responding to Student Writing*. Hampton, 1999.

Strunk, William, Jr., and E.B. White. *The Elements of Style*. 3rd ed., Macmillan, 1979.

Sunstein, Bonnie S., and Jonathan H. Lovell, editors. *The Portfolio Standard*. Heinemann, 2000, pp. 83-93.

Swerdlow, Joel L. "The Power of Writing." *National Geographic*, vol. 196, no. 2, Aug. 1999, pp. 110-133.

Thoreau, Henry David. *Thoreau on Man and Nature*. Editor Arthur Volkman, Peter Pauper, 1960.

Tress, Lynne. *Eats, Shoots & Leaves*. Gotham, 2003.

Trimble, John R. *Writing With Style*. Prentice-Hall, 1975.

Trimmer, Joseph. *Teaching With a Purpose*. 13th ed., Houghton Mufflin, 2001.

Vonnegut, Kurt. "Writing From the Heart." *Chicken Soup for the Writer's Soul*, edited by Jack Canfield and Mark Victor Hanson, Health Communications, 2000, p. 123.

Webster, Paul Francis, and Sammy Fain. "Love is a Many-Splendored Thing." Miller Music, 1955.

Williams, Joseph. *Style: Ten Lessons in Clarity and Grace*. Longman, 2000.

Younger, Irving. *Persuasive Writing*. The Professional Education Group, 1990.

Zinsser, William. *On Writing Well*. 2nd ed., Harper, 1980.

Index

A

Agreement
    Pronoun-Antecedent 143-46
    Subject-Verb 139-43
APA Documentation Format 257-59
Apostrophe 276-79
Autobiography 8-14

B

Be Specific 42-44

C

Capitalization 282
Colons 279-80
Comma Usage 267-76
Compare/Contrast 117-23, 191-94
Conciseness/Cut Deadwood 63-68

D

Dashes 280
Dialogue 54-57
Definition 133-38, 194-97

E

Editing 13-14
End Punctuation 281-82
Essay Structure
    Closings 41-42
    Middles 38-40
    Openings 34-38
    Titles 32-33
Expanded Writing Process
    Sharing Stage 45-47
Extended Writing Process 6-15

F

Figurative Language 29-31

Fragments 81-83

G

Greatest Accomplishment 16

H

Hot Tips for Writing
    Sentences 80-81

I

Italics 281

J

Journal 5

L

Letter for Change 96-97
    Samples 97-100, 185-87
Letter to Legislator 103
Letter to the Editor 100
    Samples 100-103, 187-190

M

Mangled Meaning
    Dangling Modifiers 90
    Misplaced Modifiers 89-90
    Squinting Modifiers 90-91
MLA Documentation
    Format 225-45
Modifiers
    Adjective-Adverb 104-107

P

Paragraphs 38-40
Parallelism 86-89
Parentheses 280

Peer Response 45
Portfolio
   Checklist 19-21
   Demonstration 70
   Entry Slip 18, 44-47, 130-31
   Introduction 18, 71-72
   Metacognitive
      Conclusion 19, 91-93
   Self-Reflection 18, 45-47
   Table of Contents 18, 113-14
Prewriting
   Cluster 9
   Fishbone 9
   Formal Outline 11-12
   Free Write 10-11
   Slash Outline 8
Problem-Solution 103
Pronoun Usage 108-112

Q

Quotation Marks 54-57, 281

R

Research Writing
   Citation Styles 218-20
   Note-taking 221-22
   Selecting a Topic 215-16
   Source Cards 221
   Timetable 214-15
   Working Bibliography 220
Revising 12-13
Run-on Sentences 83-86

S

Semicolon 279
Sense Imagery 28-29
Sentence Fragments 81-3
Spelling 283
Student Portrait 16

T

Thesis Statements 124-127
Time Travel 16

U

Unnecessary Shifts 68-70
   Person 69
   Tense 69
   Voice 69

V

Verb Strength 58-63
Voice
   Active-Passive 69, 127-129

W

Why Write? 3–5
Wish Granted 16
Word Usage 166-71
Writer's Profile 16
Writing a Critical Essay
   About Literature 158-65
Writing the Critical
   Essay 149-58

Y

You're the Expert 76
   Samples 76-79, 182-84
Your Significant Event 50
   Samples 51-54, 177-82
Your Significant Place 24-25
   Samples 25-28, 173-76

COLLEGE COMPOSITION

Editing Marks	Refer to Page
Frg—fragment	81
RO—run-on	83
wv—weak verb	58
pt—punctuation	267
sp—spelling	283
wc—word choice	166
SV Agr—subject-verb agreement	139
PN Agr—pronoun agreement	143
==str—parallelism	86
case—pronoun usage	108
vg—vague; be specific	42
sft—tense, person, number shift	68
MM—misplaced modifier	89
DM—dangling modifier	90
SM—squinting modifier	90
con—conciseness	63
PV—passive voice	127
adj-adv—adjective/adverb usage	104
cap—capitalization	282
apos—apostrophe	276

CPSIA information can be obtained
at www.ICGtesting.com
Printed in the USA
FSHW011454260119
55121FS